GENDERQUEER

A STORY FROM A DIFFERENT CLOSET

GENDERQUEER

A STORY FROM A DIFFERENT CLOSET

ALLAN D. HUNTER

SANTA FE

Note: The people and events described in this memoir were all quite real, but to streamline and optimize the narrative flow, I have sometimes combined several characters into one composite character, so as to not have to develop so many characters, and on occasions I've also condensed multiple similar events and described them as single events. The names have all been changed.

"In the Flesh?"
Words and Music by Roger Waters
Copyright (c) 1979 Roger Waters Music Overseas Ltd.
All Rights Administered by BMG Rights Management (US) LLC
All Rights Reserved Used by Permission
Reprinted by Permission of Hal Leonard LLC

Sunstone books may be purchased for educational, business, or sales promotional use. For information please write: Special Markets Department, Sunstone Press, P.O. Box 2321, Santa Fe, New Mexico 87504-2321.

Book and cover design › R. Ahl
Printed on acid-free paper
∞
eBook 978-1-61139-584-6

Library of Congress Cataloging-in-Publication Data

Names: Hunter, Allan D., 1959- author.
Title: GenderQueer : a story from a different closet / by Allan D. Hunter.
Description: Santa Fe, New Mexico : Sunstone Press, [2020] | Summary: "A
     personal coming-of-age memoir and coming-out of a genderqueer male from
     a conservative family growing up in the U.S. Southwest in an era of
     political, social and cultural transformation"-- Provided by publisher.
Identifiers: LCCN 2019049386 | ISBN 9781632932907 (paperback) | ISBN
     9781611395846 (epub)
Subjects: LCSH: Hunter, Allan D., 1959- | Gender-nonconforming
     people--Southwestern States--Biography.
Classification: LCC HQ73.8 .H86 2019 | DDC 306.76/80092 [B]--dc23
LC record available at https://lccn.loc.gov/2019049386

WWW.SUNSTONEPRESS.COM
SUNSTONE PRESS / POST OFFICE BOX 2321 / SANTA FE, NM 87504-2321 /USA
(505) 988-4418 / ORDERS ONLY (800) 243-5644 / FAX (505) 988-1025

To my parents, Raymond and Joyce Hunter. Because home was safe.

CONTENTS

PREFACE

This book is the coming-out and coming-of-age story of a gender nonconforming male. Set in the late 1970s, it's a work of nonfiction and highlights the realness of an identity that is not gay, bisexual, lesbian, or transgender, but isn't cisgender and heterosexual either. It's something else. It's my story.

In 1992, I wrote a feminist theory piece, titled "Same Door, Different Closet: A Heterosexual Sissy's Coming-out Party." I've also given talks and done presentations to women's studies students and gender theory devotees, and at one such presentation I was asked to talk about my personal history, growing up as I did before there was any such word as "genderqueer" or any social awareness of such an identity. As I responded to that I began to realize that a personal narrative could make some fairly complex social concepts accessible to people who aren't regular readers of political and social theory.

In 2019, we have the word "genderqueer," but there still isn't a coming-out and coming-of-age story about people like me anywhere to be found. And that means anyone like me who is in their early adult years and trying to sort this out would still have to do so largely on their own.

I want everyone to know what it's like to be made aware of this kind of identity, but the most important people I write for are the ones who are like me. The people who are my own younger self. So I wrote the book that I so desperately needed but didn't have when I was nineteen and twenty.

I am also a blogger, writing about gender and other relevant subjects. My posts are available in identical form on these platforms, all current at the time of the publication of this book:

> LiveJournal: www.ahunter3.livejournal.com
> WordPress: www.genderkitten.wordpress.com
> DreamWidth: www.ahunter3.dreamwidth.org
> Blogger: https: www.genderkitten-echo.blogspot.com

I can also be reached by email: ahunter3@earthlink.net

I would like to thank Cassandra Lems for reading rough drafts and making corrections; Barbara Rogan and my other "classmates" in her workshop and the other authors in Amateur Writers of Long Island for their feedback; Alice Klugherz for moral support; Anne Doyle for her many suggestions; and my publicist John Sherman.

PART ONE:
SCHOOL

AT A PARTY: 1979

I guess I'd shot my mouth off. I was second in a line of people walking down the trail to the evening's bonfire party. From in front of us, a couple other guys from our town suddenly loomed up out of the darkness, coming back in our direction. The person in the lead was startled by our presence, I guess: he crouched and raised his fists. A tall blond guy directly ahead of me held up his hands in a warding-off gesture and said, "Whoa," and everyone relaxed.

I laughed and drawled lazily, in my best wasted stoner voice, "Like yeah, man, it's too heavy to get into that aggressive shit when we're already stoned and stumbling around in the dark."

The blond guy spun around and punched me hard, cocked back the other fist and whacked me again and said, "You want a piece of this? Huh?"

I repeated the same open-palmed warding-off gesture he'd used a moment earlier. "Hey, sorry, no. I apologize, I'm a little buzzed. I totally didn't mean anything by it." He said okay. We went on, and I walked a little slower as soon as the trail widened enough to let others pass me. Maybe those two guys had some kind of history, and Blond Guy thought I was trying to get involved in their ongoing feud. I didn't know, didn't care. I don't do this violence shit, man, I've got better things to do at a party.

A couple hours later the same guy came over to me where I was standing with a dozen or so other partiers, in a little flat spot between low hills with cactus growing around us. He said "Hey. Hey, man. Look, I'm sorry about that back there, okay?" I reiterated that I was sorry, too, for running my mouth. "No hard feelings?" He held out his hand. I went to shake it and damned if he didn't punch me again.

He'd knocked my glasses askew and I straightened them up. He came at me again. I backed and tried to circle to an angle where I could see him better, when suddenly I was blinded by glare: a couple of the other people in our area there had turned on flashlights and were shining them in my face. The blond guy punched me in the nose, which hurt but didn't catch me solidly enough to break anything or give me a nosebleed. I could see his silhouette, but the flashlights were making things really difficult. When he lunged at me again, I caught his arm with both hands and spun and dropped to try to bring him down to the ground.

Almost immediately I had someone *else* on my back, pinning my arms long enough to force me to release the blond guy. Now I had a third flashlight aimed into my eyes. I felt an ineffectual kick to the ribs. Was this guy trying to be Bruce Lee or something? The second kick caught me squarely in the crotch, way down low. It hurt bad enough to make me suck teeth. People were laughing. "I don't think he has any," I heard someone say. I put it together: my assailant was deliberately trying to kick me in the balls and people were actually egging the guy on. I realized I had to get myself out of there. Despite a profound perplexed curiosity about what the heck had motivated all this, and a belated flash of outrage, I wanted nothing to do with this.

I blundered away from him and in the direction I thought was the trail back out of the canyon. I ran straight into a walking stick cactus, which impaled its green length of needles all along one leg. Hurt like hell and I couldn't do anything about it. I had to hop and limp away.

Perhaps that gratified them sufficiently in a way that my successfully dashing off might not have, I don't know, but I made it out of the immediate area without further pursuit, still hopping, until I found a stick to help me pry the cactus off me. With dozens of needles still jammed into my right leg I limped a bit more effectively until I came to a large flat rock about twenty yards off the trail and worked my jeans down and spent the better part of the next hour catching my breath, recovering from my shock, and pulling cactus needles out of my skin.

As I sat there, yanking needles and branches of walking stick out of my thigh by the light of the moon, I had time to think. Okay, making fun of the cult of male fighting back there hadn't been a good judgment call. The pot party scene wasn't really the benevolent nonviolent hippie love-and-peace sex-positive dream world I wanted it to be. But there was more to it than that. I had lulled myself into thinking I wasn't so weird and different these days and that here among the town's pot-smokers I was accepted and had found a place to belong. Yet back there those folks had acted like my getting a serious ass-kicking was something that was way overdue, and they'd been enjoying the spectacle.

I thought about how I had come to see myself as different and how it had all led up to this.

A TIME BEFORE

There had once been a time before I first felt like a misfit, back before everything had gotten complicated.

In 1966, I had gotten a lot of praise from my Valdosta, Georgia second grade teacher, the very pretty Miss Adams, for being smart and being really good in reading and spelling. At home my parents had also been proud of me for being good in school. I had liked all that admiration, so I competed with the other kids for good grades and for other things that adults tended to praise and admire, like behaving well and being polite and thoughtful and kind of dignified, the way adults were.

Have you ever heard people say that girls mature faster than boys? Teachers and other adults certainly expected girls to be more mature—more social, less antagonistic and violent, more patient, far more self-disciplined, smarter, better at classwork, and more sensitive and aware of things.

Well, I was competing with them. I could keep up, and I wanted the quiet approval and acknowledgment the girls got. I was showing them I could be as good as any girl. I had pride in myself, and also group pride, as if I were representing the Boys' Team. I admired and respected the girls but some of them definitely had a sort of smug attitude toward boys in general, an assumption of superiority, so in this competition I was very definitely out to show them, to prove that a boy could be just as good as they were.

I had friends back then and I played on the playground with them during recess and sometimes went to their homes to hang out after school. I had no sense that I didn't fit in. By third grade, some things were already shifting. Other boys didn't regard me as a hero for holding up the boys' side in this competition. Instead, they made fun of me and they made it plain that they didn't see any worth in the things that the girls and I valued. Especially when it came to conduct, they acted like the only reason we behaved ourselves was that we were afraid of what would happen if we didn't. This wasn't how the girls saw it at all. They saw anyone who could not behave properly as weak, unable to hold themselves up to a standard.

The boys seemed to want to do whatever the adults told us not to, which got all of us, all the children, yelled at by adults. In other words, our reputation as children was mostly being ruined by boys. And boys were proud of this, proud to be bad. I found them embarrassing, so I tried to dissociate myself from them.

For instance, I went totally nonviolent, even refusing to fight back if attacked. *BOYS* fought, and fighting tagged them as discipline problems. I decided I was above all that.

Then there was Karen Grey. Karen became my girlfriend during third grade. She was my best friend and liked me even though sometimes she got teased about being with a boy. The other boys called us both names and sang insulting songs at us during recess and even tried to get me into fights about it. Not only that, but one of the playground supervisor teachers acted like we were doing something inappropriate and said we should know better and tried to separate us.

But we cared a lot about each other and we promised we would not let these people split us apart. It felt special and wonderful to be girlfriend and boyfriend. We loved each other. We talked about things at home and about our friends, and sometimes passed notes in class, and we walked to the school bus together and sat next to each other and held hands, not caring what anyone else said.

Gradually, inside my head, other boys stopped being the rest of the Boys' Team and instead they became *them*. Sometimes they annoyed me and made me mad. A lot of the time I just ignored them and avoided having much to do with them, and a lot of the time I went to extra trouble to avoid being seen as one of them because I didn't want to be thought of as being anything like them.

I still continued to have friends—more often girls and not as often boys at this point, to be sure, but that wasn't a problem. My little sister Jan was fairly popular and had friends over on a regular basis. There was some crossover: some of Jan's friends liked me, and my girlfriend Karen liked Jan, so we played together a lot. Jan occasionally complained that she didn't want her friends to be my friends, that I should get my own friends, that her friends had come over to play with her. But upon determining that I wasn't forcing myself on Lenoir or Tracy against their wishes, my folks pretty much left us to sort it out. The girls enjoyed playing dress-up and they liked dressing me up in taffeta and sequins and tying ribbons in my hair.

During recess at school, I'd often hang out with the girls I knew, playing jacks or jump-rope. They mostly accepted me. Some, like Lenoir and Grace, said it was a good thing for a boy to join in and not just be coming over to disrupt them and bother them. Others, like the twins Rhonda and Wanda, were more suspicious at first but shrugged and let me be a part of their group when they saw that I was willing to turn the rope and after a while they didn't treat me as if I were any different from the other girls.

Meanwhile, I had my own secret perversion, something I wasn't telling anyone and never would, which was that I liked looking at that part of girls, between their legs in front, where they were shaped differently from boys. I could see it when they wore pants. It made a distinctive V shape. This was one thing I never told anyone about, not even Karen, even though it mostly seemed like we could talk about anything together. I was too afraid that she'd think it was creepy.

Karen Grey's family moved away during the summer after third grade, and in the fall my family put me in a different school system when I started the fourth grade. That's when everything changed for the first time. I didn't know many people in the new school system and I had trouble making new friends. Several kids were hostile and ridiculed me.

I didn't just passively accept my new status. In fifth grade I made a real effort to come out and be social and popular. It was a disaster. Other boys picked on me pretty badly and girls didn't seem to want to be friends with me. People invented mean-spirited nicknames to call me—Boogerface, Greasehead, Queerio—and both boys and girls mocked and taunted me and said I was weird. For the first time I began to worry that something was wrong with me. I would sometimes see a cluster of girls and overhear them talking and it made me feel lonely and left out.

Junior high was a little better. I still didn't have friends and people still made fun of me. But the teacher was better at keeping order and I was mostly left alone. By this time I had learned about sexual appetite and realized that certain feelings I had had about girls and their bodies were not some secret perversion unique to me that I had to keep hidden forever but were actually normal. And that girls and boys were expected to start being attracted to each other this way and would start dating. This would be good. In elementary school, girls had often been reluctant to be close friends with boys because they'd be teased about it if they did.

Meanwhile, home was a safe refuge. Neither my mom nor my dad ever expressed discomfort that I wasn't a sports-loving roughhousing coarse-mouthed boy, nor did they seem concerned that I preferred girls as my friends. My dad was a scientist, an intellectual, and he was a good alternative role model who in turn saw a lot of himself in me, a quiet well-behaved kid with my nose in a Nancy Drew book, a boy who kept to himself a lot.

Valdosta Junior High School was run very strictly, with corporal punishment for talking in the hall or being anywhere but in your classroom once classes had started. The strictness stopped a lot of the bullying. I had been a believer in the rules and a respecter of adult authority all along, so I felt vindicated that there was enforcement and that I would be protected. I embraced the world of obedience and rule enforcement. It was going to be okay.

During seventh grade, I spent more and more time looking at girls and eagerly waiting for the chance to have a girlfriend again. I was surely going to be favored by the girls as their interest in boys and boyfriends increased. After all, I'd always liked girls and shared their values and respected them as colleagues, whereas most boys were abrasive loud unimaginative clods who had never liked girls before and had not paid them much attention aside from expressing their contempt for them.

Then our family moved from Valdosta, Georgia, to Los Alamos, New Mexico, and that's where I started eighth grade. And once again, everything changed.

NEW KID IN TOWN

I had managed to break my arm. It was the late summer immediately before school began and I was sitting in our venerable swing set, in the canvas seat, preparing to bail out in classic style. I had decided to let go of the chains early, to just float back on the backswing with my hands sitting easy on my knees. I figured that when it bore me forward, at the apex of the forward arc, I'd just nonchalantly shrug out of the seat and keep going along the same arc and float down to the ground as the seat swung back behind me. What happened instead was that at the apex of the backward arc, the canvas seat stopped going backwards and I just floated right on back, feet over face, doing what was probably a rather elegant backflip except that I didn't tuck and get my feet back down under me. I landed on my left arm.

We were now in Los Alamos, temporarily living on 42nd Street while our new house was being built, and I was due to start eighth grade in a week or so. I was a skinny kid and having a broken arm meant making my debut at Cumbres Junior High School twice as fragile and half as composed as I should have been.

Jan and I got up from the table after breakfast, said "bye" to our folks, and went out the door. Jan went down the block to join other sixth graders headed for Mountain Elementary and I headed the other direction around the corner toward Pueblo Junior High. I stood there by the flagpole, listening to the flag cord rattling, waiting for the bus from White Rock. When it arrived to let the Pueblo students get off, I got on, the only student boarding. Because our family planned to move to White Rock during the school year, the school administrators decided that I should start at Cumbres, the junior high at the far edge of town where all the new White Rock kids attended.

The principal at Cumbres, a somewhat rounded fellow with the unfortunate name of Cockey, held an assembly in the gym to welcome us all and start the year. He laid out his expectations of us and then segued into warning and hectoring us collectively about the kind of misbehaviors he really hoped not to see this year. The students around me mostly ignored him. Nearby, a freckled kid mocked the principal. Every time the principal paused at the end of the sentence, he replied "Itty-boo!" and "Cockey suck!" and imitated the principal's gestures and the boys next to him laughed. I rolled my eyes, wondering if I were going to be surrounded by obvious discipline problems like him.

Soon the assembly was over and the students dashed for the doors. The halls were noisy with shrieks and joking around. I examined my printed schedule and the map showing where the classrooms were and found my way to my first class.

The teacher, Ms. DaanHorzen, introduced herself, spent ten minutes getting everyone to be quiet enough for her to take roll, then explained that eighth graders were to choose "mini-courses" and work on a selected subject this semester. She passed out a list of mini-courses and asked us to put our names under the one we wanted. When it came to me, I chose Media and Television. Before the sheet had finished making its way around, the bell rang and people sprang up and began talking and heading for the door. Ms. DaanHorzen waved her arms and raised her voice, pleading with us to write our names on one of the courses before we left.

My science class turned out to be biology. Our textbook was handed out and the teacher, Mr. Carmichael, asked who had had Ms. Jones last year and took roll and talked a little bit about the difference between botany and zoology and then the bell rang again. It didn't seem like classes lasted long enough to get started before they were over.

I got up and headed for my math class. Mr. Peters was a tall man with a skinny face and a shock of light brown hair. After handing out the textbooks and writing his name on the board and calling roll, he explained that we would be doing algebra this term, and he asked who had been in which teacher's class last year, and wrote a couple equations on the board and asked, "Did you do that?" after each one.

In the afternoons, riding home on the bus, the other kids began cutting up and roughhousing. A short boy in a red shirt with a loud voice had some other boy's textbook and was threatening to beat him over the head with it instead of giving it back. A moment or so later he and a big guy with long brown hair were telling a smaller kid he had to move to another seat or they'd give him "noogies." This was my first year riding a school bus since third grade, and eighth and ninth graders were a lot louder and far less under control. People poked and attacked other students and insulted each other and generally turned the bus into a rolling zoo. Animals without leashes. The bus driver didn't seem to care.

After the first couple weeks, I learned that the freckled boy I'd seen in assembly on the first day was named Calvin Beems. He started taunting me in class, calling me Big D and when the bell rang, he came up behind me in the hall and smacked me in the back, knocking my books out of my arms. There were no teachers in the halls keeping order. Later, when I was at my locker, dialing the combination to switch books for the next class, he snuck up behind me and watched over my shoulder as I dialed my locker combination and then called it out: "fifteen, forty-eight, forty-five, huh?"

Back in Valdosta, I had drifted toward a retro-1950s look, with narrow-legged pants and slicked-back hair. Now students were harassing me, making fun of my short hair and my clothes. "Hey man, where did you get those pants? Did you take them from your grandpa's closet?"

My dad had advised me to say something sharp and snappy back when this kind of thing happened, so I asked, "You sure you have the official cool clothes that everyone needs to wear to be an officially cool person?" A boy named Vinnie Esperanza repeated back what I'd just said in a nasal high-pitched squeaky voice and they all laughed and one of them said, "What a fag!" and they left me there fuming.

By October, a big guy named George Hodges started calling me "pansy" and Vinnie Esperanza shot spitballs at the back of my neck in English class. People would come up to me in groups and someone would ask me some insolent question and whatever answer I gave, they'd make fun of and repeat to each other.

One of the required courses was physical education (PE) which I quickly came to hate. I had to put on gym clothes in the locker room then come out and sit on a bench, where we'd wait for the coach to send us out to play sports or do exercises.

Several of the boys in my gym class were athletes on intramural or varsity teams and the coach, Mr. Eggerton, knew them and bantered with them, all casual insults and put-downs.

"Okay, okay, get yourself seated if you can figure out which part of you goes on the bench. You, McAllister, that don't mean your head."

The jocks in the class snickered. "Yes, sir Coach Eggerton sir!" replied the boy he'd addressed as McAllister, grinning.

"Aah! Damn fool basketball player. When your coach said dribble down the court you thought he wanted you to drool. Wipe your chin."

More snickers from the athletic guys. "He don't know how to wipe yet," suggested George Hodges.

Coach Eggerton glanced at me in my cast and said, "What did you do to get that thing? I suppose you can't do chin-ups. Great." He acted annoyed about it and the other boys laughed. He addressed a boy on the next bench: "Robinson! You trying out for basketball this year or what?"

"Yes sir, Coach Eggerton."

The coach pretended he was going to throw the ball directly at his face, then selected someone else. "Griegos, you gonna let Pueblo outrun you again in the 880?"

Eggerton didn't make any effort to teach or coach the rest of us who had to be there, those of us who weren't sports-oriented students. He'd blow his whistle and wave us onto the gym floor or out into the football field and let the athletic boys take over dividing us up and starting the games.

They called me pathetic and invented nicknames for me and yelled if I did anything wrong and made fun of anything I tried to do. I had my dignity, fragile though it was, and I hated being mocked and spoken to this way. They could tell I was fuming even though I kept my silence, and my anger just encouraged them to taunt me more.

Soon enough I was the target of enough mocking and hostile name-calling to become tired of it. I went to my teachers—Ms. DaanHorzen and Mr. Peters and Mr. Carmichael—and asked them to do something to make it stop.

Ms. DaanHorzen shrugged and said she was always trying to maintain order but one could only do so much with so many students. Mr. Peters behaved as if I were annoying him: "I'm in my classroom trying to teach math, and when I'm not, I'm in my office seeing students or grading papers. I don't know why you think *I* can do anything about it or why you think it should be my problem. Can't you handle this on your own by now? How old are you anyway?" Mr. Carmichael said "I hear what you're saying, but if I were to hear their side of the story are you going to claim that they wouldn't be saying that you insulted them first or started the roughhousing? Tell the truth. I don't believe in angels."

A short and aggressive boy named Jason Britten kept calling me "fag." He and his friends circled me and Jason began singing "Derek Turner naa naa naa, Derek Turner naa naa naa, he always takes a boner, Derek Turner, naa naa naa." George Hodges wanted to fight me. "C'mon, you pansy, put up your fists, I'll kick your ass."

I opened my spiral notebook and began writing down names. Jason Britten. George Hodges. I soon had an "Enemies List" of people I considered to be harassing me. I became convinced they were all in communication with each other and conspiring ahead of time about what they'd do to me next. There was so much similarity in their behavior toward me, and they seemed to use a lot of the same language, so I assumed that they all knew each other.

Since I had failed to get any help from any of my teachers, I went to the guidance counselor's office and stuck my head in. There was a man at a desk shuffling papers. A plastic nameplate identified him as Gilbert Walker. "Hi, do I need an appointment?" I asked. He shook his head and beckoned for me to sit.

"I'm new in town. My family's from Georgia. I know new kids always get picked on, but there are some boys here who never stop, and the teachers aren't doing anything about it."

"What sort of behavior are we talking about here?" he asked, pushing his glasses farther up the bridge of his nose.

"There's a guy with a nasty mouth, Jason Britten, who keeps calling me 'fag' and 'queer bait', and Vinnie Esperanza, who shoots spit wads at me in the classroom, and a big guy, George Hodges, who keeps calling me 'pansy' and trying to get me into a fight, and there's another boy, bit of a smart-aleck, named Calvin Beems..."

I recounted my problems, who had said what and done what.

"Well, that's not very mature behavior on their part, and I'm sorry this is happening to you," he replied at the end of my litany of insults and injuries.

"I appreciate your sympathy. I haven't been getting much of that. In Georgia, if I told a teacher, she'd put boys like that out in the hallway, and the assistant principal's staff would come by and paddle them."

Mr. Walker rested his chin in the palm of his hand. "We don't go in much for corporal punishment here."

"Well, something needs to be done. It's not fair that they can tease and harass me and no one does anything about it."

"I may be able to intervene if they step over the line significantly. But meanwhile, try not to escalate the hostility. As you pointed out, you're the new kid. You know they're testing you. Try not to react to them, and report the behaviors to me and we'll document the pattern of abuse."

So I agreed to continue taking notes on who had said or done what, and periodically I took the list in with me, tattling my earnest and offended heart out, hoping for some kind of protection.

In one of Ms. DaanHorzen's English mini-courses, we had to get up in front of the class and make a speech. As it approached time for me to do my presentation, I was nervous, my stomach clenched, and I had to pee. I wasn't sure I could talk. I was not looking forward to being center stage here at school where I was so often singled out for ridicule. I had become a shy snob, still convinced of the overall superiority of the contents of my head, proud of the ways in which I was an individual instead of a conforming sheep, but socially reclusive and far from being at my best in front of people.

I did my speech about women's liberation and equal rights between the sexes, urging support for the Equal Rights Amendment because it was fair and because people should not be treated differently because of what sex they are. I stammered and flushed and stumbled my way through it, but I felt good about what I'd said.

A girl in my class with short pixie-like brown hair, freckles, and a cute elven face that came down to a little chin whispered, "That was a good speech. You said that well." I quickly learned her name: Tavia Wycliff.

I was almost instantly obsessed with her and, as I observed her over time, I found her kind, witty, and highly intelligent. I came to cherish her appearance and to crave everything about her. I wanted to spend time with her and talk with her, but she was nearly always with a friend or two and I had a hard time coming up with an excuse to start a conversation.

In the afternoon, I had band class. I retrieved my French horn from the instrument locker and sat down in the French horn section. Tom Land and Jeremy Michaels were chatting away and cutting up as usual. "...because you can't bear to be parted from your sweet wee bee," Jeremy was taunting.

"*Me?* You're the one who has a poster on the wall worshipping the great..." I hadn't the vaguest idea what they were babbling about. I took out some valve lube and began oiling up my horn's valves and getting ready for class.

"Derek, what is that stuff, kickapoo Joy-gia juice?" Tom asked me insolently. I glared. He often teased me about being from Georgia.

Jeremy interposed, "Tom wants to borrow it to rub on his wee bee."

"Oh shut up!" Tom replied, rolling his eyes.

The conductor tapped impatiently on the music stand, scowling in the general direction of our section.

I was oversensitized and irritable from so many people picking on me and making fun of me, and I didn't really care for Tom and Jeremy adding to it, but I was starting to realize that their teasing was qualitatively different. They picked on me the same way they picked on each other. And although it seemed to amuse them to see me getting annoyed, it didn't have that ugly undercurrent of real disgust and contempt that I felt from people like Calvin Beems and Jason Britten.

The "wee bee" turned out to be a collection of Warner Brothers comic books in Tom's bedroom that Jeremy had seen and started making fun of, which only increased in intensity and silliness when Tom made the mistake of defending them. They knew each other from Boy Scouts and lived close to each other on Barranca Mesa.

I was in the cafeteria sitting by myself eating and George came up from behind me and squirted me in the face with a squirt gun. I stared at his stupid mocking face. *Seriously, this too??* I refused to react. Apparently that wasn't satisfactory to him: he squeezed the trigger again and again, squirting me repeatedly, the water running down my shirt and puddling in my food, and my fury flowing fast along with it. George grinned, as if daring me to do something about it. I wanted to: I wanted him dead.

I stood up slowly, carefully and deliberately picking up my plastic cafeteria lunch tray, and suddenly smashed it down upon his head with a loud *CRACK!* It shattered into green plastic shards, spilling my ruined meal all over him and knocking the gun away in the process.

George wasn't grinning now. He punched me hard in the stomach and then shoved me to the floor. All conversational chatter had died; we were the center of attention. I heard adult kitchen staff voices. So did George, apparently, and he said something about me being dead this afternoon then stalked off. I got to my feet and stalked off toward my next class, ignoring all the stares and whispers.

Alan Snyder, one of the boys on my Enemies List, was boyfriend to Chris Bundy, and they emerged from Mr. Carmichael's class holding hands. I was jealous, and it was part of a disturbing pattern: girls were connecting with boys, all right, but boys like *that*, the coarse and loud ones, the sort of boys for whom I felt contempt. It wasn't fair. Boys like that had never been interested in girls before. Well, I'd just have to be patient. Girls would find out that boys like that weren't very nice, sooner or later.

I really hated PE. Historically through my life the only times I'd been undressed with other people in the room had been when going to the pool, where the other people were strangers. The one notable exception had been an awful YMCA summer camp after fifth grade, when all the boys in our cabin had been taken to a natural outdoor pool and were expected to strip naked and swim. I'd been very body-shy and embarrassed about taking my clothes off in front of people who were not very friendly.

And now I was in a similar situation. Every day, at fourth period, PE was more or less the same: Bang, a locker slams close by my head. Someone snaps a wet towel at someone else, and people are yelling and clowning. There is talk about bodies, ribald and crude, in that same "dirty and we like it that way" attitude and tone of voice, familiar and contemptuous. They talk about girls, and girls' bodies. *Tits, pussy, ooh, unhook that bra strap ha ha ha. So and so is such a slut, she'd let anyone fuck her, should put a coke bottle up there instead. A tightly rolled towel held between his legs like a giant phallus, isn't that funny, ha ha ha. Hey Derek, do you want to suck Beverly's tits? Naaah, Derek sucks something else, don't you, ha ha ha.*

There was a constant undercurrent of threat, of potential for being picked on in ways ranging from verbal harassment to immediate violence. The PE coach wasn't going to protect me. He seemed to like boys behaving this way and considered that anyone on the receiving end of all this hazing and horseplay to have brought it upon ourselves.

"Okay, you remember from yesterday we were doing 'FOIL', like this," began Mr. Peters, rapidly sketching in chalk on the blackboard that $(x - 3y) (x - 2y) = x^2 -5xy + 6y^2$. I stared at it and tried to remember what it was that made it somehow true that multiplying then adding "first, outer, inner, last" as he had shown us was mathematically valid, and also trying to understand what was "better" about $x^2 -5xy + 6y^2$ than the original $(x - 3y)$ $(x - 2y)$, why we were doing this in the first place.

Then I realized he'd written out several more lines with a different mix of letters and numbers and people were raising their hands calling out answers. I realized I'd missed something critical that he'd said. He assigned a couple pages of homework and got up at the end of the lesson. I followed him into the hallway and asked him to explain the process again. "Oh," he said casually, "you just 'unFOIL' it, get the factors, if they have valid factors. Some of them don't." I was appalled to find myself not doing well in this class. I'd been bored in math for years in Valdosta, doing the same old arithmetic year after year, but this algebra was leaving me in the dust.

I got transferred out of Mr. Peters' math class into a slower-moving algebra class. Ms. Chavez, my new teacher, pointed to an unoccupied desk in the back and said that would be my seat for the semester. Directly in front of me was a girl with long blonde hair and a perfectly symmetrical oval-round face. Beautiful. Cheryl Dionet. I didn't develop a crush on her as I had with Tavia Wycliff but she was so pretty I always felt nervous talking to her, and it was tempting to just stare at her for the duration of class. At least it made math class more pleasant. Ms. Chavez did a better job of covering the concepts and I did adequately well in math class for the remainder of the year.

My mishap with the algebra class had caused me to doubt that the main factor making me different from the other kids was that I was considerably more intelligent than average. I still considered myself significantly intelligent but there were a lot of non-stupid kids my age and they were not subject to being singled out for social ostracization and mistreatment as I was. Some of them were pretty popular, in fact.

The business of being more like a girl than one of the boys also occurred to me, of course. It was a difference that people were often hostile about and brought to my attention. But it was one difference among many, and people often acted like *all* difference was bad, like being from the south or liking different music, even things like being lefthanded (I was) or having eyes of different colors (mine were).

Mostly I thought in terms of my tendency to value individuality over conformity. But I was doing a fair bit of thinking about myself, and whether maybe I was perpetuating my own isolation in ways that were not really making me happier and didn't really mean being true to myself. Perhaps being a "shy snob" wasn't entirely avoidable but I was becoming aware that in retaliation for judgmental hostility I had become a rather judgmental and hostile person myself, radiating my own disapproval of people for their trendy fashionable mannerisms, their music, and their appearance. I realized I had unconsciously combined those things in my head with their harassment of me, and reacted to them all as "characteristics of The Enemies." I was starting to long for peace or at least a truce.

One day when I got off the bus at Pueblo Junior High to walk home to 42nd Street, two guys I didn't recognize began taunting me and they followed me the entire way home. They insulted me and laughed at me and mocked me and imitated me and pitched rocks and pine cones at me. There was such a deep hate in me all the time now, I was always feeling pretty close to the edge. As I walked home everything seemed to be colored all black and red. I wanted to hurt them badly, but because I hadn't participated in fighting since around third grade I didn't know how to hurt someone by hitting them.

I got to our house with them still following me, and felt unsafe even in the house with them right outside. Furious and miserable, I went into the kitchen and snatched the largest of the razor-sharp butcher knives down from the magnetic knife rack and ran back outside to confront them. Their laughter got thinner and they backed away and kept their distance as I advanced on them, and then they ran away. I went back in and realized how ready and willing I was to kill someone if people would not leave me the hell alone.

I often watched girls out of the corner of my eye and listened to them even though I couldn't really count any of them as friends. I was tired of always feeling like I had my nose pressed against the glass, wanting to be with them and wanting to be accepted by them, loving their shapes and the way they moved, but feeling like there was always this barrier in the way keeping me out.

Girls had once been my main friends; they'd mostly accepted my hanging out and playing with them on the playground and after school, and I'd befriended several of Jan's friends before we got to an age where that got awkward.

But that was a long time ago and it was time to stop clinging to that as a sense of identity. It wasn't getting me anywhere. It looked like if I wanted to have any friends at all, I needed to learn how to be around boys...and to stop thinking of boys as *Them*.

"So, Derek, are you going to come to the troop meeting?" Tom asked. I was considering joining their troop even though Barranca Mesa was at the far edge of town.

"Thursday night at seven-thirty?" He nodded. I'd mentioned it to my parents. "I think that's a great idea," my dad had said.

"See?" added my mom, "I told you if you gave it a little time you'd meet some other people at school that you'd get along with."

The meeting was called to order. I stood in the line as part of Tom and Jeremy's patrol as we chanted the Scout Law and recited the Pledge of Allegiance. After a couple announcements, we met as patrols, sitting on the gym floor in clusters. The boys in the patrol began socializing and trying to shoot folded paper triangles through the basketball hoops. A pair of them grabbed another boy's jacket and he chased after them down the hallway. Jeremy was mock-insulting Chris, a freckled redheaded guy.

I turned to Tom and asked, "Is this the patrol meeting or is this the part where we relive our kindergarten years?" I sounded prissy and disapproving to my own ears.

"Give it a rest, will you?" Jeremy said, exasperated with me.

After a few minutes, the Scoutmaster came over and introduced himself as Chip Deavers. "Boys, can I see your handbooks? Let me see which requirements you're working on. Okay, you need to get these two signed off next time we go camping."

On our first camping trip, I woke up to the morning reveille bugle call, went to the crackling campfire, and got in line with my mess kit plate for breakfast. Somebody named Matt was the designated cook, and he plopped down a big spoonful of lukewarm grey glop on my plate. "What's that?" I asked.

"Instant oatmeal."

Jeremy mocked me: "Sorry, Derek, we don't have any Jaw-ja grits."

I had to do dishes because I was on KP. I went to Ed, the patrol leader, and asked if I could be on cooking duty the next day. I knew about campfire cooking from going camping with my folks.

I twisted my gym locker combination lock through its sequence and opened it. With my back to the rest of the changing room I peeled off my clothes as quickly as possible and flung the gym shorts and shirt into the back, then grabbed my towel and slipped past the other boys to the showers. Joey and Tony were horsing around, spraying each other by jamming their thumbs into the shower heads, but fortunately I was being ignored for once. I could wash up quickly, dry off, then dress and get out of there.

After the shower, I slipped onto the wooden bench and put on my glasses and reached in to retrieve my street clothes. *Uh oh. Here's my socks, shirt, pants, but where the hell's my underwear?*

"Hey, something wrong, Big D?" *Calvin Beems. This can't be good.* I took a deep breath and tried to assemble a neutral face. Not a face of outrage, not amusingly upset, and not scared.

"Derek Turner isn't getting dressed. Why aren't you getting dressed, Derek Turner?" mocked Jason Britten.

"He's looking for his nuts," suggested George Hodges.

"What's the matter, Derek Pansy, can't find your panties?" chanted Calvin. He made his voice high and nasal and whiny. "Has anyone seen my little pink undies?"

"Yeah you're funny," I said flatly. "I never knew you were so interested in other guys' underwear or I would have brought an extra set for you to play with. If you're done with them for now, how about letting me have them back." Trying to act mostly bored, a little amused. *My voice is shaking too much. Dammit.*

"Look over there. I think I might have seen them somewhere over there," Calvin suggested helpfully, pointing toward the coach's office.

"No," contradicted George, "I'm pretty sure they're tied to the flagpole out front."

Seven or eight other boys watched the interaction from their places on the changing bench, faces showing various degrees of amusement. One of them pointed back toward where I'd just come from. "Might want to look back there."

Jason said, "No, go check out the girls' locker room. Go on, they haven't had anything to laugh at all morning."

I glared at them all. *C'mon, quit prolonging it.*

"Seriously, Derek, I think you should check back there," Calvin said, pointing toward the showers and toilet stalls.

"Go on. Take a look," Jason concurred.

"Where are they?" I demanded, trying to keep my voice level and calm.

"I don't know. Why would I know? But I think you really should go take a look back there," Jason persisted.

"Yeah, Derek, go fucking look for them," added George, also waving in that direction.

I wrapped myself in my towel and stalked across the tiled floor. No soggy wet clump of fabric anywhere in the showering area. "Go on," they called at me. "Keep going, keep looking."

I found them in the third toilet stall, floating in a filthy unflushed toilet bowl.

"The school most certainly doesn't condone this kind of behavior," Mr. Walker stated when I reported the incident. "I can have all three of them called in, if that's what you want. We can do that."

I glared at the guidance counselor. "I want them expelled. Or at least suspended."

Gilbert Walker sighed. "That's probably not going to happen. You said yourself that you didn't see them do it. And the thing is...the thing is, you said your goal is to stop this harassment and get them to leave you alone. Do you think that's more likely to happen if we call them in and ask them questions about this incident?"

He rotated his office chair so he was facing me more directly and rested his palms on his thighs. "It sounds to me like you handled it well.

You didn't let them get you angry. And when these boys...they're immature bullies...when they see that they can't get to you, they'll go find someone else who is more fun to pick on. If we call them in...do you remember what I said about escalation?"

"So if I report them for what they've done and get them in trouble and they come after me for it, that's my fault?"

"I'm not saying that. I know it might sound that way to you, but I'm not. I'm just saying you have to pick your battles. If they do keep hassling you, sooner or later they'll screw up and do something that will get them in real trouble. Until that happens, your best strategy is to try to grow a thick skin and show them they can't manipulate you into getting angry and entertaining them with your frustration."

To be honest, I wasn't without a fair amount of ambivalence about authority and related issues. The attitude of authoritarian adults toward kids, especially toward boys, seemed to be that if and when we were being good and not getting into trouble, it was exclusively due to our fear of the consequences. So they always exuded an attitude of "Even if you are not currently doing anything wrong, it is a good thing to frighten and intimidate you as well as the ones who are currently misbehaving because we know you would misbehave if you had the courage and the opportunity and thought you might get away with doing so."

All my life I'd assumed that the world was run fairly and responsibly by good citizens, and that as I got older I'd join them, along with my well-behaving peers, with the immature and ill-behaved ones left behind if they didn't change. But the older I got the less certain I was that my peers as a whole were ever going to unify around any behavioral code or belief that I'd want to be a part of.

Jason Britten's dad was John Britten and his contracting company was the one that was building our house down in White Rock. The project kept slipping and months went by and we were still staying in the house on 42nd Street. The weather played a role in the delay, as that winter was one of the snowiest on record. Finally, though, the house was ready and we packed up everything and moved down off the hill to the split-level stucco ranch house at Shirlane Place in White Rock.

My younger sister Jan began making friends in the neighborhood immediately. As usual, I was more reticent. I had just received a box of books I'd mail-ordered and I lay sprawled on my bed reading. My mom said, "Go call your sister for supper." I stepped out the front door and found Jan standing in the driveway talking with Jay Schirmer from the house to our left, and whispering and laughing with Tina and Terri Bond from the house to our right.

I met many of the neighbors as a side effect of their clustering around Jan. Soon I was once again being mocked for my taste in music, my hairstyle, how I dressed, and so on. "Don't you have any pants that have a little flare in the leg?" Tina Bond asked. "No one wears those pipe stem pants anymore."

"No, I always wear this kind. What's so special about having them flare out? If it becomes the style to put a bone through your nose, will you all be saying 'Hey Derek why don't you have a bone in your nose' and offering me one to use?"

She didn't find it funny. She shook her head and told Jan, "He's hopeless. C'mon, let's go."

Jay Schirmer and Kyle Stankowski from farther down the street asked about my hair. "What do you put in it anyway? Brylcreem?" Kyle's face twisted with revulsion. "No," I replied with an annoyed glare, "I use Vitalis." Jay asked if I'd consider letting my hair grow a little longer, enough to come over my ears, and let it hang forward some over my forehead instead of combing it directly to the side. "Why do you care?" I asked.

It was a serious question. I was genuinely curious. There was the familiar whiff of dismissive contempt in it, but Jan's friends seemed determined to get me onboard, as if they were trying to rescue me. They kept explaining that it was 1973 and I had my feet planted on the wrong side of the generation gap. Did I really have to be against them and allied with the adult generation all the time?

I was tired of this protracted antagonistic fight with virtually everyone my age, and of being ostracized and made fun of. And I was less and less impressed with the rightful authority of parents and teachers and other adults. So although I was pretty stubborn about retaining my chosen appearance and other superficial differences, I became less judgmental and less intolerant of them and their choices and behaviors.

I even stopped openly disapproving when they broke rules that adults emphasized as pretty serious things, such as smoking. I knew many of the other kids were doing it. I was the target of many sidelong glances and behind-my-back signals when the other guys and girls were talking and was pretty sure they didn't trust me not to keep my mouth shut about it. Not without good reason, really, as earlier the same year I would have told on any of them, so allied was I with the adults and the importance of being a good citizen and doing the right thing and so on.

But now Jay Schirmer or Terri Bond would ask on behalf of the cluster in general if I would tell any parents if they smoked cigarettes in front of me, and I said I would not, and there began to be some mutual relaxation.

One outcome of having to undress in PE class was that everyone in the school seemed to know that I wore boxer shorts. This was 1974. No one else under the age of forty wore boxer shorts. All the other guys wore jockey shorts. One day the other kids in the neighborhood invited me to go down to Pajarito Springs where a small local creek joined the Rio Grande and formed a natural swimming hole complete with waterfall. Jay and Jan and Tina and Terri were inviting me along. It would involve swimming in our underwear.

I didn't want to be pointed to and hear comments made about my underwear fashion sense. On the other hand I thought I would like to see Tina and Terri in wet underwear. I had a couple pairs of jockey shorts given to me by some clueless relative as a Christmas or birthday present so I went in to change first. Then we headed down the trail, down the canyon to the pool.

I was shy about taking off my street clothes but I managed. Being badly nearsighted I had to choose between wearing my glasses and being somewhat curtailed in what I could do in the water or else not wearing them and not being able to see things in focus. I figured it would be pretty obvious what I was wanting to look at if I left my glasses on so I decided to take them off. We splashed around and took turns standing directly under the waterfall, and we had some water fights. Jay teased Tina some when she was adjusting her bra strap, pretending to think she was taking it off, but it was actually a pretty G-rated day, although it was exciting just because of the idea of the kind of things that might happen, even though they didn't.

That summer, the neighborhood cluster of kids encouraged and pleaded and begged me to go with the rest of them to White Rock community center dances and let them make me over and dress me for the event. They taught me how to dance to rock music and made me practice with them in the living room and, in fits and starts, with intermittent reversals and changes of mind, I went along with it and began to come out of my isolation.

Jan had become involved with Jay. I don't think they were especially serious about each other but Jan did claim him as a boyfriend and they were in each other's company fairly often. She was also close with both of the Bond girls. Toward me they would sort of oscillate between trying to include me and make me over as someone who looked and acted more as they felt I should (conforming) and making fun of me or leaving me out of things as a wet-blanket square nowhere-man that they didn't want around. I oscillated between being amenable to being made over and pulling back from it and reasserting my individual different self.

28

Upstairs in the guest bedroom, we had a second TV set and an avocado-green hide-a-bed sofa, and Jan and her friends had taken to hanging out up there to get more privacy from parents (and perhaps from me). One day they invited me to join them and I did so. They turned on the TV and turned off the lights. Jan sat with Jay and Terri Bond sat next to me. In the semi-dark she slid up next to me and leaned against me. I put my arm around her tentatively and we sat there for a little while like that. Jan and Jay were whispering something and kissing.

Terri turned around more to face me and pulled the bottom edge of her t-shirt up a little and took one of my hands and placed it on her waist. *Is she daring me to try to make out with her? Does she want me to make out with her? Is she going to embarrass me and make fun of me and act like it was all my idea and say I'm a perverted creep?* I didn't know but I was sufficiently intrigued to be willing to find out. Cautiously and slowly I extended my hand against her skin under her shirt, back to where her bra strap was, then couldn't make myself believe this could be real. Since when did Terri feel that way about me? Would that be the triggering moment when they all laugh?

After a moment Terri said she had to go to the bathroom. Jan followed her and I could hear murmurs and suppressed giggles. *Okay so they are talking about me. Well I don't know as how they can make all that much fun of me since I only followed her lead.* They came back and again she sat next to me. This time she tucked the tips of my fingers under the edge of her jeans waistband.

An entire lifetime of being fascinated by the delicious shapes of girls, the V shape in their pants, how they looked in jeans panties bikinis...yes, those shapes, right there. The ultimate craving. And now my fingers were inside her pants. *Inhale, exhale, slip fingers a little farther down. Inhale, exhale, slide fingers a little farther down. WOW this is really happening, I don't know why but please don't stop me yet. A little farther.* Terri began to move her hand and I anticipated her removing mine or otherwise ending this but instead she undid her jeans button and lowered the zipper a little.

Quick glance into the murky semidark to see if Jay and Jan were watching me but they weren't looking in our direction. A little farther down. *Her skin is so warm. How close am I to reaching her pubic hair, to touching her there?* A little more and my fingers encountered panties elastic. *Oh yeah. Oh wow girls are so long in the waist. All that distance I've covered and yet I'm only now down to where her underwear starts?*

"Oops, bathroom break, excuse me," said Jan, and Terri quickly shuffled and composed herself and went off with Jan again to the bathroom and again there was muffled conversation and stifled giggles before they came back.

Terri again sat next to me. Hesitantly I nudged her jeans snap with my fingers and she again unbuttoned and unzipped. Slowly and deliciously I recaptured all the lost ground and got my fingertips under the elastic. And kept going. Fantastic. And yes. Through and past the glorious land of girl hairs, down into the beginnings of the cleft. Her clitoris. Her place that would feel to her like mine does to me. I wanted to make her feel those feelings. It was a small bump, sort of, and slick, and I started to rub it very lightly and slowly.

Terri shifted and called yet another bathroom break and she and Jan again went off to whisper. When they came back they switched the lights on and Terri sat farther away.

I didn't care what they might attempt to make of all this; they could make fun of me if they were so inclined. I couldn't believe this had happened. This was so great. *So...it's real then. Girls do like to do this.* Even if this was just to have some kind of fun at my expense, this could never have happened unless girls do this sometimes. I wanted more.

CONNECTING

My parents had not been oblivious to the agonies of my eighth grade year. I had told them about the people picking on me throughout the year as it had happened, and had asked them to meet with the counselor Gilbert Walker, which they had done. But unless I brought it up, neither of my parents ever spoke to me about my being different from other kids or being picked on for being different. Mostly I think they felt that their hands were tied, that they could not protect me forever from my peers, and that any authoritarian/systemic intervention they pushed for would backfire against me.

My mom urged me to laugh with the people who were laughing at me and said that once they saw I had a sense of humor it would not be as much fun for them to tease and torment me. My dad recommended clever replies that would turn the tables on them verbally. I don't think either of them had a sense of the intensity of the emotion directed toward me by the other kids, or the intensity that I felt in response to it.

Not that every waking moment in school was awful. In ninth grade English I ended up being placed behind Tavia Wycliff. I could look at her from behind and think about her. She had short enough hair that I could see the back of her neck above her collar and I would often visually trace the outline of her body from there down each shoulder and then to where it tapered in at an angle to her waist.

I wondered what it would be like if she were in love with me. I wondered what sex itself would be like. I knew where the intensifying feelings I was having were headed, but actual sex still seemed like a very clinical and invasively personal thing that I wasn't sure I was ready for. And to be honest I wasn't entirely sure about posture and what limbs went where, although I was aware in a basic sense what parts had to come together to make it work.

I wanted more touching like what had happened with Terri in the guest bedroom, and I wanted a girlfriend to care about me and to be in love with. I wanted tenderness. And I wished it would all happen with Tavia Wycliff. I looked at the back of her neck and imagined kissing her there and putting my hands in her hair. We could figure out the sex thing over time.

"Hey everybody? This is Denise Spears," Jan introduced. "She's in our church youth group and she's having supper with us tonight." Denise said hi to the family as we gathered around the dinner table. I recognized her from the youth group. She was physically in transition, just getting breasts and still with baby fat around her face but totally cute with a real sweet smile. She was a bit younger than Jan, who was just turning twelve this year herself.

"There's this hay ride thing that the youth group is doing next weekend," Denise told us. "Jan said she'd go if it was okay." She was including me with her eyes and her smile. "It's kind of silly, I think they're hooking a wagon full of hay to a jeep and we all ride in the wagon while they pull us around Rover and other streets in White Rock." My parents both said it sounded like fun. "You could come too, if you wanted," Denise informed me. "It's not all sixth graders, there'll be some older kids."

Jan didn't always appreciate her friends asking me along but she didn't seem to be bristling at the idea. Well, this was nice. I hadn't been able to get much of a conversation going with Tavia in English class—she'd been pleasant but closer to cordial than friendly. Now here I had someone who seemed interested in me. Of course she was only eleven or thereabouts, but I enjoyed talking with her. She looked directly at me and included me when talking with Jan or my folks.

So on Saturday I went on the hay ride. It was cold so we all dressed warmly in sweaters and then got up inside wagons full of hay to be pulled through the back streets. After a while, Jan got into conversations with some of her other friends, and Denise ended up sitting next to me. She sat close to me and I somewhat shyly put my arm around her shoulders. "My arm's too heavy to hold up, so I'm going to have to rest it here," I said. It sounded lame and silly to me as I said it. She leaned against me and smiled happily and said she couldn't help it if she liked boys. It felt great to have my arm around her and the sweet weight of her head against my shoulder.

Finally having made it to advanced band on the French horn, I was also necessarily in the marching band, because the advanced band was the marching band. We were out on the practice football field, freezing in the cold autumn wind while the conductor yelled out the cadence, learning how to measure off five yards per eight steps. "I don't see why we've got to do this," I groused to Tom and Jeremy. "I want to be a musician, not to march around entertaining people who came to see the football game. I don't care about football."

The other two French horn players shook their heads. Derek was at it again.

"Seriously, though, it's like we're cheerleaders or something. No one comes to the games to hear us play. Or watch us march around for that matter. Are the football players going to come be ushers for our band concert?"

Jeremy laughed and leaned forward with his arms dangling and adopted a dull bewildered face and rasped out "You! Sit in chair!" and mimed throwing someone into a chair.

It bugged me though. Many of the football players had been heavily represented on last year's Enemies List and they still weren't my favorite people.

"Hey, French Chef. Hey, Julia Child," Tom interrupted. "Are you ready for the weekend camporee? Got your frying pans ready?"

I was now getting some respect in Boy Scouts. Everyone wanted to eat my meals. I was permanently absolved from doing KP or waking up early and gathering wood in the cold and starting the fire. "You know, the best chefs are usually men," Scoutmaster Deavers had commented. I was even awarded a special uniform patch proclaiming me "Bull Chef."

They needed someone to head up a patrol, and I agreed to serve as patrol leader. I had the rank and experience for it now. Several of the other boys said they'd quit before they'd be in my patrol and were accepted as transfers to some of the other patrols. I began trying to conduct patrol meetings in an organized manner, but two or three of the younger scouts were incessantly playing games and not participating. I told them they had to straighten up and take it seriously, and when one of them continued to clown around, imitating my voice mockingly and becoming belligerent, I went to Deavers and told him I didn't want that boy in my patrol. He was appalled. "You can't just go around kicking boys out of your patrol. You need to be a leader here. If they see they can push you around, they will."

I often complained at home about boys perpetually challenging and harassing me and always being in a hurry to settle things physically. One day my Dad decided he needed to intervene.

In the living room, he picked up a sofa cushion to use as padding and showed me, as if it were a principle of science or a proper technique in packing a backpack, how to throw a punch. He was right: I didn't know.

He showed me how to pivot and get my body's weight behind it and had me practice punching him while he clutched the sofa cushion.

I still did not want to be in fights and did not think I should ever have to, but unquestionably thinking of myself as someone who *couldn't* fight was not helping me cope. Psychologically, I think this exercise reawakened a sense in me that if I were nonviolent when confronted it was because I chose to be. And that I could choose otherwise. It was also of course a tacit permission to get into fights if in my judgment doing so was necessary.

Because of French horn sectional band practice I stayed late after school and then ended up riding the activity bus home, which took a slower and more convoluted route to drop people off at a wider assortment of destination points. The other French horn players lived on Barranca Mesa so I was essentially by myself, not riding with anyone I knew. The activity bus always took the long loop around Rover Boulevard, and right around the time we made the first turnoff a couple of boys I had never seen moved to the seat directly behind me and began talking about me, saying I was a fucking pansy. They took turns asking me nasty insolent sarcastic questions. They kept this up as the bus made its way around the Rover Boulevard circle.

Finally the bus got to their stop and they got off. I got off too although it was still a long way from my own stop. They realized I'd gotten off with them and suddenly they seemed nervous. I asked, "Do you have some kind of problem with me?" They denied it. "Do you want to explain why you were saying all that shit back there on the bus?" Oh we didn't mean anything by it. "Don't you ever start in on me again. I don't need it. I'm sick of it. Do you understand me?" They nodded and promised they would not mess with me again. I walked home the rest of the way around the loop. That felt good.

Marijuana had always been described by my Dad, just as it had been described to most kids by parents, teachers, television, and church, as one of several DRUGS each of which was addictive, would incapacitate you so you could not function normally, and you would not be able to do schoolwork and would flunk out and end up destitute and ruined. You would get hooked on it. It would turn you into a pathetic waste of a person.

All drugs were discussed as interchangeably equivalent, equally bad. Marijuana, cocaine, heroin, LSD, they were all like this. My eyes and nose told me that a pretty large cluster of the junior high student body, including the majority of people who got on and off at the same Grand Canyon Drive bus stop that I used, were apparently smoking pot fairly regularly and then going on to function in their various classrooms. They weren't flunking out. They did well enough within their home and school environments to not get in serious trouble, and time went on and none of them seemed any the worse for it, really.

Tina, Terri, Jan, and Jay decided that for my fifteenth birthday I needed to throw a party, with rock music and girls and boys from the neighborhood invited and to play spin the bottle and dance the way they'd taught me to dance. I would have to agree to wear clothes they'd pick out for me and let them fix my hair. They made up my guest list, inviting Lisa Waters and Alan Snyder and Chris Bundy and Kyle Stankowski and many other people that, if I no longer considered enemies or members of some unified Them, still weren't exactly my friends. I was amused that I was to have so little say in what was to be my own party, but I went along with it.

My parents approved. I think they were very glad to see me included in any kind of group activity. They diplomatically absented themselves for the most part, going upstairs and letting us dim the lights and put music on. I still felt somewhat as if I were being made fun of with the spin-the-bottle game or, if not me directly, then whoever was called on to kiss me. Yes I wanted this as a factor in my life but no I didn't appreciate being a spectacle by kissing Lisa Waters who was very resistant to the faintest suggestion that I was a person she'd kiss under normal circumstances.

I felt like a clown trying to dance, too. But actually, mostly people seemed to be enjoying themselves and they really did seem to be trying to include me, not just setting me up for ridicule.

I had found a book in the school library that I quickly got sucked into, a book named *Carrie* by a new author named Stephen King. In the book, Carrie, an overwhelmingly unpopular girl, is at a certain point invited to the prom. The people directly involved in inviting her actually have good intentions or at least the absence of bad ones. But a different student conspires to have her elected queen of the prom, and then dumps pig blood all over her as she's being crowned.

I had the fear that something like that could happen to me at any moment. I sensed that the people going to so much trouble to get me to dress like they dressed and to listen to their kind of music and so on, to make me one of them, had at least relatively benign intentions.

I figured that a lot of it amounted to a belief that their way of being in the world was fundamentally right, and I would make them less uncomfortable if I were pulled into it rather than kept out of it. They seemed to feel something more like exasperated frustration with me, rather than anything warmer and more fundamentally compassionate, but they seemed sincere enough about trying to "fix" me.

But as with Carrie in the book, this opened up a lot of possible opportunities for someone with a bit more malice to set me up to be made a fool of, to be laughed at. And *again* as in the book, if they did so and succeeded in humiliating me, I sensed that the others would be more likely to laugh with them than to get outraged on my behalf. Participating in all this made me feel vulnerable and I remained wary.

Jan invited some friends over for a sleepover party of her own. Terri was among those invited. The girls got a Mexican piñata and took turns being blindfolded and whacking it with a stick until it broke open and spilled out all the candy. In the evening, they brought in some of our camping-trip sleeping bags and arranged them on the living room floor.

They all stayed on through part of the next day. During a lull around mid-morning when other people were taking showers or talking on the phone, Terri Bond and I ended up being the only people in the living room. I began teasing her about how they should have invited me to participate in the sleepover portion of the party. Terri said "dream on" and then stuck her feet down into one of the sleeping bags, then lay down and zipped herself up in it.

I kneeled down and began wrestling with her for control of the zipper and got it unzipped and behaved like I was going to get into the sleeping bag with her. Suddenly she stopped giggling and struggling and just lay very still. *What's she doing? What does she want me to do, is she inviting me to go ahead and do exactly that? Does she actually like me or is she going to giggle about me to her friends later on? Where's this going?* I got flustered and let go and backed away from her.

Our church participated in an interdenominational youth workshop on adolescence and sexuality, which gave us several topics to discuss and an opportunity to ask personal questions anonymously by writing them down on slips of paper and adding them to a question box.

I thought about Denise and Tavia and Terri. I didn't know how to make anything start happening with Tavia, who was my own age. The other girls, with whom things *had* happened or seemed like they *might* happen, were just turning twelve or thirteen, and there was a definite attitude among parents that girls that age were too young to be dating yet. Meanwhile, lots of girls my own age were with boys who were older, in high school already.

I wrote: "People say girls mature faster than boys. If this is true, how can I get involved with someone at my own level when I'm just fifteen?"

When the advisor got to my question, he read it out loud. My face felt hot; I was self-conscious, thinking everyone would know who had written it. "Well," he said, glancing around, "it's important, at your age, to take safety precautions when you meet boys, especially older boys. Always have them meet your parents. If he's a nice person and genuinely interested in you, he'll understand why that's important. And don't be afraid to ask your folks their opinion of him." I wasn't about to correct him and explain that the question had come from me.

Denise Spears came over to visit. She and Jan were cooking supper for everyone. I parked myself at the dining room table, far enough away to not be considered underfoot but close enough to be social. "Now we need to goosh this sauce up with the broccoli and the cheese," said Jan.

"Eww, it's more than a bit gooey," said Denise. Giggles.

I glanced from my vantage point and chimed in: "Ooh, *yummy* paste!"

Denise put her hand on her hip and said boys who were going to get their delights from icky things needed to grow up. "Yeah," I pretended to agree, "because girls don't deal with any icky things."

Denise and Jan exchanged a glance and Denise said "Not that *you'd* know anything about, at any rate."

I raised my eyebrow. "Really? I'm surprised that *you* do."

She returned my glance. "Oh, believe me, I do."

Following dinner, the three of us went downstairs to Jan's room, chatting about parents and their unfair curfews and house rules. After a little while, Jan stared at me and sighed. "Denise and me are tired and we're going to lay down on my bed and take a nap." My cue to leave.

"Well, I'm not actually sleepy," Denise countered. "I'll lay down with you, but you don't have to chase Derek out, do you?"

To my amazement, Jan conceded. "Fine, but he can't get on the bed with us. If he wants to lie down on the floor and wait, I don't care."

So there I was, on the floor next to the side of the bed that Denise was resting on. She reached down over the side of the bed and we held hands for a while. Then I figured I had a girl's hand and what had worked for Terri with me might be fun from the other end of the experience, so I slipped her fingers under the edge of my pants and waited.

She positioned herself carefully to get a better angle without Jan seeing what she was doing and then slid her hand down inside. I was fully aroused and erect, and soon I was fully aroused and erect and in her hand. But with her arm already awkwardly extended there was no way to really do anything more. After a while Denise decided to try rolling off the bed and onto me, which was quite nice except that Jan woke up and asked what the hell was going on. Denise said that she fell off the bed, and that was pretty much the end of that for the time being.

One day Jan did not show up for supper. "Where's Jan? Go down to her room and tell her supper's getting cold," my mom said. I went downstairs but she was nowhere to be found. My mom was angry at her for going out without telling us where she was going and for how long, and ruining supper. Anger turned to concern when the Bond parents called to ask if we knew where Terri was. My folks were in between calls to other parents of Jan's friends when the phone rang and Mrs. Bond told us that Lisa Waters' parents reported that she was also missing. Enough things were missing from their rooms that they decided that the girls had run away together, destination unknown. The police were called and phone calls were made to nearby relatives.

I was worried too. What would happen to her? Where could she have gone? There was nothing useful I could do and I mostly felt like I was in everyone's way. By breakfast time the next morning, something had happened at the Bond house, and we were waiting to hear details.

It turned out the three girls had hitched across the state to where Terri's aunt lived, and they had hoped to stay there but it had not worked out as planned. They had gone to the police station to report themselves as runaways. The police had let them call Mrs. Bond but said the girls could not stay at the station while waiting for someone to come pick them up. Mrs. Bond had then said she would instruct Terri to break a window so they could get arrested, if that's what it took. They let them stay. By midday the girls had been brought back to Los Alamos, debriefed by the local police, and were being grilled and yelled at by parents in various houses.

Our church pastor Jake Scully came to our house to talk to our family as a whole about what had happened and why it had happened.

My parents sat together on the sofa, Reverend Scully took the tall-back red leather chair, I plopped down on an ottoman, and Jan perched on the fireplace hearth. "So, Miss Jan, I hear you took off on an unadvertised vacation," Scully began. "Got your family a bit upset, but you know all that. They'll survive. Tonight I'm more interested in knowing how it came about that our little bird flew the coop."

"Jan probably misses Valdosta, where she was more popular," my mom interposed.

"I do!" Jan confirmed. "You made me move away from all my friends." She glared at my parents.

"And when you're trying to make friends in new places, it's easy to get pulled along into what they want to do," my mom said. "But I wish you'd given some thought to how worried we'd be when you agreed to run off with Terri and that Waters girl."

My mom had given Jan an easy out, but she wasn't taking it. "No. You don't understand. That's not how it was," Jan said, scowling. Her hands gripped the edge of the bricks where she sat. "You never think I have any problems; no one ever thinks to be concerned with me. Lisa and Terri ran away with *me*."

Interesting. Wonder what's going on with her. And why doesn't she ever think she could talk to me about stuff?

My mom looked poised to speak again but Scully made a dissuading gesture. "It may seem that way sometimes, but we're all in this room because people are concerned for you," he said.

"Honey," my dad said, "I'm sorry I'm sometimes busy and I miss signs and signals I should be noticing. You know we love you, right? Even if we don't always do a good job of it?"

Jan's eyes were brimming; her mouth tightened and her cheeks flushed red. She'd always been one of those people who got even madder if being upset made her cry. She nodded, a curt acknowledgement. "But I hate it here. Everyone teases me and makes fun of me at school." She whipped her head in my direction; tears were streaming down her face now, "... *because of Derek*. They laugh at me because Derek is my brother and the whole school thinks he's a *freak*, he doesn't even *try* to fit in, and no one wants to be friends with me. They just come up to me and ask what it's like having him for a brother. And I *knew* you wouldn't understand if I said so because

38

you always take up for him; you don't care if my life is ruined."

I felt ambushed. *What the hell? No! Not here too, not at home.*

My mom and my dad were talking on top of each other before I could say anything. Jake Scully held up both hands, protesting. "Let's hold on."

I slapped the top of the coffee table and everyone quit talking. "Oh, so you get teased," I repeated back to Jan. "People pick on you. Did it ever, for one moment, occur to you to wonder what I go through every day? Do you have any idea how mean the kids are to me?" I lowered my voice to a flat snarl. "And how would you like it if...if I found you to be an embarrassment, some kind of *problem to solve*? Thanks. Nice to know I'm welcome at home." I was crying now too.

"Hey, hey, okay, this is why we're having this chat," Scully said, getting us all settled back onto our cushions and bricks. "Jan, let's start with you. What do you think your family could do differently? What do you suggest?"

Jan glanced between faces, still scowly, her tear-wetted hair clinging to her cheeks. She looked thwarted, cornered. My suffering at school was transparently worse and she was coming across as selfish and unsympathetic, and I figured she was probably realizing that. "Well, Derek could try to be more normal, like other kids," she sniffed.

"Jan, when other kids tease you about Derek, why don't you try standing up against them?" Mama suggested. "If they find they can't embarrass you, they'll leave you alone and maybe reconsider how they think of him as well."

The discussion continued on that note, with the adults defending my right to be my own person, while I claimed to be making some attempts to get along with other kids, which even Jan eventually acknowledged.

But later, when we were alone, Jan again stated that I was weird and that something was wrong with me and that everyone knew it. She said, "The other kids once asked Mama and Daddy what is wrong with you and then said that you weren't normal, and Daddy said 'We know'. So Daddy and Mama think so too. They just won't say it to your face."

In English class, assigned to write a poem, I turned in a multi-stanza rhyming poem in iambic pentameter about a guy who hears something in the basement and goes down, gets scared and convinces himself there's an actual monster down there. He runs back up and from then on ignores sounds from the basement. The English teacher really liked it and begged me to submit it to the creative writing journal of our school, which I did, and they published it.

I was in the house by myself and heard the doorbell chime. Denise Spears. "Umm, Jan isn't here at the moment, but do you want to hang out for a while?" I asked, hoping she'd say yes.

"That's okay because I actually came over to see you," she explained, smiling at me. She came in and I closed the door, which latched with a resonant chunk in the quiet room. I was feeling pretty tongue-tied; I couldn't think of anything clever to say. Denise looked a little nervous herself.

"I'm glad you came over. I like it when you're here." We hugged. After a couple moments I realized I should be acting like a host. Or at least not just staring happily at her and not saying anything. "Do you want anything, like to drink?"

"Not unless you want," she replied.

Denise was smiling shyly, eyes down. She was wearing snug jeans shorts, with the legs rolled up to make cute little leg bands. I thought about how nice it would be to get my fingers inside that denim. This was maybe my big chance, if that's what she had in mind. I wondered if she'd known that we'd have the place to ourselves when she'd decided to come over.

Maybe she did.

"I've been thinking about you and that hay ride," she said, then blushed, "and, umm, you know."

"I think about you too. And yeah..."

It wasn't like how it was with Terri, who was always sort of challenging me to do stuff. I totally trusted Denise and I knew there was no risk that she was trying to set me up for embarrassment or humiliation. But somehow it felt serious and not like playing around the way it had been on the hayride or in Jan's bedroom. "It was funny when Jan caught us on the floor that day," I said, just to have something to say.

Denise chuckled. "I know, right? Like she couldn't decide who to be mad at."

I gestured to the living room couch, and we sat there, our backs to the big window.

Denise seemed fragile and somehow younger today and I was a lot more conscious of the age difference. It felt wrong somehow to try to start making out. As if she wanted me to like her and would therefore *let* me do things whether she *wanted* to or not. It hadn't felt that way before, and maybe she was actually impatient for things to happen. But how it seemed was like we were both uncertain about what to do.

We kissed and held hands and talked on the couch for a half hour, then she said she'd better be heading home.

Later that week, I rode by Denise Spears's place a couple of times and finally stopped and knocked on the door, hoping to catch her in. Her dad, Bill Spears, opened the door and did not seem particularly friendly or happy to see me although we knew each other from church. He suggested that it was more appropriate for me to call ahead and make a date rather than showing up unannounced, and I apologized. He called Denise out and we talked a little while, but she said she had homework she had to finish and could not go out. Mr. Spears was friendlier after having made his point and offered me a soda or coffee, and then after a short time I told Denise that it was nice seeing her and we said bye and I left.

The Singing of Canaries

Tenth grade started with a shorter bus ride, a new campus (high school), and an important new class: choir. A couple times over the years, in elementary school or church, there had been girls who sang together in harmony, and it had always sounded beautiful and made me feel left out, as if boys were too crude to be able to do something as delicate and sensitive as choral music. There had never been many opportunities for boys to sing music that was divided into voice parts like that. I had sung a couple times in the summers with the adult choir in church though, and I could read music and stay on my own part's pitch pretty good. So I had signed up for choir when I saw it was offered at the high school level.

I had band fourth period, then lunch, then choir. Band was more of the same familiar scene. Director Greg MacEvoy would come in, thwack the music stand with his baton, pass out sheet music. The French horn parts were still dull and redundant. I was once again sitting with Jeremy Michaels and Tom Land. Drilling on the music until we got the notes right. Getting yelled at as a section or as an entire band for doing things wrong or sloppy.

Choir was different right from the start. Maybe it's because there's something more personal about making music with your own voice instead of through an instrument, but I think mostly it was our choir director, Andrew Olson. He talked a whole lot more about the type of sound he wanted from us, and about attitude toward the music and nearly everything he said was emotionally supportive, finding things to praise or to point out as worthy of reflection or celebration as musicians.

One thing that came with being a high school student was open campus rights. We were considered old enough to leave the high school campus at will. It was our responsibility to get ourselves to classes on time. We could go across the street and shop in stores during our lunch period if we wanted or, for those students who had cars, perhaps drive off and do errands elsewhere. Smoking was not allowed on campus but students who smoked could cross the street and smoke off-campus. A student who wanted to take fewer than a full roster of classes was not required to sign up for a study hall but could instead just leave the period open and not have to be anywhere in particular during that hour. Spectacular! We were finally being treated somewhat like actual people.

There was a new girl on our block. Next door to where Jay Schirmer lived were the Blacks, an older couple. There had never been anyone close to my age living there before, but now suddenly there was a girl, often standing outside on the sidewalk with a cigarette in her hand. I'd seen her there a couple times and then one day she waved at me to come over.

"Hi, I'm Gail Clinton. What are you looking at? You checking me out? No, don't be like that; it's okay. How old are you? Yeah? That's cool. I'm fifteen too." She nodded toward the Blacks' house. "That's my uncle. I don't think he likes me very much. I'm a lot of things he doesn't approve of. Can't blame him, really." She rolled her eyes, then smiled a weird giddy sort of cross-eyed smile. "Does it bother you if I smoke? Thanks. Want one? You don't smoke? Okay that's cool." She took a couple of puffs. "I got busted for not going to school. My mom couldn't handle it. I mean things were getting pretty bad at home. I thought I could do better on my own, you know? But then I got it for being a runaway, too young to leave legally, and they put me in juvie. I nearly got raped by two security guards but I was getting my period and it freaked them totally the fuck out. Good thing because they had me pinned down."

Our front door opened and my mom summoned me for supper. "Nice meeting you, Derek. Catch you around, okay?" I smiled and waved.

I would see her from time to time after that and we always fell into conversation. She seemed to like talking to me. I hardly ever saw her with anyone else. She didn't seem to make friends with the other people on our block. She had a boyfriend, Tommy, who lived uptown in Los Alamos proper, and I met him eventually when he came by to visit. She seemed very blasé about him. She'd do things like be on the phone with him in the Blacks' living room (having invited me in) and would hold the phone away from her ear and roll her eyes and smile as if she were amused by him and didn't take him very seriously.

"One time I was sure I was pregnant, I mean really fucking sure. Sorry, you don't mind if I cuss do you?" Gail winced.

I made a waving-off gesture. *Doesn't bother me.*

"I didn't have my period for shit, man, three months even, and then one day I was going down the walkway and it was icy and I slipped and grabbed the rail but I went over hard like this because I couldn't stop sliding." She leaned over her arm, which she tucked hard into her gut, "...and later that night I finally got my period and it was..." She took a drag on her cigarette. "...chicks' periods they aren't all the same. I'm sorry if this grosses you out or anything but it wasn't like it usually starts out. It had more stuff in it, and I think that was it, that I knocked something loose in there and I had a miscarry and wasn't pregnant any more."

Gail invited me, along with her friends Margie Peak and Ann Cavaglia and Tommy, to her Sweet Sixteen party. We went ice skating. Someone offered me a cigarette and I took it. I puffed on it. Later I accepted another and this time Gail saw me with it and said "You're not doing it right, you're not getting anything." She showed me how to pull a little bit of smoke into my mouth and then after I'd gotten it there to inhale it. The nicotine hit me like a fireball. I got pleasantly dizzy, my body felt nicely different. It was intoxicating. *Wow! All my life, people have told me about how cigarettes are not good for you and also about how they are addictive, but they sort of left out the part about how nice nicotine makes you feel.*

Over the next few weeks, Jay and Alan Snyder and others were surprised when I accepted a smoke when someone offered cigarettes from a pack. It went a long way toward convincing them that I'd loosened up and joined my own generation and was no longer a square and a representative of the parental generation and the school establishment and so on. I was a rulebreaker now because with rare exceptions no one's parents wanted them smoking.

The neighborhood changed. The Bond family moved to Texas and we said goodbye to Tina and Terri. At Cumbres, Jan was starting her eighth grade year and had new friends she spent time with. She wasn't unfriendly with the people on our block but she had broken up with Jay Schirmer, and with Tina and Terri gone there was less of that sense of a cluster of neighborhood kids.

Jan had straightened out and was doing well in math and also in sports, where she played on intramural teams. She was tall and strong and had far better aim than I ever did. She took up a band instrument also, the oboe. We didn't interact as much but when we did it was less hostile. Jan was amused to see me taking up habits and hanging out with the crowd she used to, now that she was not doing those things.

I started listening to rock music more of my own accord. I borrowed some albums from Jay and recorded them on our family's reel-to-reel tape recorder. I borrowed some from Gail too, and Jan had a couple of albums, one of which was *Fragile* by Yes, which I had become quite fond of so I recorded that one also.

Deavers wanted to see the scouts make advancements in rank. He started going over each scout's record of what he had earned and what he needed in order to progress, and what the troop as a whole was deficient in. Our troop had become a solid group of camp-proficient and outdoors-capable scouts and we usually did well in intertroop competitions.

I got my Star Scout rank and continued to earn merit badges. I was mostly accepted among the scouts, although there were times when I felt odd among them.

One evening a bunch of us were staying up late around the campfire. Bill Young told a joke about a priest and a nun stranded in the desert with a dead camel, and the two of them deciding they'd like to see the opposite sex naked at least once before they died. The nun points at the priest's penis and asks what it's for and he says "It gives life," and she says "Well, put it in the camel so we can get out of this damn place." It was a cute enough joke but from there the other boys started telling increasingly dirty jokes about sex and sluts and prostitutes. Jack Thompson asked me if I knew any to tell. I said I didn't. "Big shocker," he replied and the other boys laughed.

Deavers would sometimes come over when I was by myself, like when I'd finished putting my cooking stuff away and was sitting around reading, and urge me to go spend more time with the other scouts, but I wasn't sure that letting them learn more about me and get to know me better was such a good idea. They liked me okay now and no one was picking on me.

Our church youth group decided to participate in a regional retreat that would be attended by similar youth groups from all over the state. This took place at a retreat lodge called Glorieta Assembly. We had communal motel space with three or four people per room, and one of the people I drew as a roommate was Terry Scully, the preacher's kid. We were unpacking our suitcases and bags. Terry paused, then announced to us all, "Listen, you guys, now, you all got to promise me you won't laugh at my underwear."

Then he displayed a pair and they were neither jockey shorts nor boxers like mine but instead... "Yeah, I wear bikini underwear," he confessed.

Of course I was tuned into the conversation because I'd received my share of teasing about my own undies. Terry was a person who was far more relaxed and confident and the notion that he too wore an unconventional choice had me watching how much better he handled the issue in front of other people than I did. I saw how he defused it by drawing attention to it himself and virtually making sure we *would* laugh by extracting such solemn assertions that we wouldn't.

But aside from that, I liked his choice itself. I didn't really want to wear what all the other guys were wearing—jockey shorts just reminded me too much of sports and athletes—but I wasn't liking boxer shorts so much as I got older. They don't have any support and they make lines if you're wearing snug jeans. I had never disliked my own body. In fact I was secretly rather vain about it, both my body and my face, even if I did not at all resemble the cultural image of what a "cute boy" or a "sexy man" should look like. I might have been skinny but I thought I had a nice shape and was inclined to want to wear clothes that showed it off, not baggy clumpy clothes that hid the body.

So...bikini underwear, huh? I associated bikini underwear with girls. With sexy girls. With girls being photographed or displayed specifically to be looked at appreciatively. The idea of that applying to *me*, if I were to wear that... Why *shouldn't* my body be sexy? That such underwear was produced and sold for guys to wear made it authentic. And if Terry could do it, so could I. I couldn't be laughed at any more than I was already. I filed all this away for future shopping and then unpacked and went out to see what events were taking place where.

I discovered that Tavia Wycliff was attending. She must have been a member of the Los Alamos congregation, the First Methodist on the hill. I went to discussion groups and music groups and hung out with various clusters of people but all the while I kept an eye out for Tavia and hoped to end up in groups with her, to have a chance to talk with her and get to know her. Unfortunately, she didn't show up in any of the groups I'd selected to attend.

Still, the people attending from Los Alamos all knew each other. And when it was time to drive back, we departed together, so I ended up in a car immediately behind the one in which she rode. The radio was on and a silly song was playing on the radio, the singer telling a girl she was sexy enough to make him believe in miracles.

So I took out a sheet of paper and a magic marker and inked the radio station frequency along with "Dedicated to Tavia Wycliff" and stuck it in the dashboard window. The people in the vehicle in front of us saw it and saw me pointing and waving, and laughed and got Tavia's attention and she read it and laughed too.

This continued, with all the people in our car getting in on it with each new song being dedicated to someone else in the car up ahead and the people in our car discussing who was the best person to dedicate each song to. Well, I'd finally found a way to tease and send hints to Tavia, if she had any inclination to read between the lines and realize the initial salute had come from me to her... and that maybe I was trying to tell her something.

Although my main musical interest these days was choir, I had been taking piano lessons since first grade. My piano teachers found me frustrating because I learned by ear and they wanted me to depend on the written music. But my method worked for me. I took out Rachmaninoff's C# minor prelude and began to pick it out. Although it took a long time for me to decipher the sheet music and memorize the notes, the actual things my fingers had to do to make those beautiful sounds were not much more difficult than what I had been playing before. Once I had plowed through it a few times sight-reading, I was playing it by ear and wasn't actually reading the sheet music when I was playing it.

I continued to hang out with Gail Clinton, especially in the evening. These days I was buying my own cigarettes. I had chosen Viceroy as my brand (not wanting to smoke what everyone else was smoking, of course) and I limited myself to exactly four cigarettes per day. I figured even if I got addicted I would not be damaging my health too much at a rate of four per day. After supper was one of my primary times for a smoke so I'd step outside the house and would generally meet up with Gail, who would often be outside for a smoke herself.

I threw my *own* Sweet Sixteen party when I became sixteen and invited Gail and her friends plus Jay Schirmer and my sister, and we went bowling. As with the Bonds and Jay and the local neighborhood crowd I had hung out with the previous year, I think Gail's friends probably found me naive and strange and still more than a little bit square. Nevertheless, they had not known me back when I was so much more of an adult-centric self-righteous prig, and they seemed to accept me.

Gail continued to talk to me about all kinds of things in her care-worn sultry jaded way. She seemed lonely; it felt as if she'd long been ill-treated, and she sought me out and drew me into her orbit. I was her confidant, whether she expected me to understand and relate to all that she was telling me or just wanted someone to be there to listen.

I didn't think she and her boyfriend were all that close, and I daydreamed and fantasized quite a bit that she would get upset with him or otherwise dismiss him from her life and, thus free of her arrangement with him, select me. And introduce me to sex. And let me take care of her. I could love her and be tender with her and make up for all the bad things that had happened to her already in her life.

One day she called me over and explained that she was running away, right then and there, and needed my help. Mr. Black was too strict and did not care for her and she had to get out of this house and strike out on her own. I agreed and went with her and since she was worried about the police already looking for her as a runaway, I made a phone call for her to her boyfriend Tommy. She was nervous and worried and I chose a place (parking lot of a church fairly far from our neighborhood and deserted this time of night) for us to hide in until Tommy could get there in his car.

Tommy rolled into the church parking lot with a crunch of gravel, his lights already off. "C'mon, I don't like this place," he hissed.

"Well, where are you taking me? We need to figure some stuff out," Gail shot back. They argued about where she should go and could go.

"Well," I interjected, "I should get back, I guess. Good luck, okay?"

"No, don't leave," Gail told me.

"Dude, umm... Derek, right? We may need your help to get some stuff out of my apartment. If I go, they may already be waiting for me," Tommy added. So I climbed into the back seat, shoving empty beer cans out of the way.

We were on Diamond Drive headed back down away from Barranca Mesa when the police lights went on behind us and we were pulled over and all taken down to the police station. I expected to be in deep trouble of some sort with the police and with my parents, but they came to get me and I was released without comment. Although my parents said all this had hurt Mr. Black who had tried to make a home for Gail, they didn't stay upset with me about it.

I never saw Gail Clinton again.

Someone else had disappeared from the edges of my life while I wasn't paying attention. Denise Spears did not come around anymore. I did not see her at church and eventually I asked around and was told that she was staying with an aunt and attending school there for the time being.

One day, after asking me and making sure I was "cool" with it, Jay Schirmer and Bob Diaz took out rolling papers and a baggie of crumbly greenish ochre stuff and rolled a joint and lit it up in front of me. They took turns inhaling deeply and then trying to hold in the smoke without coughing. I watched them for obvious and compelling changes but mostly they simply became sort of sardonically amused, as if they found something to be absurd. Even after watching them "take drugs," as my folks would have put it, so that I knew for sure they were under the influence of the stuff, they didn't seem greatly changed. They could still have conversations, make plans, walk, ride motorcycles, have coherent conversations with adults who said hello...

A few iterations later, I was hanging out with Jay and Alan Snyder and Lisa Waters and Candy Humphrey from a few blocks over, and someone mentioned that Alan's girlfriend Chris Bundy was coming and had pot for us to smoke. She showed up and brought it out, apologizing for it smelling like perfume because she had kept it in an empty perfume bottle. They put it in a small metal pipe and lit it and passed it around. When Jay finished taking a hit, he found me looking at him and asked if I wanted some. I nodded. It didn't go unnoticed.

Chris Bundy said, "You smoke pot now? That's cool. I thought you were too straight to be hanging out with a bunch of heads like us."

Someone else said, "Far out, man." I was given basic instructions: Inhale it straight in—don't puff and then inhale as you would a cigarette. Then hold it in as long as you can. I took a deep hit and it made me feel like coughing but I managed not to. In due course the pipe made its way back around and I took a second hit, this time coughing my brains out. I wasn't the only one. The perfume had gotten into the stuff and apparently made it chokingly harsh for the others too. I waited for something to happen, for something to change the way that drinking a beer or even smoking a cigarette would have an impact on you, but nothing happened. After a while we dispersed and went back to our homes for supper.

After that, whenever it was being passed around I would smoke pot along with everyone else. Sometimes it was in the form of a joint, and sometimes it was smoked in a pipe. Whatever the mechanism, I found that marijuana didn't actually DO anything. Or if it did, it was very subtle. I decided this must be some really spectacular in-joke: that this substance, so demonized and feared and rendered illegal, did not actually have any significant effect at all.

I was waiting for the bus in the morning at the bus stop when Bob Diaz and Alan Snyder waved me over to their van and asked if I wanted a ride to school. I got in. Once we were out of White Rock and on the road, they lit up a pipe and passed it around. The van began climbing the hill and I found myself daydreaming. A very very long time later I realized I was still in the van and we weren't there yet. School must have started already; what happened? I said "How far we how long has it been?" *Whoa that wasn't right.* "For school. What time now is it?" I managed.

The others glanced at me, looked at each other, and then pronounced, "You're stoned." I remembered I was in a van. I was going to school and it was a long time ago and I was still here. *Oh boy. I am stoned.* The vibrations from the wheels were inside my head like a machine, droning and drumming against the walls, suspended on a long cable attached to the middle of my brain and spinning heavily around. I remembered *I am in school today. I have to get back to that. We are in the parking lot. When you leave the van it stays behind in the parking lot and I have to be somewhere. I need a somewhere. I don't remember a good somewhere and I have canaries in my head cheerful chirping while the vibrations are still thrumming against the walls rumbling against my head. Oh boy. I am stoned and school. I can't with that rumbling wombus wombus brumbling wombus in my head, not with that canaries. Kill the canaire, kill the canaire, kill the canary wombus. Thrummm. Oh boy. Stoned. I guess that works. This is stoned. Whoa.*

I was, at this time in my life, seeking new experiences, seeking new meaning to things. My old worldview, which had developed and then sort of ossified into a stubborn stodginess between third and eighth grade, was now being thoroughly questioned. I was trying to loosen up and catch up on the fun I'd been missing.

It did not take me long to decide that getting formidably stoned just before first period, and facing high school classrooms as my introductory venture into the world of the pot-altered was *not* a good idea. But I had not expected anything to actually happen. It was not like this was the first time I had tried pot. My judgment wasn't excellent overall but I would not have smoked my first bowl as preparation for history class, and when I had tried it under safer and less volatile circumstances the weedy stuff had seemed toothlessly benign. And yet although I had gotten off to an awkward start with marijuana, I wasn't averse to maybe trying it again. Cautiously.

Some kind of very linear and very right-angle-cornered thinking in my head had just gotten bent. Everyday things had seemed unfamiliar and new and different, if not so much so that I could not recognize them. My own unthinking automatic everyday familiar reaction to things had been suspended, if not quite to the point that I couldn't remember how I would normally behave. It wasn't like alcohol. I had familiarity with alcohol. Drink beer, wine, or spirits and you get cheerfully giddy, silly, happy, a bit dizzy. But the world doesn't become any more fascinating. Marijuana made the external world around me and my own internal mental world definitely more fascinating. Dramatic. Potentially darker and more ominous but also chockfull of portent and promise. Yeah, I would try this again.

My dad had taken Jan and me out to teach us the basics of how to drive when I was fifteen and she was thirteen. First he had taken us out in the Pontiac and gone down a rutted dirt road and had us each take the wheel and (slowly) steer around the tight corners and aim the big car, operating brake and gas pedal, inching along at no more than five miles per hour. Later he had taken us out in the Datsun and had us practice starting off from stationary then going through the sequence of gears, bringing the car up to thirty-five or forty mph in fourth gear. It was fun and was a wonderful feeling of power and control to operate the machine and be in motion.

Now at sixteen I took and passed my written exam and practical exam behind the wheel and got a full-fledged driver's license from the State of New Mexico.

I knew where the Wycliff's house was located, and one day I gathered my courage and drove over there. After sitting behind the steering wheel for a few minutes, I got out and knocked and asked if Tavia was around. She came to the door and I asked if she was involved with someone, and if not would she go out with me sometime. Tavia smiled kindly and said that she did have a boyfriend at the moment but thanked me for the invite. We chatted briefly and (at least on my part) awkwardly for a few more moments and then I took my leave.

I hadn't really dared get my hopes up very high, and now instead of being disappointed and depressed about it, I actually felt elated that I had at least managed to make the effort and ask her. I figured most guys in my position would have managed to bump into her and get to talking to her at school. But short of following her around all day long it seemed that I'd never encounter her without other students around and that intimidated me.

I worked odd jobs occasionally to earn extra money, most commonly either mowing folks' lawns or babysitting. I was pretty conscientious and tried to do a good job whenever I was hired, and I had always gotten along with young kids pretty well. My parents kept an ear out for people looking for help in either capacity (Jan also did work of this nature) and it was the kind of work where customers are usually repeat customers.

I came into the choir room early. A cluster of sopranos and altos and a couple of guys were standing around the piano, chattering, and I joined them.

"... work so hard on something that's just going to sound like noise." Kate, one of the altos, was saying.

Luisa shook her head. "I've learned a lot from music I didn't originally think I was going to like."

"Are you talking about that Daniel Pinkham thing?" I asked. I was already on record as thinking Pinkham's *In the Beginning of Creation* was deliberately silly.

"No, that new piece," said Tavia. "*All the Ways of a Man*, with those strange chords and the spoken parts in the middle. What do you think of it, Derek? Too weird for you?"

"Oh...it's kind of winning me over. I admit I thought it was another one like the Pinkham piece, but it's got these delicate shimmery parts where the notes of the chord just sort of step down, and it floats. It's odd but very pretty. I like it."

Twice during the second semester we saw letters to our director Andrew Olson taped to the door for the whole world to read. One from Greg MacEvoy (head of the music department and director of the symphonic band) said something akin to "Dear Mr. Olson, in contrast to what you said, I did place those orders in a timely fashion. I'd like to remind you that your allocation sheets have not been received and you are holding up the process on your end." One from a parent said, "Andrew Olson—I was here for our appointment. I waited for you. Where were you?"

I didn't read much into the content of the letters so much as the public way in which they had been posted. He had an office and presumably a telephone and an inter-office mailbox like every other teacher. It was really rare to see teachers speak ill of other teachers and not common for parents to openly imply dissatisfaction with a teacher where students could see it occur. Apparently our director Andrew Olson was stepping on someone's toes.

The second time I got high on marijuana was down the street at Bob Diaz's house. *After* school this time. We smoked a bowl from his pipe and he introduced me to a new album by the German group Kraftwerk, *Autobahn*, giving me headphones to hear it really well and turning the TV to a channel showing motocross races. The album's main side is all one long track and contains compelling electronic sound effects that evoke the impression of high speed highway driving.

Under the effects of marijuana, I found the music powerfully vivid and I also found myself astonished and fascinated by the synesthesia of what I was seeing and what I was hearing. I could not get past the impression that the TV was visually interpreting the music or that the sound was coming from the TV channel, which was somehow broadcasting prolonged footage of motorcycle racing set to interesting music. Every few minutes I'd recall that the music was definitely from the new album and that record albums did not send signals to TV sets to create visual impressions, so how was this happening?

Afterwards, I went on over to our house. My parents weren't home yet and Jan was doing something in her room so I turned on the television and lay down on the couch. I have no recollection what I watched, but the shape of the TV set itself kept representing itself to me as a shape abstraction, as if its sides had no texture or features but instead existed as translucent red mathematical planes that would stretch at will, deepening to become a glowing cube four or five feet deep front to back then snapping back to conventional dimensions. I was hungry so I got some pretzels from the kitchen and the taste of the pretzels (delicious and very satisfying) was the same taste as the color of the deep brown wood paneling in the room, which all smelled like pot smoke and was very warm and cozy and had sweet-sad nostalgic overtones.

Over the months to follow, I began going to parties on Friday and sometimes Saturday nights nearly every week, borrowing one of the two family cars (my parents being glad I was going out and being social) and driving up the hill to the downtown section of Los Alamos. A certain parking lot was the perennial planning ground for impromptu parties every week. "Where's the party?" people would say in greeting. Party's at American Springs. Drinker's Point. Baja. The Pines. Rendija Canyon...

I joined the throng. I got out of my car and followed the glow, entering the circle around the bonfire. As usual, someone had brought firewood sufficient to get a blaze going, and logs and branches were being dragged from the surrounding area to feed it. Someone had a pair of speakers up on the roof of their car and was blasting Led Zeppelin, probably from their tape player. Sometimes there was a keg and we'd be asked to toss in a buck or so to whoever had bought it. Tonight I'd merged my money with some from Alan Snyder and a couple other kids I didn't know by name and Alan had gotten an older guy to buy some six-packs, Stroh's for me, Bud for Alan, Coors for the others.

The smell of burning pot came to my nose and I followed it. When the curly-haired guy in the jeans jacket took a hit, he passed it on to me. "Hey, ain't you Derek Turner from Cardova's first period history? You party now, huh? Fuckin' A. Gimme five." We slapped palms. Our parties were outdoors and not on private property, so no one needed an invitation, and the people there made me feel welcome. After so many years of my being an outsider, people were including me, welcoming me, and it felt so good and right to stop holding myself aloof and separate and let myself be a part of it all.

On TV and in books and movies, authority-challenging countercultural boys were portrayed as cool, and girls apparently found them sexy. Guys like that weren't like jock boys, all belligerent and aggressive. They were peaceful and mellow, and instead of the nasty pushy approach to sex and girls, they espoused a different attitude, where girls and boys could all be joyfully free with sex. I began more and more to aspire to that kind of identity for myself.

Not only was I no longer thinking of boys entirely as *Them*, I was actually starting to think of these boys, at least, as being *Us*. The hip mellow laid-back countercultural guys.

Whenever I looked back, I didn't think of my earlier life as girl-identified so much as authority-embracing. Square. But a major shift was taking place in how I saw myself, because for the first time in my life I was embracing an image of myself that was shared by other males.

Word had really gotten out about Andrew Olson's choir. Jocks who had never participated in music tried out. All the Key Club and Phi Beta Kappa types came in droves. People whose music career had been in band or orchestra up until then auditioned for choir, and more than a small handful dropped band to be in choir. Jeremy Michaels and I were among them. Jeremy was placed in the bass section, and once he began also showing up at pot parties we spent even more time together. We'd get stoned and then share insights and impromptu philosophies and observations, often to our mutual amusement, cracking up laughing at the world and feeling quite profound.

I was now one of the oldest and most high-ranking scouts in our Boy Scout troop, closing in on my Life Scout rank and discussing possible Eagle Scout projects with my dad. I got a telescope for Christmas, a small reflector with a set of eyepieces and extensions and little thumbwheels for fine manipulation. I learned how to read right ascension and declination and in the clear skies of New Mexico found some of the major sky objects and got them to focus. I took it with me and showed Tom and Jeremy and we stayed up playing with it in the evenings.

Tom Land was being awarded his Eagle Scout badge. I was hanging out with Jeremy outside before the ceremony started. "Look, they sent the newspaper reporters and everything. We should have made our own award so this doesn't all go to his head," said Jeremy.

I nodded, amenable, and we walked around the building until Jeremy spotted a speckled feather from a large bird. "Perfect. Now, let's find some ribbon or something. Oh, good, here's a blank index card."

We stood at attention and gave the salute with the other scouts during the ceremony, then after the congratulators thinned out a bit, we accosted Tom. "Here. We felt you haven't been sufficiently honored, so we're awarding you the rank of Turkey Scout." Jeremy handed him the adorned feather with the card.

"Oh, you guys, you goofy idiots!" Tom laughed, shaking his head.

In my own scouting career, I had started reading the handbook and picking out obscure merit badges that were hardly ever seen on local sashes, and I would call the local council for a list of area people who were certified to pass someone on them. In this fashion, I got merit badges for bookbinding, for beekeeping, for gardening, and so forth. Although I was one year younger than Brad Williamson and Reggie Brand, the senior patrol leader, I was treated as one of the old hands in scouting and was especially renowned for my cooking on campouts.

At the end of the year, there was prom, and I was encouraged by my family to invite someone to go to it. Jan and my mom took me shopping and when they had finished with me I was the reluctant owner of a pale peach leisure suit and a gaudy printed nylon shirt with big wide shirt cuffs designed to stick out past the leisure suit coat. I didn't have anyone in mind to invite except Tavia Wycliff but I'd already explored that option. In fact, although it had been the best year of my life since as far back as I could remember, a time of optimism and fun and the virtual end of being a picked-upon outsider, the one thing that had not developed was any kind of a girlfriend relationship.

I was confident that it would happen, that I would meet a hip and sophisticated girl in school or at one of the weekend parties and things would begin to get started, but it had not happened so far this year. Jeremy Michaels suggested Luisa Velez, from choir: "I've seen her looking at you. Maybe she thinks you're hot." I hadn't noticed anything of the sort, but I called her and asked if she would be interested, and she agreed.

Luisa was cute and animated, with dark hair and a round face with dark eyes. We danced to the music and said hello to other students who knew one or the other of us.

She seemed to me to be sort of posing—she'd strike a posture then glance back to catch me looking at her, then smile and lower her eyes, and I thought "maybe she likes me looking at her." And I did like looking at her. She was cute and curvy, all delicious girl-shapes, and I wanted to touch her.

I asked if she wanted to go somewhere where we could sit in the car for a while, to which she was amenable. I found a good off-road location under some nice trees and we talked for a while, then tentatively kissed a few times and I put my arm around her. I didn't know if she expected or wanted to go further but she was pleasant to be with and pretty, and it made sense to try and find out.

I let my hands travel and she soon caught my wrist and put a stop to that. We swung by a soda fountain called Peterson's for a dessert and coffee and then I took her home. I called her later in the week to see if she would like to hang out but she wasn't enthusiastic and said she had to study.

I heard later from Jeremy Michaels that a girl who knew Luisa told him Luisa did not want to go out with me because I was one of those boys who was only after one thing. Things like that made me more cautious about initiating anything overtly sexual with girls. It was an attitude I encountered often enough to be wary of it. I was not, after all, "only after one thing." I was totally happy to become someone's boyfriend.

YEARNING TO FLY

Junior year. In front of me in my trigonometry class there sat a new guy, Kevin James, whose family had moved in from California. He had long hair—*really* long hair, longer than any other boy at school, hanging all the way down to his shoulder blades.

Back when Tina and Terri Bond and Jay and Jan had been pressuring me to conform to the other kids' styles, I had sort of gone along with some of it with an inner exasperated eye roll, but their attempts to get me to grow my hair out had gradually sparked something. Girls had long hair. It was something I'd never contemplated for myself, something never considered as an option. I'd been resistant at first, preferring my individuality to their creepy sheep-like conformity to current fashion, but increasingly I found myself wondering what it would feel like. Not just the bangs in front and hair down to the collar like many of the boys wore, but long down the back like many of the girls had. In the name of fairness, why couldn't I, if I wanted? My dad would be furious but...after I graduated and moved away...maybe.

My dad called me aside and informed me that my grandfather's old Pontiac could be mine if I could earn and save $500 to pay my grandmother for it. I began looking for an after-school job. I saw a sign at the Taco Bell that they were looking for help, and I applied and was accepted.

Starting the next Saturday, I went in and was walked through the routine. "These items are bean items and all sell for forty cents. Beef items are more. Memorize the prices. Here's how you make a tostada; here's how to make a burrito. *Dip, fold, fold, wrap, wrap, done.* Here is how you do the cash register, repeat back the order, listing each item and the quantity while jotting them down on the overhead for the steam line workers to read. At the end of the sentence you should know the total for the order. Count change back: cents, dimes, quarters to the next dollar, dollars and fives to the amount they gave you. Wish them a good day then say 'Hello may I help you' to the next person. If you're on steam, by the time the person on cash register repeats back the order and price you'd better be handing it forward to the delivery window."

I enjoyed the work, I felt good about the food itself (I liked Taco Bell), and the boss treated me well. Unfortunately I wasn't fast enough to suit him. I was better on cash register than steam but I sometimes became flustered during rush hour if someone gave me a long order. After a week of it, he thanked me for trying and wished me luck but said he could not keep me on.

I think my dad was decently impressed that I had found the job opening on my own and had made the attempt. He might have called in a favor on my behalf or he might simply have asked around and heard through his own networks about anyone looking to hire a high school student. Either way he told me Peterson's Pharmacy, which was linked to the soda fountain and was directly across the street from the high school, was looking for a worker.

I went in and spoke with the proprietor, Ronald Peterson, a somewhat sour curmudgeon whose entire staff except for his mom consisted of kids like me. My job would involve stocking shelves ("Antacids along here, as soon as it's not flush to the front of the shelf, grab at least two, never just one, from the box in back and fill them up flush. If you have an extra lay it down over the top..."), running the cash register, sweeping the floor, emptying the trash from the bathrooms ("These ladies, sometimes they leave a 'tamale'. You gotta make sure it isn't smearing the can, okay..."), and sweeping the parking lot with the big push broom.

In the early fall, my dad ran for and won a local political election for municipal judge. The municipal judge is the person who handles traffic cases, things like barking dogs and ordinance violations, and is also empowered to marry people who want a civil service.

One effect this had on my life was that in order to eliminate any possible appearance of favoritism, the local police kept an unusually sharp eye on my driving habits. At Peterson's Pharmacy, I worked until after ten one night and afterwards got into the car to drive home. Diamond Drive was totally deserted and I rolled through the stop sign to make the turn at walking speed and got ticketed for running a stop sign.

Recurrent draconian enforcement of motor vehicles laws, including speeding less than five mph over the posted limit, left me with a rebellious attitude that was probably already predicated by my outlaw status as a marijuana smoker and underage drinker. It increased my impression of authority as a bad model and law enforcement as a problematic practice overall. Meanwhile, the posted speed limits seemed ludicrously low. Cars and drivers were obviously safe at considerably faster speeds, and driving faster was more fun. The speed limits seemed to have been set with ticket revenue rather than the public good in mind.

I was spending a fair amount of time considering society and authority and the question of social order. In my lifetime career as a nonconformist I had started out identifying with the adult world and my nonconformity had consisted of wanting to be a good citizen at the expense of fitting in with other kids my age. Then I had gone through a period where I sought out the protection of enforcers of rules to protect me, as a nonconformist, from hostile kids who mistreated anyone perceived as different. Now, increasingly, I was rejecting the notion that the "right people" would necessarily end up in charge of an authoritarian system or that human behavior should be regulated by punishing those who deviate from the rules.

I had been introduced to rock music and marijuana because kids my age had put a lot of effort into trying to "normalize" me a bit. I had gone along with it largely because I was lonely and isolated and tired of being so polarized against everyone else my own age, but I was warmed by a pretty genuine acceptance once I'd done that much. My previous allegiance to the world of teachers and parents had been seen as an allegiance to rule enforcement.

I was also aware that there were certain cultural associations between rock music, marijuana smoking, long-haired guys, and questioning authority. I decided to learn more about the philosophies and beliefs of the social movement that had swept all this in. I went to the library to read up on "hippies." I found and read books like Charles Reich's *The Greening of America* and Lewis Yablonsky's *The Hippie Trip*. I read books about people who had lived on communes, about California in the late 1960s, the antiwar movement, the counterculture, and anything else I could get my hands on, and I began clarifying my own thoughts on the matter as I read.

"Hey, Squeaky Clean," Jeremy shouted through the car window of the rusty 1965 GTO. "Dude. Check it out! This is my new ride."

"Hey yourself. Not bad. Moves on its own power and everything."

"This is a cool car. It's got class. Like me. Everyone who sees it will say 'Oh baby, I wish I could be like Jeremy and drive such a cool car.'" He grinned, waving at me to get in.

Jeremy twisted the wheel and aimed us down the street and punched in an eight-track tape. I'd never heard anything quite like it, delicate eerie stuff that was overwhelmingly powerful at the same time, awesome sounds. "What's that music you put on? "

"Pink Floyd. Speakers sound great, don't they?"

My own tastes in rock were developing. I was finding that I liked what at that time was called "album rock" or sometimes "progressive rock." They overlapped in a lot of ways with what I liked about classical music: long motifs, recurrent themes that build and are elaborated upon, complex chords, counter-themes, and textured harmonies. At the same time, most of them were starkly passionate, angry, fraught with dire warning or ominous overtones, and the overall mixture was powerful and evocative. I didn't stop listening to classical but my liking for this was genuine.

We rolled down Diamond Drive with the windows down, *Dark Side of the Moon* singing our presence as we went.

Jeremy liked to talk about girls and sex more than I did. He was more giggly-naughty about it than lewd and filthy like lots of other guys. I was kind of secretive about what I felt. "So have you ever had your hand up a girl's skirt, or down her pants yet? Did she make sounds? What color were her panties? What do you do with your dick in your pants when you get hard? I slide mine over like this." He demonstrated. "I like Melissa, from choir. When she's singing she looks so nice with her mouth open like this, it makes me get hard. Do you get hard a lot when you're in class and stuff?"

Jeremy did talk a lot about getting hard and he was kind of voyeuristic about my experiences and what it was like for me, wanting to compare notes. "Do you use baby oil or do you just spit on it when you jack off? Aww, c'mon, everyone does it."

"I was doing it before I knew what it was," I acknowledged. "I discovered it when I was, I dunno, in second grade or so. I thought it was like tickling myself or something. No, eww, I don't like to put stuff on it. It feels better dry."

"Doesn't it get sore?" he asked, making jerky pumping motions.

"No, not like that. I like to do it slow. Sometimes I use the inside of my wrists. If you were touching a girl's breast you'd be soft and gentle and make it feel good, not be trying to milk her, right?"

"Can I watch? I thought everyone did it the same way I do. C'mon, I need to learn techniques. Just show me a little bit, then you can stop."

In choir we were learning dozens of Christmas songs and cantatas, plus several simpler carols, and when Christmas rolled around we went caroling door to door in different parts of town, showing up on folks' lawns singing in eight-part harmony. We had something special, and I was part of it. In the hallways, when someone else from choir saw me, I'd get a warm smile and a wave, and when I saw a choir member I'd go over to hang out.

Once we went to the state capitol building in Santa Fe, filing in amidst the lunchtime commotion, and interspersed ourselves under the dome in clusters. One of the altos produced a pitch pipe and in moments we were humming our starting pitches. Mr. Olson gave us our cue and we opened up, bouncing the lively phrases of Da Viadana's *Exultate justi* off the marble and glass at full volume. Visitors and politicians and public employees came to a halt and stood there looking amazed, caught by surprise by the unannounced concert. After we'd performed three numbers, Olson waved us onwards and we next invaded the shopping plaza in the old historic part of town.

From then on, sometimes we'd accidentally end up somewhere in public, some assortment of members of the choir, and would pick a song and just start singing it in public on our own without Olson.

My earlier reticence about going all the way sexually was pretty much over. I figured that if the opportunity came along I'd enjoy the full experience. I was attracted so often to so many girls it was a world of perpetual promise. I'd be working at the cash register at Peterson's and a couple of girls would come in with those little middy tops that showed their lower waist and navels and, below that, jeans so tight they looked like an organic part of them. It was hard not to stare at their bodies instead of treating them like customers.

At the same time, though, Luisa Velez's feedback about my behavior had only been the most personal and direct version of something I'd been hearing in a more general way: lots of girls did not like to be with guys who only seemed interested in sex and were otherwise uninterested in the girl herself. I could easily understand how that could be. The way so many boys talked about girls, all that hostility and contempt, why would any girl want to get intimately close to that?

I had thought my own attitude toward girls would make me appealing as a boyfriend. That hadn't exactly panned out that way so far but it was still important to me to be seen and recognized for who I was. I did *not* want to be perceived as akin to those guys. Yes, I wanted sex, but I'd been wanting a girlfriend for a long time, ever since the days of Karen Grey in third grade, in fact. The thing to do, obviously, was to meet girls in a context where, if you *did* have a boyfriend-girlfriend relationship, being sexually active with each other was typical, not unusual. Where people weren't uptight about sex. The girls all looked delicious and sexually enticing, so it was mostly down to finding one who was easy to talk with and who liked me.

The pot-party scene was marked by an easy relaxed sexuality, with ongoing couple arrangements and casual sex both accepted as normal and commonplace. As I circulated and chatted, I got to learn the names and faces of the girls and figured that in this environment, where the girls apparently often hooked up with a guy just because sex felt good and they were in the mood, I'd sooner or later get lucky. Just by my being there on a regular basis, sooner or later one of the girls would realize she'd like me as a boyfriend, and things would take off from there.

"So," said Jan one evening as we were both arriving home for supper, "you're now the one who comes home smelling like smoke. It could just be that you spend your time with Jay and Chris and their smoke gets on you, but somehow I don't think so."

I nodded with a smile. "Yeah, it looks like we crisscrossed. Is it fun being the squeaky clean straight kid in the family for once?"

Jan hmmphed. "It probably would be if our parents had noticed. Well, that isn't really true. Yes. I could never be more good than my brother. When I tried, no one would notice. Now I am, and I know it even if Mama and Daddy think you're still perfect." She started to open the front door, then looked back at me. "That's not going to last, you know." I nodded again.

My parents actually weren't totally oblivious to my change in direction; they knew I smoked cigarettes and it was the subject of many arguments. I handled them mostly by refusing to engage. I would be told in no uncertain terms that I was absolutely forbidden to smoke as long as I lived in their house, and I would listen and not argue, and then I would get up from the supper table and go outside and light a smoke. I was seventeen and there was a limited amount they could really do about it.

Peterson wasn't easy to work for. Sixty seconds after a customer had paid up at the cash register, he would say he didn't understand why he was paying me to stand there with my hands in my pockets when I could be stocking the shelves. Oh, so I did that already? Well why wasn't I sweeping the floor then?

So I would sweep the floor aisles, all the while watching for customers coming in so that the cash register would not sit unattended due to my sweeping up. I'd finish and go back to the cash register and he'd say why wasn't I finding something else to do? Why didn't I show any initiative? I could be picking up garbage from the parking lot. He always acted like any employee of his was constantly looking for ways to cheat him out of the labor he had paid for, and nothing anyone did was ever really satisfactory.

At home, often while stoned, I would sit at the piano and try to create sounds like the motifs in the rock music that I liked, big bold dramatic sounds. Although I didn't really know what I was going to play until the second I played it, it felt good and I was starting to think maybe it sounded good, unless I was just so stoned that anything would sound good. My parents didn't much agree with my assessment: "Do you *have* to bang on the piano like that? Can't you play something nice, something pretty, something softer?" One day after getting stoned with Jay, I asked him to listen and he said it sounded pretty damn good.

I also discovered that I could pick out lots of existing songs. Essentially if I could "sing" them inside my head, I could play them with my fingers after a few tries to get the patterns sorted out. All those years of playing by ear (despite the efforts of piano teachers to get me not to) were paying off.

The word was out: the school system was *not* going to renew Andrew Olson's contract and this would be his last year at Los Alamos High. I couldn't believe it. It wasn't fair to him and it wasn't fair to us. I couldn't believe there were any legitimate reasons that wouldn't look silly if said out in the open. Why *wasn't* this process taking place in the open? Shouldn't decisions of this nature take place in meetings that parents, administrators, teachers, and students could all take part in and each of us speak our piece?

I got the address of the office of the superintendent. In the hallway, I found Kate and Don from choir and after a moment's discussion they decided to come with me. We all walked down Central to the superintendent's office and asked to speak to him.

He wasn't available, we were told, but we could leave a message. The receptionist offered us a pad and a pen and we wrote a letter and asked that our concerns be heard. We stated that it wasn't fair to make such decisions without airing the reasons and listening to all the viewpoints. We said that Andrew Olson had taken a typical decently good high school choir and in two years created an outstanding musical group, and that the ability to do that ought to weigh most prominently in any consideration of a choir teacher.

We never got a call back. It was simply a done deal, something that could not be fought. Andrew Olson was not happy but told us this kind of thing happens and that despite our youth it was a hard lesson but one it was important for us to learn along with choral technique. I never did learn the official reasons; I'm not sure they need any when a teacher doesn't have tenure. I guess they can just say "We decided not to renew your contract" and leave it at that.

Terminated or not, we were going to go out in style: this year it was the choir's turn to do a big trip. Our choir was going to California. We all piled into the big bus and rolled off down the highway to Albuquerque and points west.

We were put up in host family houses in Los Angeles while we performed several works such as Jean Berger's *Magnificat*, Michael Haydn's *Tenebrae Factae Sunt in A flat*, and William Schumann's *Four Canonic Choruses*, and got standing ovations. We also had a day off to ride the rides at Disneyland.

Being together on the bus all day, being bound together in the shared experience of performing our music and our pride in the quality of our musicianship, and being collectively set upon by the forces that had led to Andrew Olson's termination as choir teacher, added up to a powerful shared emotional experience. The choir was my family, had become the group of people I identified most closely with, a place I felt I was truly accepted and participated in as a full member.

Then, on the first night of our return trip to New Mexico, a sort of collective mood seemed to erupt on the bus. New couples formed before my eyes, boys and girls kissing in the seats, a bacchanalian orgy of sex and joy and fun and mutual caring. Everyone seemed to have someone new to kiss. Except me.

I sat in my seat watching all this happening all around me, feeling very left out. There were many girls in choir I found attractive, including, of course, Tavia Wycliff in the alto section, but everyone always seemed to be going steady, the girls all having boyfriends already.

But now here, on this day, it seemed like our shared emotional experiences in choir were breaking those existing connections with boys and girls back home and, whether it was only for the moment or something more permanent, our bus was following the advice of Crosby Stills and Nash's "Love the One You're With." But no one seemed interested in claiming *me* for a boyfriend.

What I felt toward someone when I was wanting an involvement with them seemed to be all serious and tender. In contrast, all the flirting behaviors I was familiar with, that I had seen other people use when they wanted to get something started or explore whether or not that was a possibility, were all about teasing and also creating an equivocation between sincere sexual overtures and pretend ones. To me, perpetually serious person that I basically was, teasing was not going to come naturally unless I already knew the person pretty well.

The bus pulled in at our motel and the cheerful choral students piled off and headed to their rooms. I was absolutely in a mood to *party*, hoping for a wild night and a chance to throw every caution to the wind, pull out all the stops. I really wanted to open the door to the possibility of something happening tonight. I wanted a good time. I sought out and found sources for alcohol and pot and became unusually loud and effusive. I drank a lot and tried to engage everyone in conversation, I was manic and fired up with the desire to be a part of things happening. If there was still an urge to find new companions to kiss and celebrate with, I wanted in on it. In fact I'd like to get laid. I was ready to not be a virgin any more.

I continued to make the rounds of the motel rooms where multiple people were hanging out in sociable clusters until finally Don Glass and Bill Delaney indicated that they really wanted to go find some coffee, and would I come along with them? Sure, good idea, caffeine means being able to stay up longer and party harder. Lead on. They didn't seem very excited or enthused as I chatted up a storm while we sat in the diner drinking several cups of coffee. When we got back they just wanted to go to their motel rooms and go to bed. I continued to try to ferret out whatever rooms exciting things might be happening in, but the activity quickly faded and vanished.

I gradually realized that Glass had been trying to sober me up with the coffee, but now I was an alert and stimulated drunk-and-stoned person looking for some action. I even glanced around at the surrounding area, briefly considering looking for some kind of action "in town" but we were pretty much away from any metropolitan area and there was nowhere to go. I went back to my room and my mood gradually collapsed into a lonely aching emptiness. The sense of connectedness to the rest of the choir seemed illusory now. I was in choir and was accepted in choir as a member of it, but not necessarily accepted by the people in choir as a person they wanted as a friend, as someone to be included. As a potential boyfriend. As a sexual possibility.

We did our final concert in Los Alamos. We belted out our numbers and put our all into it one last time for our families and relatives to hear. Then the semester—and the Olson choir—was finally over.

I started the summer, doing my usual rounds of lawn-mowing and babysitting and various other odd jobs while continuing to put in my hours at Peterson's Pharmacy.

Ronald Peterson started having me come in for full days, and ordered supplies with which to tar his building's roof. I was warned to bring clothes that I did not care about, including shoes, and something to sit down on for the drive back home to prevent getting tar all over the car seat, or else a change of clothes. "But it won't be easy to wash up in the bathroom here so you might want to wait until you get home so you don't get tar on your other clothes."

I spent many days up on top of his roof. First I swept up all the loose gravel and detritus with a broom and carried it off in buckets. Then I began dumping gooey black synthetic tar onto the roof and spreading it in a thin layer with a big shop broom. Finally he had me covering the tar with a layer of new gravel and sweeping the extraneous loose gravel and picking it up with shovels and dust pans and returning it to the gravel buckets. I was only earning the same hourly wage as I'd been receiving to work at the cash register and stocking shelves, but with the long hours I was amassing a growing bank balance and making more progress toward owning my car.

I got tar under my fingernails, in my hair, up my nose, and generally all over me. By the third week my clothes stuck to themselves and I had quite become the tar baby, squelching with every movement I made and spreading additional tar every time any part of me brushed against any surface.

I got my car when our family was back in Georgia to visit relatives. My dad agreed to front me the rest of the money and I would pay him back from my wages from the pharmacy. We got a couple of minor mechanical problems fixed and then drove back west in two cars, our family car and my own elegant Bonneville.

I took the opportunity to drive by myself a bit around town. I was, of course, curious to see what kind of acceleration the car had. I found a highway entrance and waited until it was deserted then floored it.

At first the car almost stalled. After a couple beats it decided to burn gasoline instead of drowning in it and the back of the car lowered and it took off most impressively. Yay, I had a powerful car. Felt like it needed a tune-up of some sort but if anything it felt like it might have a little bit stronger acceleration than my dad's car once it got going. I was happy with it.

Around August, we had visitors from Massachusetts. The Sorrens family had lived on the same block as my parents in Boston back when I was a baby. Their two children were the same ages as Jan and me, and we'd all played together as young children. The Sorrens had stayed in touch with my parents over the years, exchanging postcards and Christmas cards, and were currently vacationing in the western states. They stopped in to spend a couple days with us on their way back east.

Linda was fourteen, red-haired with a smattering of freckles and very cute. Although she wasn't an extroverted talkative person I found her looking at me a good portion of the time when I glanced at her. Most interesting was that even when the adults started teasing us about the possibility of us latching on to each other, as adults tend to tease their kids, she continued to look over at me and really did seem interested.

I had a lawn-mowing job so I somewhat reluctantly left and spent the afternoon shortening a neighbor's grass. I came back and hung out on the periphery of the kitchen where everyone was sitting, including Linda. After a bit, my dad needed a package of mushrooms for supper and asked me to pick it up and suggested that Linda ride along if she wanted. And she did.

Linda seated herself in the passenger's seat and I started the car and backed out of the driveway. Several blocks slipped past while I sat there in nervous anticipation: was I imagining her being interested in me?

"How long have y'all been on the road so far?" I asked.

She put her hand to her forehead and did an exaggerated eye-roll. "It hasn't been that long, really, I guess, like two weeks and a couple days, but it seems like forever. It's the way all the days are sort of the same after a while. Car prison."

"The being cooped up for so long, or the way it stays the same and you can't get away from it?"

Linda nodded. "Both, but not being able to get away from it is the worst part. I mean, I chose this, my parents didn't kidnap me or anything, but it feels like I don't get to make any choices now."

"Your vacation predestination."

She grinned. "Exactly."

There was a pause in the conversation. The car rolled past a handful of suburban blocks. I glanced at her. She was looking back, and she smiled and then glanced away. As I returned my eyes to the road, she shifted to face me more directly and it seemed like she was about to say something. I felt my face heating up like I was about to blush. Or maybe I actually was. *Oh please, don't let me act dorky.*

"Sometimes school is that way," she eventually said. "Not being able to get away."

God yes. "And feeling trapped and like you don't get to make choices," I added, nodding.

We were almost instantly comfortable and talking about aspirations and worries and factions in schools and favorite music and so on. It felt great.

After breakfast the next morning, we took the Sorrens family to see Bandelier National Monument. Together the families roamed the trails up and down the volcanic ash cliffside and in and out of the weathered and crumbling cave ruins and the reconstructed Native American great houses down below.

After a while, Linda and I slipped ahead of the others in order to be together.

"So," began Linda. Picking up where we'd left off like there'd been no interruption. "What you were saying yesterday. I *do* like boys and sometimes I wish I could say so or act like it, but it's like if I do, then that means I want to..." she rolled her eyes and pretended to be fanning herself. We giggled together.

"It's one thing to want that to happen," I said, "and another thing to be saying 'Right now, baby, let's unzip'. I hate the way everyone makes it sound, I don't know, mean, and crude."

"Yeah. Or, if you don't act interested at all, 'Oh, she's stuck up and thinks she's better than everyone else'. So you have to be really careful to be just the right way. And then it feels like you're trapped and can't get out. Predestination again."

"Or if you even stand next to someone of the opposite sex in the hallway and you talk with them, people might think it's sexual, and sometimes people don't want to be talked about like you're a couple, so they pull away from even talking to you."

"How are your parents? Do they ask a lot of the time about whether you're popular and ask who your friends are?"

I shook my head. "Not really. They just want me to *have* some friends. How about yours?"

She shrugged. "Mostly just my mom. She'll say, 'Oh, so Stacey's in your art class? Isn't she the one who asked you if you go skiing, do you talk with her between classes and go places after school and does she have a lot of friends?' And so on. She wants me to have a good social life, I guess, but it's like she's, how would you put it, it's like she's checking my Neilsen ratings."

Linda smiled. She had the cutest freckles right around the bridge of her nose. Her hair was coppery-red in the sunlight.

In contrast to all the times when I had had some interest in a girl and had found myself tongue-tied and unable to figure out how to get started, being with and talking with Linda was just effortless. We understood each other so well it was like reading each other's minds. There was no awkwardness about negotiating whether or not she was interested in me romantically, or I in her. We hadn't said a word but we both knew and we both knew the other one knew. And we couldn't stop smiling.

The next morning, while we were sitting around sipping our coffee after breakfast, my mom suggested that I drive Linda around and show her some of the local scenery. I glanced at Linda and she nodded enthusiastically, so we got into the car and I drove around and pointed out a few things as we talked. I concluded by driving down DP Road and then off onto a dirt access road to get to a point that overlooked the canyon and the neighboring mesa across the way.

I put the car in park and switched it off. "Let's get out. There's a really nice view of the canyon just up ahead."

Linda remained stationary. I assumed she was pausing to check out the scenery through the window. I also assumed she shared with me the joyous giddy delight I was feeling, my happiness at being with her like this, and with a flare of playful mischief I reached over and unlatched her seat belt, which had the added effect of bringing my hand in rather immediate proximity to her. Only then did I realize she was sitting really stiff and her formerly warm and animated face was sort of white and closed off, her lips thin, her head hunched over, not meeting my eyes.

"Hey...are you okay?"

"I guess."

I sat back on my side of the seat. "You look really worried and uncomfortable. Can you talk to me? I'm sorry if I did anything to make you feel... I've been enjoying how things have been, being able to talk to you, and I don't want to do anything that would make that go away."

She gave me a wobbly smile, "Sorry. I'm okay, I just... when you drove off onto the dirt road, I...I started thinking I had made a bad mistake. I mean we've been talking about... you know, how things are with boys and girls, and...I thought 'uh oh, now he's taking me somewhere hidden where no one can see'..."

I shook my head, no. Linda caught my reassurance and her smile firmed up. She gestured to the windshield and continued, "Then...when you said we should get out of the car..."

"Oh God. I'm so sorry. It never crossed my mind how that would be."

"I'm okay now. Really. You don't seem at all like that, it's just that I thought I'd misjudged. I...really like talking to you too. I feel safe with you. I know, that sounds silly after I just...but that's why it was so...I don't think I've ever talked with a boy this way, and it was like I forgot to pay attention to things and then all of a sudden...I'm not usually so jumpy."

"I think it's horrible that girls have to worry about things like that happening. It must be creepy, to always have that to deal with. I've seen boys being really pushy and I know stuff like that happens and it's not fair."

"It must not be very nice to have someone suspecting you would do something, either. If you want, I'll get out and you can show me what you came here to show me."

DP Road was along the edge of one of the many Los Alamos canyons, and there was a nice overlook on the side of the cliff just a few yards from where I'd parked the car. Piñon pines and cactus grew among the apricot-colored tufa rocks that spilled down from the mesa top, and a few ravens cawed from tree branches down below. We found a place on the edge of the canyon where we could continue talking, and sat down there, side by side.

Linda picked up a small stone and began turning it over in her hands, as if examining it. Looking at the rock, not at me, she said, "What you said before, 'Let's unzip baby', it's like deciding to jump from the diving board into the pool and once you've jumped you don't get to change your mind." She moved the stone to the other hand "It's like you're consenting to be assaulted or something."

I sighed and nodded. "I know." I wanted to talk about some of my own feelings that I didn't often talk about. About how it was for me. I felt self-conscious. I picked up a stone of my own. "From back when I was a kid, seeing girls... I would sometimes want to do something, touch, I don't know how to explain it, but kind of the way you feel if you're thinking of tickling someone, like there's a little bit of mischief and attack. But *playful* attack, not that nasty hateful stuff the way so many boys make it sound."

Linda said, "Girls talk about boys and what boys want to do. That boys want to do things to us, make us do things, and that boys are always desperate for it." She pitched her stone down the cliffside. It bounced and rolled and disappeared down below us. "One time I was at my friend Amy's and we stayed up late talking about what we sometimes daydream about doing to boys. So...we do it too. We think about stuff like that." She risked a glance at me and then selected another small stone. "You should be feeling *pret*-ty privileged right now. Girl secrets."

"It can be so weird when you feel something and you don't really understand what you're feeling," I said.

"Yeah. You know how so many girls when they're twelve or thirteen really get into horses? I was. They're beautiful and so powerful and it feels good to have that and to feel that close to a living animal. Anyway, sometimes when I was in the saddle it started feeling so good. Maybe that's why girls like horses a lot more than boys, I guess it wouldn't be quite as much fun for a boy."

I tossed my stone down into the canyon and watched it bounce, and selected another one. "Well, you know how boys tend to like cars so much? It's a personal space, something a guy can fix up, make it so that it's like a reflection of himself, and it's where you can bring your friends and entertain them, right? So it's like an apartment. It's home. I don't really know why so many guys like small cars with bucket seats. My car zips around as well as theirs do, but I like to imagine that if I were dating, my car is my bachelor pad, and it's comfortable to sit side by side and..." I felt my face going red, "... well, there's plenty of room."

And so we sat there throwing little stones down into the canyon, blushing, telling our truths and our confessions, revealing stuff to each other that we had never told anyone of the opposite sex and in many cases had never shared with anyone at all before.

We kept on sharing intimate feelings and stories, intermittently breaking into surprised laughter or scandalized giggles.

On the way back home, at one point she looked over at me and said "You know, what I was afraid you wanted to do back there? Well...if you said you wanted to, I would." My heart started beating harder and I wondered if she meant she wanted me to pull off somewhere else so that we could. Or if she meant that even though it wasn't something she was ready for yet, she liked me so much that if I wanted to she would anyway. I wanted to.

But we had used up our time and were expected home. She wasn't saying anything more. I wanted it to happen but not rushed and I didn't want to scare her again if I took it the wrong way. The car kept rolling and the minutes ticked and I didn't say anything or do anything and the moment passed.

I was partly convinced that I had blown an opportunity but yes, this was how it was supposed to be, how I wanted it. Linda would be on the road tomorrow morning with her family and she lived in Massachusetts so it wasn't like we could keep on seeing each other. But it felt like I had her in my life, in a very special way, and we'd always have this connection. And in the larger sense, it was reassuring that yes, it could be like this. I wanted this in my life.

Linda Sorrens was beautiful and wonderful, and no matter what else happened, other boyfriends and other girlfriends and miles and years, I would always know she was out there. We would know that we had this between us and that we would always be very special to each other. My most special secret dream had finally come true.

Endings and Beginnings

Soon, school was about to start again, and I was to be a high school senior. I had finished tarring Ronald Peterson's pharmacy building roof and was back to working on cash register one day when Peterson came behind the counter and picked up a handful of loose items in little boxes from below the counter and demanded to know what I was doing with those things. I explained that apparently they were items belonging to various cashiers who worked here, although I didn't know which boxes were whose, but that none of them was mine.

He accused me of breaking the rules and taking items out of standard inventory stock and making little stashes of them and said it was stealing from him, which was a rotten way to repay him after he had given me this job. I said I did not do that, that any time I wanted candy or other items I paid for them, that I was not a thief, and that these items he was holding were not mine and had been there a very long time.

"You're supposed to charge anything you want, and have it deducted from your paycheck. You haven't been doing that. You say you pay for things but how do I know that? I can't trust you. You're lazy and always trying to avoid doing any work but you want to get paid, and as far as I'm concerned you're stealing from me and I'm tired of it." And then he fired me.

The new choir teacher was Sidney Strassberg, a pleasant amiable man. We began learning several choral compositions. It felt strange not having Mr. Olson for choir.

One of the Boy Scouts special patches was for doing the Mile Swim. My mom, who had taught me and Jan how to swim, had all the Red Cross certifications. She was one of those people who didn't swim particularly fast but could swim tirelessly forever. Early Saturday morning, before it became crowded, we went down to the local White Rock community pool and she positioned herself at one end of the lap lanes section. "You have to do seventy-two lengths without grabbing or holding on to the sides or stopping. I'll count." Afterwards, she filled out the paperwork and I submitted it.

Linda Sorrens and I were exchanging letters. She wrote to me on Days Inn stationery while still en route home, saying she couldn't stop thinking about me, not that she was trying. I wrote to her telling her how happy I was to have met her and to have her in my life even though we lived so far apart. Some of the time when I was at the piano, I thought about her and after a while I felt like I was playing for her even though she wasn't there to hear it.

I began assembling letters of recommendation and filling out application forms for colleges. I had been interested in astronomy as far back as I could remember. It seemed like a comfortable relief to not be wondering and worrying about what I should major in, the way so many other students were doing. There weren't many astronomy programs in the US. Adams State College in Colorado was one of them, and the University of Mississippi was one. I was offered a scholarship to one school if I majored in business but I had no interest in majoring in business. My dad said I could get a scholarship simply by signing up for the ROTC at whatever college I chose. I really didn't give it much thought aside from making sure my paperwork was going out.

At home, my dad, who was always inclined to pronounce judgment on social practices he didn't approve of, condemned premarital sex and extramarital sex on a fairly regular basis. He didn't like to hear it excused as a permissible practice and didn't like to see it portrayed all the time on TV. I thought there was a bit of a mixed message, insofar as he always seemed to have an encouraging wink for either my sister or me as far as having sexual interest in the opposite sex or kissing. I guess he considered that red-blooded healthy behavior; he might tease us about it but he seemed to expect it and, if anything, to be egging us on.

But there wasn't much question that he expected us to draw the line somewhere and that somewhere was definitely on the virginal side of sexual intercourse. One evening he lectured us about how, for failure to abstain from actual sex, some girls got pregnant and their lives (and the lives of the boys they were with, at least in some cases) were ruined. I commented that there were ways of doing things that would yield sexual satisfaction without involving any risk of pregnancy and he became very angry and said, "This conversation is over. We will *not* speak any more about this at this table. Is that clear?"

I sometimes wanted to talk about sex and what was right and wrong and how I agreed or disagreed with what other folks said and thought, but home wasn't a comfortable environment for that.

I was worried about how I'd earn the rest of the money I needed to pay my dad back for my grandfather's car now that I'd lost my job, but I heard there might be an opening at the auto mechanics shop down on DP Road, Precision Imports. I went by and spoke with Darrel Mason, who ran the shop, and he said he was looking for a high school student to come in in the afternoon and sweep up the shop floor, sand down any oil spills, empty the trash cans, roll up air hoses, and do other tasks as need be. I'd get in a couple hours every day. Hours and pay were roughly equivalent to what I'd been getting at Peterson's. I had a new job.

Physics was seventh period. I sat in front of Tom Land and between two girls, Ann Hastings and Lynn Vondersee. Our first unit was optics and Mr. Hagens had us pair off with the person next to us, to experiment and record observations on the behavior of reflected light and mirrors. I was paired with Lynn Vondersee. When she did her write-up she wrote her name as "Eesrednov Nnyl." She had a sharp mind and was fun to talk to and I liked her a lot right away. I asked her if she would like to go out sometime and she smiled but said she didn't think her boyfriend would approve of that. She was really attractive to me as someone I could enjoy being with, but it looked like that wasn't likely to happen.

Linda Sorrens wrote. "How's girl hunting?" she asked. "I hope you're staying out of trouble etc. (Notice how the two connect in my mind?) You make it sound as if the entire female population of New Mexico, to put it mildly, rots. I'm happy to hear you're planning a band and I'm especially happy to hear you're sending some music this way." She indicated that she had decided she wanted to become an airline pilot.

Linda and I had never discussed being exclusive. It didn't really cross my mind to think that we should. I assumed she would date other boys in Boston. I really loved her and was fantastically happy to know she was out there and she loved me and we'd always have that, but I also wanted a girlfriend here locally, and to have more sexual experience and more fun in life.

I continued to flirt a little with Lynn Vondersee. I couldn't really help it; she was cute and intelligent and sitting next to me. One day she was half-crouched on the floor messing with a tangled strap on her book bag, and because of the angle she was leaning, her shirt hung forward. She finished wrestling with the book bag in time to catch the direction of my glance. I was looking down her neckline at her boobs. She was small and didn't find it necessary to wear a bra. I wasn't normally anywhere near as interested in boobs as most guys seemed to be, or as interested as everyone in the world seemed to assume that I would be, as if all guys were automatically totally obsessed with breasts. But...

"Umm." She flattened her shirt back against her, blushing. "Sorry, I can't blame you for that. I wasn't doing it on purpose." Lynn was quite pink and quite cute. "Listen, I've been meaning to talk to you. My sister would like for you to ask her out." I blinked. Sister?

Lynn pointed out Olivia Vondersee in the hallway. I recalled having seen Olivia before in passing but had no sense of any real interaction. I wondered how she knew me. On the one hand, I would mostly like to spend time with Lynn herself, and dating her sister didn't seem as if it would facilitate that. On the other hand, Lynn had been rather unambivalent about being in an exclusive relationship with someone else. I agreed to ask Olivia if she'd like to date me.

I called Olivia and identified myself, and asked if she would like to go out. We picked a movie to go to and then went to a diner to talk and drink coffee and get to know each other a bit. Olivia was shy and inclined to blush and look down and away a lot, and it was a bit difficult to get her talking. I did like her smile; she had a sweet smile. It was flattering to have been picked, to know that she had watched me and said to herself that she wanted to be with me. I hoped we would get more comfortable with each other and I wanted to make her happy.

Strassberg drilled the choir sufficiently well that when we performed we got all the notes right, everyone came in on their part at the right time, and we executed the appropriate changes in dynamic volume as indicated on the sheet music. We sounded pretty good. We rode to Santa Fe to perform a piece in the governor's mansion. We got a decent solid round of applause.

On the way home, on the bus, two altos who had been in choir in the previous year started singing *Tenebrae Factae Sunt* and within moments all the other singers who had been in Olson's choir joined in. The *Tenebrae* is a long, ponderously slow-moving choral piece with delicate dynamic balance and phrasing throughout. The students who were in choir for the first time this year were astonished that we still remembered how to sing it and could do a piece of that duration without a director giving us cues. We finished and we looked at each other and made our assessment: "We've lost it. It's just not the same this year. We aren't what we were."

On a regional multi-troop camporee, I was cooking for the senior tent, and the adults and senior patrol leaders from several other troops were invited. With all those scout leaders for an audience, I was showing off.

I had brought several cheeses, a little cooking sherry, and a loaf of French bread. I made a double boiler from a coffee can and a smaller aluminum pot that floated inside it on a layer of water, and in it I made cheese fondue. I melted cheeses and stirred cooking sherry into some of the cheeses and toasted little squares of the bread in a reflector oven made from aluminum foil. I also marinated squares of beef steak in a sauce made with dill and caraway seeds and paprika and garlic, and roasted it in the coals in foil envelopes and called it Hungarian goulash. I had brought sour cream and cooled it in the stream bed.

It all came out nicely and people were gratifying impressed to be eating restaurant-type food on a camping trip.

Jeremy Michaels and I made Eagle Scout around the same time. He was well thought of in the troop, both for being a knowledgeable camper and for being outrageously funny. Jeremy was insuppressible. He was always teasing me but never at all cruel with it. He'd been my friend when I first arrived in Los Alamos, when no one else wanted to be. Maybe he wasn't quite as centrally my best friend now that I actually had more social connections, but he was special to me and he made me feel like I was pretty special to him too.

We were silly together. He brought that out in me and we even had silly names for each other. I once made fun of him for his skills at being disgusting and called him Filth Monger and it stuck, and he started calling me Squeak, and those became our pet names for each other.

He wanted me to touch him, show me how I liked to touch girls. He wanted us to take turns fingering and playing with each other. When I put my arm around him, his male body felt odd there, taller than any girl I'd made out with. And thicker in the waist. It was hard to get my hand where it needed to be. He wasn't shaped exactly like I was down there either, the angle of his penis or something, it felt all different. How odd. I'd never really thought about there being variations, I guess I just assumed they were all the same.

Whenever I did it to myself, I usually looked at a magazine photo of a girl or conjured up a memory of a girl's sexy appearance, so to get started wtih Jeremy I did the same, thinking of a girl's shape within her panties and imagining touching her there. With the extra factor of Jeremy's presence, I imagined him thinking about her too and getting excited about it.

It wasn't icky. A little weird and uncomfortably personal but not icky. Being touched by someone else, rubbed to orgasm, felt nice. I'd always wanted that to happen. It was nice to be done unto for once.

After school each day I drove down Trinity to DP Road and into Precision Imports. I signed in and walked around emptying trash cans and sweeping up oil spills, using kitty litter to soak up oil where necessary, cleaning up the bathroom, putting away hoses and tools, and getting to know the mechanics and techs working there: Gene, Harvey, Mikey, Doug...

Around five PM they called it quits and went up a ladder to a hidden area above the business office where there were beanbags and low benches to sit on, and someone would light a joint or a bowl and we'd get high. They made it apparent that I was welcome to be there and join in. I liked what I saw of how they were living their lives; they worked through the day on people's cars, were paid for their skills, and at the end of the day got high with their coworkers and shot the shit, talking companionably before knocking off to go home for the evening.

I was starting to have some concerns about my intended career path. The plan called for going to college for at least four years during which I would not be economically self-sufficient, and then probably continuing in the same pattern in graduate school. I wanted to study astronomy but lately I was becoming aware that I also wanted to cut the ties of any obligation to anyone, especially my parents.

I wanted my own place, be respected for my skills (not yelled at in a derogatory manner as I had been at Peterson's Pharmacy) and basically not be under anyone's control. In college I'd be answerable to my parents for their part in paying my tuition and helping me get by, to the college itself, to the Air Force if I got into ROTC, and I'd be living in a dormitory room. Somehow these auto mechanics seemed to be closer to the kind of earthy and warm easygoing fun life that I was finding myself drawn to than what I imagined was waiting for me as a professional person or a college student studying to become one.

I pushed the door to my locker closed and felt it clang shut, hoisted my textbooks and had my mind on my impending math class when a hand gripped my shoulder and pushed me back. "You want to stay the fuck away from my sister." It was a beefy red-haired guy with acne. I didn't recall ever seeing him before.

"That would be easier if I knew who your sister was," I piped back, trying to ignore the clenching in my stomach.

"I'm Gavin O'Brien, and I'm Lori's brother. Don't go talking to her. She doesn't like you."

Lori O'Brien...yeah, I'd heard that name spoken, called during attendance or when papers were being handed back. I tried to remember any occasion when I'd spoken to Lori O'Brien and couldn't come up with anything. "I don't think I've ever spoken with her, but whether I do or don't, that's between me and her. If she doesn't want me talking to her all she needs to do is tell me so herself," I continued, hating the way my voice was shaking.

Gavin slammed the surface of my locker door, open-handed, making a loud bang. "You stay away from her or I'll fuck you up." Then he strode away, leaving me staring, perplexed.

That evening, I recounted the event to Jan. "I know that girl and she's not delicate or anything. If you *did* talk to her and she didn't want you to, she'd say so. He's got no business telling you to stay away from her. I'll go up to him and tell him to stay away from my *brother*," she threatened. Jan was taking my side; it felt good to have her there.

Jan and I were both in high school this year and we became closer than we had been in many years. A lot of the nastiness and sibling quarreling fell by the wayside. We shared an amused perspective on our parents' attitudes and behaviors and we began backing each other up in our interactions with them.

By this time Jan was involved with a guy named Jeff Maloney, who came over to our house a good portion of the time, the two of them keeping company in the living room. She was less involved in sports than she had been at Cumbres but was focused more on her classes, and she was making good grades everywhere and excelling in math. She told me her theme song these days was Chicago's "Taking Care of Business" and it did seem to me that Jan really was blossoming as an efficient and confident person who had figured out how to take care of business.

The Lori O'Brien mystery was partly cleared up for me when I walked into the choir room and realized one of the sopranos gathered around the piano was probably her. A similar cluster had been there last week before class started and I'd asked if anyone knew whether All-State auditions had been scheduled yet. So yeah, I guess in that sense I had "spoken to" Lori. I wondered whether it was Lori herself who had felt affronted or if she'd mentioned it for some reason to her brother Gavin and he'd conjured it in his head into some sort of creepy intrusive sexual advance or something.

I continued to write letters to Linda Sorrens, and she continued to write back to me. As I'd promised I would, I turned on the old reel-to-reel tape recorder and made a recording of myself playing the piano while thinking of Linda. I listened to it both stoned and unstoned and although it was a bit directionless at times and rather stumbly overall, there was a sort of wistful but powerful musical theme wending its way through it, a mood created. I transferred it to cassette tape and mailed it to her.

Meanwhile, Olivia Vondersee wanted to be with me, to be my girlfriend, to have me as her boyfriend. This was what I'd been craving for a long long time. Coming off the cusp of my brief experience with Linda Sorrens, I wanted that excitement, that joy of connection, the thrill of togetherness and intimacy and trust, to open up to each other and share and be close.

Unfortunately, I didn't seem to be able to forge that with Olivia. When I'd ask her to talk to me about things she wondered about, secret things that were important to her and so on, she'd get that shy face and say something very brief and noncommittal. And when I talked about myself, my own aspirations and confusions and other personal matters, Olivia would find something supportive or encouraging to say, but she never related what I said to anything similar from her own experience.

"Do you like to...touch, and be touched?" I asked Olivia.

"I don't care," she answered with her downcast eyes and her little smile.

I wanted sexual activity, and I hoped that it was part of what Olivia wanted and expected with me when she initiated this relationship via having her sister ask me to ask her out. I wasn't sure. It was possible she wanted a boyfriend to be intimate with in other ways but wasn't ready for much overtly sexual stuff. It was difficult drawing her out. I was hoping to recreate the close personal rapport I had had with Linda, but Olivia was quiet and remained reticent.

What did she want from me, really? I kept probing with questions, and I tried to be gentle and make her feel safe. I wanted her to feel like she could tell me anything. I wanted her to share personal material. Mostly things were not progressing very rapidly. So, well, I was hoping maybe she hungered for sexual things and wanted that in a relationship. I sure did.

We found safe and sufficiently isolated places to park and we kissed (so far, so good, she seemed to like that) and a little at a time I began touching her body. She was mostly passive but did lean her body against mine in a way that facilitated access. And she didn't pull away or protest or stop me. Now and then I asked "Is this okay?" and a couple of times reiterated "You don't have to do anything you don't want." I was being self-protective at least as much as I was being considerate. I didn't want to risk being accused of being pushy about sex, I *hated* that, and I didn't want to be thought of that way.

She was far from overt about confirming that she wanted this but as best as I could tell, she did. She felt good under my fingertips. The anticipation of going a little farther and then getting there aroused me, excited me. Soon I had my fingers where they wanted to be. I actually hadn't done this since Terri Bond in the guest room several years ago, and on that occasion as soon as I got to that point she scampered off to the bathroom to tell my sister what had happened. Now I could linger there and imagine what Olivia was feeling, try to tell from her reactions what was working.

By our third or fourth make-out session, I had learned what worked, or she had become more reactive to what I was doing, or both. I loved feeling her get wet, and I could feel her arch and hear her breathing change. I loved the heat of her, the slipperiness of her. I felt her go into shuddery little spasms and then her body sort of collapsed real warm and soft against me.

I still wondered if she was okay with this happening. I'd read about girls lonely enough, wanting to be in a relationship badly enough, that they would participate in sexual activities as the price tag for having a boyfriend even if sex-play wasn't something they wanted.

Well, I wanted sex to be in my life and Olivia had signed on to be my girlfriend and I was liking this. I really wished we had better verbal rapport and that I knew more fully what she thought and what she felt, but I liked what we did have, the making out and the hugging and kissing, the warmth of holding her and the deliciousness of her body and feeling her sexual response.

I began taking auto mechanics a lot more seriously now that I had my own car. The guys at Precision Imports taught me a little bit, I learned a little bit from other people who had cars and worked on them a bit, and I read up on things. I replaced the spark plugs and wires and the rotor assembly and points, and set the gaps and ignition timing. I paid for a carburetor tune-up. Soon it was running much better, responding without that annoying initial deadness when I first floored the gas pedal. My status as car owner made me feel even more at home working at Precision Imports.

Chip Deavers, the Scoutmaster, called me aside. "I'm going to honor these five merit badges you submitted. You'll receive them and you'll get your bronze palm for getting them, but these are the *last* merit badges I'm going to recognize if you persist in going off on your own to get them. Merit badges should be earned as a group activity. You should be earning the same ones as the other scouts in the troop."

This struck me as a very odd sentiment. What, wasn't it a *good* thing that I had the initiative to seek out things that caught my interest? I felt just the opposite, that it was a bad idea to run all the scouts through a merit badge factory, spoon-feeding everyone the accomplishments and answers one step at a time and then everyone has the same badges.

We argued a bit. The merit badges were not the only thing he was unhappy about. "I know the kind of people you spend your time with. Boy Scouts is no place for people who use illegal drugs. I don't want you bringing any of that element into my troop." Which I didn't, I never brought marijuana to any scout function. But I could sort of see his point, if that's what was actually bothering him. I knew I wasn't a vector for introducing the younger scouts to pot smoking but he couldn't know that with any confidence.

But he went on. The marijuana was not the only thing bothering him either. "What was that, with your Mile Swim, what kind of nonsense is that? You should be doing Mile Swim with the troop, when we got to it, and what did you do instead? You went to your *mommy*. What is this, Cub Scouts? Boy Scouts have no business going to their mothers to get certified for badges and awards. And while I'm at it, what were you thinking on that camping trip, cooking that, what was it, cheese fondue? That is *not* appropriate food for boys to eat on a camping trip. That is *not* Boy Scout food. You may think this is all some kind of game and you can just do as you want, but Scouting plays a role in helping boys grow up to be men. Frankly, I don't think you belong here."

I resented it a bit and felt a bit hurt by it, but mostly it struck me as just a weird, surreal conversation. The only part of it that made a bit of sense to me was the concern about me being a pothead, but I wasn't the only one in the scout troop who smoked weed by any means. This was 1977 and nearly half of the students in junior high and high school were at least intermittent smokers of marijuana. And it really didn't seem to be what he was upset about. He'd brought it up and then almost immediately shifted focus. It was all like, "You aren't one of the regular guys and you are bad for my troop." Okay, fine. He could have his troop. I was on the verge of outgrowing Boy Scouts anyway. Time to let some younger scouts take over and run things.

Jeremy Michaels and I double-dated for Spring Formal and we dressed in silly clothes (I put on that peach-colored leisure suit my mom had inflicted on me) and took our respective girlfriends to the dance. Jeremy took Lisa Monson and I went with Olivia. We ate together as a foursome at Steaksmith in Santa Fe and then split up to go parking in our respective cars.

I played around the outside of Olivia's underpants with my thumb. The other side of my hand nested in the seams of her unbuttoned jeans. I nudged, nudged, felt her swell and soften and the cotton panel fabric slowly got damp.

Touching Olivia was silky joy, so yummy and delicate and so floaty-timeless. But later, after I felt her shiver and gasp, after we dozed in warm hugginess, I was still excited and full of unrelieved skin hungers. It was always nonreciprocal. I felt that if Olivia was self-conscious and shy about talking about sex but still wanted it, that was one thing, but her shyness meant I was the one doing things, and while I was doing for her, she never touched me the same way. Not at the same time and not after and not at totally different times. She just never sought to touch me erotically. I occasionally tried doing the Terri Bond thing and putting her hand in the appropriate region and hoping she'd go exploring but she didn't.

It was frustrating: touching her, playing with her, was something I very much wanted to do, and doing it aroused me; and that made me crave being touched in return.

It wasn't that I needed someone else's help in order to come—I'd discovered masturbation on my own long before I knew anyone else had such feelings, and I was quite accomplished at making myself feel good. But it felt so normal to want to share in both directions, to expect that, so for her to *not* want to felt like something was wrong. Why didn't she want to do things to me and make me feel things? It made me wonder if I was really attractive to her or if it was different for her. I didn't understand and she either couldn't or wouldn't explain.

On our dates we went parking on several little dirt roads and turnoffs, but I never took her to the place on DP Road where I'd been with Linda.

In so many ways I was spending my senior year waiting for it to end. It wasn't turning out to be a *bad* year but I was impatient to be away to college. I thought of Los Alamos as a small insulated backwater town dominated by the Los Alamos Scientific Laboratory. I wanted to be on the cutting edge of social change, part of the wave of cultural awareness that had started back in the 1960s. I had read extensively about LSD and how it really opened up the mind and enabled people to transcend their everyday existence to see visionary truths and get insights and attain higher consciousness. I wanted to go tripping.

And I wanted an adult relationship, a girlfriend, someone cool and countercultural and sexually active. I wanted to become a nonvirgin and fall in love and be with someone who wanted to share and talk intimately and freely as I had with Linda Sorrens. Maybe an artist girl all tall and skinny with a cat and an easel, who would talk to me about her aspirations and tell me her life story and would want to have sex with me and then study together. I wanted friends, counterculture friends maybe all of us living together off-campus in a commune, cooking together and plastering posters all over our walls and dropping acid and playing rock music together and talking politics and society and ethics and stuff.

I formally opted to attend the University of Mississippi in the fall. I figured that despite the obvious reputation of the deep South, times had obviously changed. Heck, if Los Alamos, the place where the country's nuclear weapons are developed, is a pot-partying town, no doubt the counterculture I was seeking was well-established in any university setting. Everyone knows colleges are the hotbed of radicalism and free thought and experimentation.

In fact, this way I could feel like I was playing a role in the transformation of society, being part of the final vanguard of hippie folk to uproot old cobwebby social ideas instead of going someplace where all that had already been done. The philosophies and social perspectives of the counterculture as described in the books I'd read were so compelling to me I was sure the only reason they weren't in the news all the time was that they were no longer much of a surprise. Just like the way no one was horrified in Los Alamos that half the kids smoked pot fairly regularly. The transformation of society along countercultural lines was deeply in process and taken for granted, no longer generating much antipathy.

We seniors dressed in the green gowns and put on the square mortarboard hats with the tassels, listened to the speeches, and then took turns getting up out of the little folding chairs and filing up onto the outdoor stage to receive our diploma. Then it was off to the Dome for graduation party. Another big bonfire, rock music, pot, beer, and triumphant celebration. I was a high school graduate. *Life can finally begin. I'm ready.*

PART TWO
LIMBO

ESCAPE VELOCITY

Troop 122 traditionally planned a camping trip especially for new Eagle scouts. Jeremy and I decided to sit it out and go on our own trip to Yellowstone National Park. I wasn't feeling welcome or included in the troop any more and Jeremy was annoyed that the trip wasn't planned by the scouts but by the adult leaders instead.

On our first night in, Jeremy asked about my girlfriend Olivia and wanted blow-by-blow details about what we did when we parked. Then he wanted to fool around again. He wanted me to touch him and then once we had gotten started he wanted me to take him into my mouth. I'd never done that and it didn't appeal to me. I didn't really like the way his body smelled. Especially there. I thought maybe once I got started it wouldn't bother me, but when I tried it, it was pretty awful and after a moment I said, "I can't."

I was actually annoyed with the way he never seemed to stop to wonder if maybe I wasn't into this. Strange to be annoyed with Jeremy, but seriously he could be a bit selfish sometimes.

We went in eight miles the first day and set up camp for the evening. It was summertime but there were still snowdrifts everywhere, and it was surprisingly cold. We were wearing nylon windbreakers and light sweaters, and would have needed more if we had not been walking. The meadows and trees and rocks were exotically different from New Mexico backcountry landscape. Everything seemed to be on a slightly bigger scale.

On our third night in, it snowed nearly fourteen inches and was still coming down when we woke up in the morning. We decided we should get out of there and come in from the other end, because trying to hike unfamiliar trails in a snowstorm was not a good idea. We descended and made our way out and drove to the other end of our planned route and did the trail in reverse order. In the middle of the fifth night our campsite was visited by black bears trying to get to our food supplies (which were tied up between three trees, safely out of bear-reach) and we saw lots of beautiful valleys and some spectacular waterfalls.

It was August. My densely packed car was aimed east. My dad came along to share in the driving and soon we were rolling down I-40. I was headed for college.

I was a late-edition hippie. I believed in communal living. I believed in free love. I believed I would live to see the money system (capitalism, free market, the use of currency, the economy as we know it) abandoned and left to fall into obsolescence. I believed I would live to see the dismantling of nations and the end of the enforcement of laws. The Establishment represented the last gasps of some fossilized older way of seeing things that was now being supplanted by fresh hopeful optimistic ideas whose time had come. The fresh ideas seemed to have mostly been explained and promoted by the folks between my parents' generation and my own.

I was jealous of the kids who had come along ten years before me. But I felt I had contributions to make. And perhaps here in the deep South there was still work to be done. Heck, I'd probably have felt like a latecomer who had made no meaningful contribution if I'd gone to, say, California for example.

My dad and I stopped off at the home of family friends, the Rawlings: Bob and Marcia and their three kids Bobby and Sharon and Cathy. The Rawlings adults promised my dad they'd keep an eye on me and be available if I needed anything.

I was on the ninth floor of Stockard Hall, a high-rise dormitory building. I'd have a roommate, but I had arrived first. I chose the left half of the room and began unpacking my stuff. I proudly unpacked and displayed my array of homemade pot pipes like museum pieces on the shelves of my study carrel. *This hippie is claiming this pad, dig?* I put my clothes in my closet and in my drawers and made my bed and set up books in my bookcase and stashed my empty suitcases and boxes. Set up my stereo and speakers. Filled my water pipe with water and weed, put on some Manfred Mann's Earth Band and lit up. New life new freshman new day. Fantastic.

"Boy, you in the hands of the devil," pronounced Robert my roommate when he came in and saw my marijuana paraphernalia. He set up his own personal items, including an eight-track player into which he inserted his one and only eight-track cartridge, Fleetwood Mac's *Rumors*. By the third or fifth listen I was liking several of the tracks. By the thirteenth or seventeenth I was pretty insistent that we needed to listen to something from my collection for a while. I put on Pink Floyd's *A Nice Pair*.

Robert made it plain that if he was lucky the two of us would not be saddled with each other. He had done the rotations for early pledge week and hoped to be accepted into a fraternity. He said he'd be able to date because each fraternity was paired with a sorority and the system made sure you'd always have dates, and they'd help him study. I knew something about fraternities: they made you humiliate yourself during the pledge process, essentially begging to be found cool enough to be allowed in. I couldn't imagine any group that I'd ever want to be a part of expecting their membership candidates to be remotely willing to put up with that. And weren't fraternities from, like, 1963 or something?

I went to the Rawlings' for supper, and it got surreal in a hurry. Bobby Rawlings said the Christian blessing before we were to eat, and his sister Sharon asked, "If Elvis were here, he would like this food, wouldn't he?"

Mom Marcia Rawlings replied, "I'm sure he would."

Sharon steepled her hands again in the prayer position and asked God to take special care of Elvis and also let him know that we had food and would share it with him if he were to come by and be in need of food. Bobby and Marcia and Bob Sr. all bowed their heads and added their prayers for the special blessings that needed to descend upon Elvis Presley.

After dinner I slipped outside out the front door for a cigarette and Cathy also slipped out and said not to freak out too much about the family's Elvis obsession. She asked if I smoked pot and when I acknowledged that I did, she said she did too. So did her boyfriend. She complained that her folks did not like her to dress the way she did, but she had to in order to keep her boyfriend interested. "They're kind of old-fashioned. Stuck in the past. Like the rest of this town."

I had a course in German, a review course in trigonometry as prep for calculus and differential equations, an English course, and Air Force ROTC. The trig teacher was teaching the same material I'd had in high school, but not as well. In the Air Force course we had to stand at attention for long periods and they warned us that sometimes people faint and fall over from standing at attention for long periods. Oh, and they told me I had to be clean-shaven and get my hair cut so it did not touch the collar. I hadn't shaved since I left Los Alamos and wanted to grow my hair out long. I wasn't happy.

I saw signs for an event called a fall mixer, a place to meet new and returning students. I wanted to hurry up and get my social life off the ground, so I showed up in my best embroidered jeans and plaid cotton shirt. Over half of the other guys who showed up were wearing actual suits and ties and a significant portion of the others were dressed up all preppy. The girls were attired in dresses and skirts and tailored suits, lots of pantyhose and high heels, some sandals, no one in jeans and t-shirt or equivalent. I wandered in and around and tried to get into conversations.

I finally got into a rambling chat with a girl who didn't look quite so much like an ad for *College Fashion Weekly*, something about cat people versus dog people. We talked for two or three minutes and I got her first name and she asked if I had any of the same teachers I'd had last year and I explained that I was "a lowly freshman" and hence had not been here last year. She identified herself as a sophomore. One of her friends called her over from across the room but I hoped to run into her again.

It was a nice sunny early autumn day so instead of staying cooped up in my dorm room I sprawled out comfortably on the grassy lawn in front of our building to study. After about ten minutes a tall student in shirt and vest called out, "Hey, what's wrong with you, you trying to make our campus disreputable? If you want to lie down, go to your room. People sitting on the grass, that looks trashy." *Seriously?* At Los Alamos High, students had always been on the lawn studying when weather permitted. And playing Frisbee and so on.

I got up in a huff and stalked off into downtown Oxford, where I managed to find some countercultural establishments. There was an actual head shop, with rolling papers and Freak Brothers comic books and pot pipes and t-shirts and stuff, and there was a movie theater that showed avant garde films. I started spending a lot of time hanging out down there. I bought a marijuana leaf beaded necklace and defiantly wore it everywhere. I met the two guys who ran the film theater and enjoyed having some folks I was comfortable talking to.

Outside the library, I saw a girl in a blue skirt who looked familiar, and I realized she was the girl I'd met and spoken with at the fall mixer. I waved and said "Hi." She looked at me rather blankly, repositioning her textbooks against her hip.

"You were saying the dog people always have to feel needed," I prompted. "I'm Derek."

"Oh. The freshman. I remember. I'm Cathy. Well, I have to get to class but it was nice to see you again." She was cordial but didn't seem very interested. Maybe my being a freshman really did matter to her.

Fraternity and sorority rush was in full swing, with little booths and tables and chairs set up all over the place, and free flowing beer. Everyone seemed to be doing the rounds. I gravitated toward the few guys I ran into in our building who didn't seem to desire to pledge a fraternity. I discovered there was a term for us: God damned independents, or GDI. My roommate Robert claimed that sorority girls really won't date any guy who isn't in a fraternity. And that independent girls are kind of rare.

One thing was for sure: these Mississippi kids might shy away from marijuana as the devil's herb but they weren't averse to an alcohol-based party. In fact, they acted like they had never before in their lives had the opportunity to get this close to beer. On Saturday and Sunday mornings the dorm elevators were full of puke, and unconscious guys were draped over the floors in the lobby and in the halls and in the bathrooms.

Mississippi was a "3.2 state" meaning the beer that could be sold was limited to 3.2 percent alcohol by volume (very watery beer) and no distilled spirits could be purchased. I had mostly switched to marijuana because the available beer was pretty awful.

Robert was successful in his campaign to get into a fraternity and moved out, so I had the place to myself. I could now have someone over and would have privacy if I could ever find anyone I would want to invite in, and who would dare to date a freshman GDI who was in the hands of the devil and all that.

The October sun wasn't up yet, but I was. The dormitory tower heaters were roasting me and I couldn't get a comfortable position on my mattress so I hurled the covers away irritably and grabbed my robe and turned on the light. I read a couple of pages in the German textbook but I'd missed class twice and hadn't studied and kept having to flip back trying to find where the vocabulary or grammar had been introduced. I started out wanting to get it over with but I couldn't make myself care. None of this shit mattered.

This wasn't how things were supposed to be. Somewhere out there, people were connecting, talking into the late hours about relevant issues and ideas, loving, creating, challenging oppression, being real. And I was supposed to be a part of it and instead here I was in my student-cell, drudging away at schoolwork that had nothing to do with me and my life. I closed the textbook with a slap and wished I had something to read. Something to do. Somewhere to go. I clicked the light off and lay flat on the bed staring blindly at the wall. Eventually I drifted off to sleep. When the alarm rang I punched it off and stayed there, finally drowsy and comfortable. Across campus, my German class met without me once again.

My days were a blur of indistinguishable morose self-pitying blahs and I needed to get away, go somewhere, get out. Leave. I went out to the parking lot and sat behind the wheel of my car trying to think of somewhere to go, then impatiently cranked it. The big engine caught immediately and purred and thrummed. I slipped it into reverse and eased out of my parking space, then into drive and out and away, already feeling better. Who needs a destination?

I chose roadways and highways and county routes at random, sometimes chuffing along as if looking for a business or a turnoff, sometimes sailing around curves and through countryside pretending I was a space alien surveying the terrains of this odd planet. I found a long unpaved white-gravel road and as I roared down its slow easy curves, the back wheels ground and slid like a motorboat cutting through water and I fed it more gas. Faster, faster, faster, the speedometer shimmying at the far end, blasting toward escape velocity.

"Since you like Pink Floyd, you're going to like this," Joe Honegger predicted, passing me the album cover. Alan Parsons Project, it said, with a robot on what looked like an escalator or a ramp. "He was their sound engineer on *Dark Side of the Moon* and he's trying to merge classical and rock."

I went back to talking about my situation. "I thought Los Alamos was a special kind of environment, you know, small town, dominated by the nuclear weapons lab, so I was expecting the rest of the world to be more... you know, further along. I thought everything was changing. If a critical mass of people sees things a new way, it's unstoppable. I thought once I was on my own and out of Los Alamos I'd hook up with people who saw where things were headed and I could be part of the change."

"Hang on, I have to change the film reel," he said. He and Andy McManis were running Oxford's downtown alternative movie house. I took another hit on the pipe while he snapped the big reel into place on the second projector. "Yeah, I think it is changing, but hey this is Mississippi. It may not be 1964 anymore but..."

"Right," Andy chimed in between coughs. "It's at least 1967. Except here in Oxford where it's 1932."

Joe shook his head. "1832. I think it made it to 1906 once but it's been rolling backwards." I laughed but I also winced. This is where I chose to come? Well, at least I'd found a tiny enclave of people I could smoke pot with and discuss such things. Was that going to be enough?

"I really want to go acid tripping," I confessed. "I've read so much about it and I know it probably won't really be quite, you know, like a religious ecstasy event, but I need to try it." Neither Joe nor Andy had any experience or knew where to find it locally. "Maybe up in Memphis. That's probably your best bet of anything in this part of the country."

"Also," I continued, "I was expecting to meet someone. Girls. I don't mean just to get laid, although that would be nice. I was expecting to get into a relationship. All the girls I've met on campus though, it's like they stepped out of my mom's photo album from when she was in college."

They both laughed. "Women come here to look for marriage and support for the rest of their lives. That's not the only kind of women around, but the others are hard to find and they don't like being here because they don't fit in any more than you do."

There was a home football game coming up. I kept hearing people shout out a weird school cheer: "Hotty totty, gosh almighty, who the hell are we? Flim flam, bim bam, Ole Miss by damn." The campus bookstore sold t-shirts reading "Hot dogs, football, apple pie and Ole Miss." The team mascot was a Rebel, a confederate soldier wielding a sword, and he was on display everywhere.

I had essentially dropped out without explicitly planning to. I had first stopped attending ROTC classes, then German, and then after a couple of weeks I wasn't attending any of the others either. I didn't know what I was doing here.

Why on earth had I thought it would be a good idea to go to the University of Mississippi? To join the Air Force for a scholarship? To tie myself to what looked like a decade of financial dependence on my parents? To live in this stuffy old-fashioned place and never meet any girls until I graduate eons from now with an advanced degree making me a professional, since there are no jobs for people with a bachelor's degree in astronomy (they aren't going to pay you to look at the stars), learning lots of math and physics (yeah *that's* a real good fit for my talents and interests)? So that when I finally get a professional degree, after, of course, repaying my debt to the Air Force by doing a stint of active service for a year or two (oh yeah, military me, for sure) maybe some stuffy well-dressed girl will marry me if I support her financially, and then she'll let me do it to her. Sure, this is the life for me?

Oh please. Where are the communes? Where are the other hippies? Where are the clever free-lovin' organic hippie chicks playing guitar and doing artwork and stuff? I thought back to where I'd been and what I'd been doing just months ago. The place I'd felt most at home was working at Precision Imports. Those guys didn't waste years and years living like this. They might not be rich but they could afford their own places to live and they had good happy lives. No one bossed them around. They were independent and lived by their skills and basically did what they wanted to do.

I didn't need a lot of money. I did need self-determination and freedom to be who I was. Somehow I had coasted on an outdated plan for my future that had ceased to have anything to do with me a long time ago. I should have just told my folks I wanted to be an auto mechanic instead.

I made the drive to Overton Square in Memphis. I had a fair amount of money on me and some fliers and maps, and coasted smoothly into Memphis and found a place to park in the downtown area. The people I saw on the street looked interesting and some of the businesses looked hip and cool, for sure, but I wasn't at all certain about what to do now that I was here.

An animated guy with a goatee caught my eye and asked what I was looking for. I blurted out something about higher consciousness and hippies and peace and love and brotherhood. He began giving me a lecture, that What it was About was dead presidents, the kind that are printed on our currency, and how the important thing in life was to get a good hustle going.

After a while I detached from him and found someone else who seemed to be presenting himself as a guru, and tried to engage him in conversation. He neither ratified many of my sentiments nor contradicted me. Dissatisfied with the interaction, I wandered back to the goateed fellow and steered him toward the guru and asked the latter for his opinion of the sentiments voiced by the former and finally got a good debate going. The guru fellow wasn't as enamored of the flower children of the sixties as I was but rejected the materialism and emphasized connectedness and having people to care about. I was almost unbearably lonely for this kind of philosophical discussion and got a great deal of pleasure from the exchange.

Later I asked about acid and was steered toward some people hanging out in front of a coffee house sort of establishment. I hung out on the fringes of that group and eventually inquired, but no one knew anyone who had any to sell.

I left, got in my car, and headed back to Oxford. Overton Square looked like a major improvement over the University of Mississippi, but I couldn't just relocate there and it wasn't like there was a hippie underground railroad waiting to whisk refugees like me to safe communes somewhere.

"I want to drop out. I'm really sorry because I know I said this was where I wanted to go, but this was a bad mistake and I want to come home."

My dad replied that I should stick it out until the end of the semester *and then* maybe withdraw if I still felt it was what I wanted to do.

"I haven't been attending classes. I don't think continuing would accomplish anything. I'm not going to start attending classes now, and I really don't want to be here."

My parents tried to convince me that I could catch up on the work I had missed. I prevailed eventually. In early November of 1977 I was withdrawn in mid-semester from the University of Mississippi. My dad came out to share the driving to get me and my stuff back home.

Back in Los Alamos, my parents were pretty quick to sit me down and query me for an alternative plan of action. I explained my thinking. I wanted a trade, something where I could work at a very wide range of places and eventually be my own boss, one that would not take long years to acquire the training and skills. I wanted to become economically independent as soon as possible. I didn't care about a large income, just a sufficient one. And the specific example I'd seen that I liked, from what I'd observed, was the life of an auto mechanic.

My folks weren't exactly happy about it but they were willing to support me in it if it was what I wanted. We began doing some inquiries about what training programs were available for auto mechanics.

Olivia was still in town, and we began spending time together again. She expressed a strong opinion for once: she wasn't happy that I had dropped out and didn't think much of my new plans. She said she definitely thought of me as very smart and thought I really wanted to be an astronomer and she saw this as an abdication of my dreams.

Our family had always been one for togetherness around the supper table, no TV, everyone present and accounted for, opportunity to talk. My sister and my mom were discussing a sewing project she was involved in. "I don't like the new way of doing zigzag anchor points. I know it's faster but I don't want them to tear, and the old way feels more solid," Jan said.

My mom nodded. "If you have the time to put them in, that's true. But modern thread is stronger. That's why they say to use the easier method."

My dad chimed in, "That newer thread is stronger because it's full of synthetics, which means it also wants to tie itself up in knots every damn time there's any slack. Give me plain cotton thread any time. *If* you can find it anywhere. All the stores want to carry is that synthetic snarly stuff and I hate it."

"You feel that way because you embroider, so your thread is loose, but on the sewing machine it's under tension and it doesn't tangle anywhere near as bad as you make out that it does."

My dad dissented. "I don't spend a lot of time using the sewing machine, that's true, but I do on occasion. My mother was a professional seamstress, you might recall, and everyone in our family knew how to use a sewing machine, including my dad."

At this point I admitted, "I don't, actually. I'm decently good with a needle and thread, sewing by hand, fixing loose seams and reattaching buttons, and sometimes I even switch zippers out of old jeans when they derail in my new ones, but I've never cut out a pattern and made my own clothes or anything."

"Well, since you're not in school and have plenty of free time, I'll teach you how," my mom offered. I was amenable.

My mom dissuaded me from pants, saying they were spectacularly difficult and absolutely not the thing to start out with, so I picked out a shirt pattern from the ones she showed me. "Now, this pattern is intended for a knit sweater. If we measure you carefully you can still use it to make a regular shirt if you don't mind a slipover shirt." I nodded; that would be fine with me. Then we examined the bolts of fabric and I latched onto a bright bold red and gold paisley. "Are you sure? You usually wear very subdued clothes. And whenever we've gotten you more colorful and showy clothes you've resisted wearing them, like that leisure suit."

I grimaced. "The leisure suit isn't colorful and vivid. It's pastel. It's peach! And it looks ridiculous, like all leisure suits."

"Well, if you think you'd wear it," she said doubtfully. I thought I would indeed wear it if it came out and fit well. I tended to wear boring clothes mostly because I didn't often see alternatives I liked, not because I liked to be in drab colors all the time.

I pinned and cut the fabric and did most of the sewing. My mom did take over for one complicated part where the fabric had to be rotated between each stitch, saying if I did it wrong it would mess up the whole shirt. It did fit nicely and it was an unusual cotton slipover shirt and a joyous explosion of color and I liked it. From then on I wore it when I was in a festive mood.

On a couple of occasions things happened with Olivia in a way that made me nervous. The first time was at my house, when we had the place to ourselves and she followed me into my bedroom. I had twin beds, one of which I slept in and the other of which mostly just took up space, since it wasn't like I had overnight guests or a twin brother or anything. The mattress in the auxiliary bed was old and lumpy, but for some reason we ended up sprawled out on top of it, kissing and making out.

I was leaning over her, kissing her, and her shoulders and head sort of sank down into a depression in the old lumpy mattress in a way that arched her back a bit. She had small breasts but the unusual position caused them to thrust against me and as I lay against her they were compressed against my chest. After a little while she seemed to go unusually slack and got really warm and she kissed me with more enthusiasm than usual. I was quite turned on and it was tempting to try taking her pants down. I had the feeling I could do whatever I was inclined to do.

The second time was at her house when we had *that* place to ourselves and I mischievously suggested that we shower together and she was amenable. We stood in the warm shower water plastered to each other and once again after a while she was leaning against me heavily and almost bonelessly and it felt great. It seemed to me after a little while of that that if I toweled us off and then clung to her and walked her to the nearest bed she was pliable and fully cooperative.

In both cases, we didn't, and in both cases it might have been only in my imagination that she was so turned on that any sexual reticence was at least temporarily suspended. It often seemed to me as if she sort of wanted it to happen but wasn't ready to be honest with herself or with me about that. Maybe she was anticipating that I'd pull her past her hesitation and reluctance.

I could relate to that. There had been some moments with Terri and Denise when things could have gone that way for me if someone had pulled *me* just a little bit more. Not to mention Linda. But you can't have it both ways. What if Olivia accused me of trying to go too far and being only after one thing and being just like all the other boys and all that? I didn't want to feel selfish and dirty for trying.

I wrote her a letter and handed it to her for her to read after I left to go home one evening. I said that we are both adults now. I said I did not want to pose this to her verbally and put her on the spot to answer under pressure. I wanted her to think about it on her own without me staring at her waiting for an answer...but I wanted us to start having sex.

I hoped she wanted to too. I wrote that I only wanted it to happen if we both wanted it and I wanted her to be sure it felt like the right thing for her. I encouraged her to show the letter to her girlfriends and get second opinions if she wanted. Doing all this by letter felt awkward but trying to talk with Olivia had always been awkward, especially on the subject of sex.

A couple days later I called her and she said come over, and we went for a walk so we could talk without being overheard by her family.

"I talked to my friends and I showed them your letter, and they all agree. You're just trying to use me for sex, and if you really cared about me you wouldn't have asked me to. You only care about one thing and you would be taking advantage of me. So, no."

"I don't see why. It should be mutual if both people want to and I was hoping you wanted to. And that really hurts. You make me sound horrible, and I asked in the least...the least pushy way I could think of. So you think I'm like that."

It disappointed me that she didn't want to and it stung that she considered me to be selfish and just trying to use her. And when I thought about it, we really didn't have much going on between us except for making out.

"Well...I guess I'll go home now..."

She looked back. "Okay."

I took a drive down DP Road and dropped in on my old boss Darrel Mason. "Hey Derek, how's it hanging?" he asked me. "You doing all right?" I explained that I was back in town for a while and was wondering if he could take me on as an employee.

"Well, you know, I could always use someone to come by and spiff up the bays, sweep, empty the trash cans, that sort of thing. And we might be able to come up with some additional stuff to keep you busy."

I began coming by after lunch and putting in four or five hours each day doing the same kind of work I'd done there after school before. Darrel made good on his promise: "You finished up for the day? Go down past the fence and go into that quonset garage, looks like a can of tomato sauce turned on its side, and ask for Steve. He could use some cleanup down there too." From then on I was lent out to them sometimes to clean up their floors and throw out their trash as well.

I discovered that Denise Spears was in town. In retrospect, I felt I'd been foolish not to pursue a relationship with Denise with a lot more vigor. Compared to how things had been with the uncommunicative Olivia, my memories of my interactions with Denise were considerably more joyous. I got in touch with her, and she was warm and yet a bit guarded. Understandable since we hadn't spoken in quite some time. I hadn't given her sufficient signals that I was genuinely interested in her, and she might be well aware that I'd had a steady girlfriend for over a year. We set up a date.

I was with Denise and we were talking, in part about people we both knew and reminiscing about when we first got to know each other. I had been in the habit back then of sort of teasing her about things, to get a pretend-indignant response or maybe a smile and a blush, and so I fell into that pattern again. "So you were gone from around here, I haven't had the chance to see you. People were whispering, 'I bet she's pregnant.'"

Denise looked at me with older and sadder eyes than I remembered and said, "I don't spend a lot of time worrying about what people say about me because people talk about all kinds of things when they don't know anything about it."

We had gone out to a movie and I had enjoyed having my arm around her a bit and holding her hand but we'd actually watched the movie, not ignoring it to make out or anything. Now, in my car, I turned toward her and opened my arms. She came over but within a few moments as I began nibble-kissing on her lips and letting my thumb start to stroke her breast through her shirt, she repositioned herself a bit. She said she had learned some lessons about whether someone was actually interested in a girl or was only interested in the opportunity for sexual favors. I didn't understand why it should have to be just one or the other when I wanted both.

Well, I'd managed on fairly short notice to say and do all the wrong things and give the impression that I was just looking at her as an easy sexual mark, and I really wasn't like that, or didn't think I was. But the truth was I *did* want sexual experiences. I was sorry about the stupid quip about being pregnant. I hadn't for a moment considered it a real possibility. I had been teasing.

I wanted a sexually active relationship, even if one where we only did things that didn't get people pregnant. Neohippie and free love advocate that I was, in my fervent belief systems, I wasn't really looking for a relationship with someone who wanted a long chaste test drive and perhaps, if I was correctly reading between the lines, a commitment to permanence and fidelity and all that. It was awkward. I took her home and we smiled fondly and a little sadly at each other and she got out.

Darrel at Precision Imports told me he knew a guy down the road, at the North American Van Lines center, who needed a worker and that they could use me for more hours than Precision could. I went down and introduced myself to Mac, who ran the place. It was the furniture storage warehouse where the long distance vans would unload furniture and it would sit there until time to deliver it to someone's house; or, inversely, where the furniture from a local person's house would be kept until a long distance van came to take it to the destination.

They had a small fleet of local trucks, not the articulated semi-trailer trucks but the solid-bodied smaller ones. The big concrete floor was full of piles of possessions all covered up with dust cloths. He said to call him each morning. If there was no work for that day, he would tell me and I was not to come in. But if he said there was work, I'd get paid from the time I showed up until he said to clock out for the day, even if I was spending that time sitting in his office waiting for the truck to arrive, drinking coffee. Sounded good to me.

There were a couple other movers, grunt-work employees like me, Dan and Paul, plus a third guy Ed who came in occasionally, and we hung out with Mac in his office a fair amount of time. Dan and Paul were often telling stories like crazy nutty homeowners wanting to dig back into their things once they were all boxed and packed and then complaining it was taking so long, or difficult moves like getting a grand piano up a curving flight of stairs. "...and when they got there, the couple was these two *guys*, right? And so the driver says 'Which one of you is Mr. Kinderson, or are both of you?'" Dan recounted, snorting in derision.

"Yeah," noted Mac, "You know, I once knew a fag truck driver, drove regular from Seattle and El Paso. And he didn't try to hide it or anything. Like he didn't care what you thought. These guys at the depot were ready to beat the shit out of him and he just looks at them and says 'Yeah, I'm gay, I'm a fucking fag. You want to make something of it?' And he could fight. I'm telling you, some of these fags can fight."

A few days later, it was misting rain and the van we were set up to unload was late. We were hanging around drinking coffee and chatting. "It was late and we were from out of town," Paul reminisced, "and BAM, the door flies open and about nine guys came in. I thought we weren't gonna be heard from again. I was fuckin' scared,"

Mac said. "The thing about it, any time you got several people you got to deal with and they all want to take you on, they expect you to be afraid of them because there's just one of you. The thing you got to do is convince them you're totally bat-shit crazy and just don't care. Blow your nose, blow snot all down the front of your face, spit on the floor, and yell at them."

I had strong legs from the hiking I had done, and although my upper-body strength wasn't so great I could still carry a lot of weight and move fast with it. I learned how to stack things efficiently both on the warehouse floor and in the truck. Sometimes I was asked to drive the truck, and I learned how to use the red knob that switched the variable speed differential from low range to high. The regular stick shift was the same as any other standard, and I was used to driving a big Pontiac so the truck, although obviously a lot longer, wasn't much wider than I was already accustomed to.

I was in the parking lot uptown in Los Alamos, where the beer store was, where all the partying teenagers gathered on Friday and Saturday nights scoring ten dollar bags of weed, getting a person of legal age to buy the alcohol, and awaiting word through the crowd of where the party was going to be. I noticed a girl named Renee, who'd had a reputation as a "slut" back when I'd still been in high school. In fact I remembered Jay Schirmer once responding to a mention of her with, "Oh, slut Renee..." as if it were part of her name. I'd never understood the contempt for sluts, meaning girls who were not reluctant about sex and did sexual things with different guys and so on.

Renee and another girl strolled over to me. "Are you driving up to American Springs for the party? Can me and my friend here have a ride up with you?"

I said sure. It was always nice to have female companionship in my car. I wanted to be thought of as cool, and my car as cool, and to be less on the periphery and more in the center of the high life. Maybe we'd talk some. Get to know each other as people. Presumably she was not sexually reformed like Denise and yet maybe, as a girl who was so often being derisively called things because she put out, as they say, she'd be interested in a guy who would maybe want her for a girlfriend and who didn't think anything bad about whatever she had done.

I drove down the rutted dirt road to the parking area close to the party's bonfire. The girls got out, six packs of beer in hand. "Thanks for the ride," Renee said. "You can go on ahead if you want," she added, motioning toward the crowd around the bonfire. "I have to pee." The other girl said she did too. "So you should go on to the party unless you get off on watching girls pee or something."

I gave a good-natured okay and a wave and went onward toward the party. Later I saw them standing around with other people but they didn't make any effort to hang out with me and I figured I'd be making a nuisance of myself if I acted like giving them a ride meant I was welcome to go hover around them.

On the last week I was working there, my boss at North American, Mac, said, "I'm in the mood for a chili burger with those big waffle fries. I'm going to go to the Los Alamos Inn lounge when I lock up. If you're not doing anything you're welcome to come along." Sounded cool to me. I'd never forgotten how miserable I had been working for Ronald Peterson and

I really liked working for employers who treated me like a human being, like even though I work for them it's fundamentally a friendly relationship and not some kind of adversarial thing.

I let my folks know I was eating dinner with the boss and would see them later. We ordered dinner and sat and chatted. At some point we talked about some of the other guys he had working for him. He seemed to respect all of his workers but made some wry observations about some of their behaviors, like one guy who would chain non-smoke. He was trying to quit, so he'd light a cigarette and hold it and not smoke it except for an occasional puff, then he'd light the next one immediately. "By the end of the day he's inhaled as much cigarette smoke as your basic pack-a-day smoker, but he's paying four times the cost."

Mac noted, "I've seen how you don't join in laughing when Dan starts talking his shit."

It was true, I acknowledged. I considered Dan to be another one of those clowns who always have to be obscene. Anything round or any destination, was "Put some hair around it then I can find it," and any casual passing mention of anyone with a female name was followed by a dissertation on what kind of cock she wants, and so on.

Mac waved his hand dismissively. "He's got this thing about queers, you know, and wants to make sure everyone knows he likes the pussy. The thing is, he thinks all fags are sissy. Weak little fairies. Hell, I know some fags that lift weights and kick butt and have cast-iron balls and you better think twice before disrespecting them."

Mac paused a moment, then continued. "There was this drill sergeant in the service I once heard about, and he'd been going pretty rough on the recruits, which was standard, except he started really leaning on this one, yelling about how some cocksuckers can't be tolerated and going vicious on him, kneecaps and teeth and kicks to the gut, really over the top, trying to break this guy, trying to break this green kid. So he gets called over by this crusty hard ass colonel who tells him flat out, he said, 'I been shot at in Iwo Jima, and I swam with sharks in the Pacific during the war, and anyone wants to question my authority had better be prepared to die for the privilege.' Then he told that drill sergeant, 'I like dick. It's nobody's business but that's how it is. If I hear again that you're singling out that recruit I'm going to gut you and watch you die slow and then report that you committed suicide in front of me. Any questions?'"

I thought it was totally cool that Mac was so comfortable with himself that he could admire gay guys like that. I'd never really thought of it that way but it made sense.

FRUSTRATIONS AND CONFRONTATIONS

It was 1978. I was nineteen. College dropout. Piano player. I was starting to take my piano playing and compositions seriously. Maybe I could play along with a guitar player and a singer some day or something. Horny virgin.

And now I was an auto mechanic trainee. I was in Albuquerque to start my Vo-tech training. The course would run through the year, break for Christmas, then continue the next spring and wrap up in May of the following year. They didn't offer any official certificate but they had placement counselors who would help us get jobs when we finished.

They had listings of other students who wanted to split the rent and living costs. My parents were paying my tuition and would be paying my living expenses, so we met with the placement counselors and all agreed that an older guy named Donald S. Skyler, recently out of the Army and attending on military grant money, was a good person for me to partner up with. He was enthusiastic and confident and impressed upon my folks that he had lived on his own. My folks emphasized that I should be sure to budget, bought me cookware and plates and bowls and cups and saucers, and donated some old pans and silverware. Then they hugged me goodbye and headed back home.

"So," said my new roommate, "let's take a load off, shall we? What do you say we get some pizza? That your car I saw, that big brown one?"

I nodded. "Pontiac Bonneville, 1965. It looks kind of Sunday go-to-meeting but it moves. Yours is the Plymouth Duster? That's sort of the sporty version of the Valiant, isn't it?"

He waved off that suggestion dismissively. "Same underframe maybe. This baby has serious shocks though, and a 318 with a four banger. Holley carb, baby. And you saw my tires, right? Fifty series on the rear, just like a real racer."

We talked cars for a while. He was just as proud of his as I was of my old Pontiac, very chauvinistic about the superior characteristics of Chrysler products to anything else. He rolled a joint then retroactively asked, "You okay with pot? You look like maybe you take a puff now and then, but tell me if you'd rather I didn't light up in here."

"See that cardboard box sticking out on the edge there?" I said proudly.

"That's my supply of homemade pot pipes and there's a bag of decently good Oaxacan bud in there."

He lit up and sucked in a good lungful of smoke and passed it. I reciprocated. "You from around these parts? I'm from New York myself, and I'm attending Vo-tech on an Army bill. I done my stint in the service, good times I tell you. But when I signed up for Vo-tech auto I didn't expect I'd end up in New Mexico, ay compadre moocho con loco, all this goat-roper music and goat-roper clothes, boots and saddles and stuff, and all this beaner no spicka da engleesh bullshit, pardon my French."

I laughed and said most folks around here listen to rock; I certainly did myself. As for the Spanish, they were here before we were.

He waved that away too. "As sure as my name is Donald S. Skyler, I'll tell you and anyone else too, this is America, I don't care who came here before; we speaka da English now. I don't have prejudice and I don't care about the color of your skin but c'mon, let's all be Americans and be an English-speaking nation unless you wanna be told your eyes are crossed, you smell funny your feet don't match and you don't even believe in the good lord."

I couldn't tell if he was partially being serious or not, but he was amusing and didn't seem to take himself excessively seriously or expect me to either, as far as I could tell, so I grinned and took the joint again.

He took me for a drive in his car. He had done some odd things to it, in my opinion: he had decided that power steering didn't belong in a sporty car, so he'd cut the fan belt and drove without benefit of power steering. Yet he had replaced the stock steering wheel with a smaller black metal and chromium sports wheel. It made it difficult for him to steer, especially at slow speeds. He had installed a super-strong clutch pedal assembly with a spring so stiff that he had to be very careful releasing it to prevent the car from jolting. He had an aftermarket camshaft in the engine so it always idled fast and roughly.

Like me, he had a chromium air cleaner under the hood and bright yellow spark plug wires and liked to rev his engine, and had glass pack mufflers so you could hear the thrum and boom as he drove by. Yet he drove timidly, cautiously, never choosing to accelerate or peel out. And as he had pointed out, he had put big fat 50-series tires on the rear wheels, the alleged purpose of which was better traction when you peeled out, which as I said he never did.

Donald S. showed me his approach to cleaning up a messy apartment: most clutter that isn't clothing or garbage is rectangular, just pick it all up, square the edges and lay it down and it's in a neat pile. Take a matchbook, open it, and use the edge of one side to scrape up loose stuff into the ashtray. Done. He derided the notion of either of us cooking, and insisted we could eat fast food and microwave food more cheaply. He was Donald S. Skyler, never just Donald Skyler, and he had an opinion on everything and he was going to share it with you.

Finally it was my opportunity to go acid tripping. "Shit yeah, acid is good stuff. You see pretty trails; it's fantastic," Donald S. Skyler had asserted, and said he'd already made connections for obtaining a variety of drugs and that we could pick some up for the weekend, and so we had.

"I want to take it because I've read so many accounts from people who say they attained a higher consciousness and really understood life and saw what matters."

Donald S. Skyler laughed and said I'd been reading too much hippy dippy bullshit and that acid was just a lot of fun and felt good and let you see trails and stuff. I hoped he was wrong. I wanted to be moved, to get in touch with inner truth, or whatever real thing corresponded to those lofty descriptions. I was worried that the acid he'd gotten us wasn't the same stuff all the books I'd read had talked about, but I was still excited, anticipatory.

We swallowed the tiny squares of paper and we waited. Donald S. Skyler put his feet up on the table and leaned back in his chair and bade me do likewise: "Relax, kick back. You're going into orbit and you're going to like it."

After about an hour, the initial excitement lifted off into an enthusiastic joyous fast-thinking giddiness, but I still couldn't tell if I was just excited to think I was going tripping or if it was starting to have an effect.

I wasn't seeing any of Donald S. Skyler's advertised "trails" but as I continued to talk about and think about ideas, I seemed to understand them more sharply and clearly. I made new connections and drew new conclusions or added detail to things, which made me pleased and more excited.

An hour later the same thing was happening except with even more intensity. I'd clarified my thinking about many things and the rate at which I was becoming clear on things was itself increasing. War and punishment and frowns. What they had to do with the failure to requestion a decision. Why uncertainty is actually certainty and vice versa. Donald S. didn't find it of compelling interest, but that didn't matter much to me. *He can go see pretty trails if he'd rather. I guess each person gets the trip they seek or something like that.*

After several hours the understandings got a little crumbly. I was tired in the head and had trouble holding on to all my new knowledge and understanding. I didn't worry overly much, figuring once I was rested, all that material was, after all, in my head. Even if some little parts danced beyond the reach of my memory, I'd be able to figure them out anew from the high plateau of the other things I did remember.

But the next day it was as faint and faded as the memory of a dream and, like a vivid dream, seemed to make more sense when I was in it than afterwards when awake. But it had been so intense and compelling that I could not readily accept that it was all an illusion with no genuine content. So I pushed my blunt non-tripping head at the same questions and issues and concerns to see if I could stimulate some recollection of what I'd understood.

The course was divided into units. First we would have tune-up. We had textbooks, sample cars to learn on, and later on in the unit some real customers' cars on which we'd do free or cut-rate work. We were also welcome to try our new skills on our own cars. After tune-up would come a unit on engines, then a unit on front end and suspension. Later on we'd have transmissions and clutches, differentials, brakes electrical wiring and gauges, automotive air conditioning, and emissions controls and safety devices.

Mr. Boggs was explaining about ignition timing. "So the piston's going down and sucking in air-fuel mixture from the intake valve. Now this valve closes, just as the piston starts to go back up, all that air-fuel mix has got nowhere to go. It's getting squished tighter and tighter, tighter and tighter, and now the piston is close to the top. Somewhere in here we want to fire the spark plug. When do we want to do that? Right when it's at the top, so the burning gas will push it down? Well actually it turns out it takes a couple moments, a couple of beats, before the flame front of burning spreads out from the spark and really gets a good push going, and at the speed the piston's moving it turns out you get best efficiency if you spark it just a little bit before the piston reaches the top, while it's still coming up. You fire *too* soon, you end up using too much of your flame front's energy pushing against the rising piston. You fire too *late* and you're chasing it, you can't get a good push against it because it's already running away from you, on its way down."

He was good at explaining things and diagramming them. And he showed us little insider tricks that our textbooks didn't cover. "Okay, here's your basic GM alternator. On this end you see where the shaft goes into this housing, there are two contacts here, with springs pressing them against the rings on the shaft. Now, GM makes some kind of seven hundred dollar gadget for assembling these. You won't be working at a GM dealership, most likely, so you won't have one of those. You can spend hours and hours trying to pry those down with a screwdriver and get the shaft past them or you can just take your smallest Allen wrench and slip it in this hole. See how it holds the contacts back? Now slide the shaft into the housing. Now pull out the Allen wrench."

Playing piano had totally become a habit at my folks' house whenever I was stoned. Now deprived of that I began walking the long walk down to UNM campus. At UNM there were practice rooms and I composed many new pieces. I carried with me a composition book and jotted down shorthand that was easier for me to write than actual bars and staves and musical notes.

I thought about Linda Sorrens a lot as I played, and I wrote some songs with her in mind. She still stood out as the one person I had really connected with, and I wrote to her a couple of times and told her a bit about myself.

She wrote back, "I've been having a small war with the family car. Would you mind terribly coming by and checking it out? I'm on cloud nine lately since I got my private pilot's license. The family is a little apprehensive about trusting their lives to my skill. I've been thinking. The nicest people I know are mechanics of some sort. I wonder..."

Linda Sorrens was thousands of miles away and sometimes I got really lonely. The halls and classrooms of Vo-tech were an all-male world. I was getting along better with other guys these days than I had when I was younger, but the fact remained that I wasn't going to meet any girls at school. Donald S. Skyler was almost a sort of caricature of a person and I didn't feel understood or in any kind of real rapport with him. Many of the guys at Vo-tech behaved as tough belligerent streetwise fellows. There was a lot of ethnic tension, low-grade but always there. Vo-tech was maybe 65 percent Hispanic. I was hurting for someone to talk to.

While in the UNM area, I discovered University Crisis, a university-affiliated medical establishment one major block north over from Central. I poked my nose in, pushing past the doors where signs advertised community mental health counseling.

"Hi. Listen, I was just out for a walk and saw this and I don't know if I belong here. I mean, I'm not suicidal or dangerous or thinking I'm Napoleon or anything. And I'm not a university student. But it would be good to talk to someone."

"Hi. That's cool. You don't have to be a crazy university student. We've got a grant to serve the community. I'm going to ask you to fill out a form if you don't mind, but I promise to listen for a while regardless of what you put on it."

In short order I explained that I had started to change my life roughly around ninth grade after years of having been sort of cocooned in an inflexible mental shell that had kept me apart from other people, but although there had been a lot of promising payoff at first, it had sort of stalled since then.

"I still don't have a girlfriend. I thought when boys and girls started liking each other, you know, at puberty, that I'd end up with a girlfriend again. I never dreamed I'd be nineteen and still be alone like this. I don't make friends easily. There are a lot of things about being with people I don't think I learned properly from being cut off as a kid, and I need to make more progress. Break down barriers. Things were going good for a while."

I had in my head the notion that if these folks could analyze me and my situation, then as people with counseling credentials and so on, they could do in a professional way what Tina and Jay and Terri and Chris and Alan had done; that they could prompt me and direct me toward the changes I needed to make in order to fit in better. I wanted to be a part of it all. I was tired of being partway outside and lonely and not doing whatever things normal people learn to do in order to connect with other people well.

I was ready and I was willing, or at least at the times that I came there feeling achingly lonely and desperate, I certainly was. *Fix me. I'm tired of this, I'm totally fucking tired of this, please fix me.*

"I see. I hear a lot of frustration, and I understand why that would be frustrating, to feel so cut off. I'm not so sure you need 'fixing', though. You don't seem so broken to me."

I nodded. "I don't necessarily think something's...*wrong* with me...but I need something. Skills or better understandings. Or knowing where to go. You listen good and it feels good to say all this, but I still don't know what to do or where to go."

I came back to the Albuquerque Crisis counseling center from time to time, and they never made me feel unwelcome there. They'd listen and make some responses. I felt their kindness but they didn't give me much in the way of answers, and the next day I would not be in the same mood and although they sometimes gave me a referral to some kind of outpatient program, I didn't follow through.

Engines were where everyone's head was at. It's the power plant of a car. And we all craved acceleration and speed and responsiveness and the engine was where it came from. Unfortunately, our engine class instructor, a man named Kingshead, was dull and not particularly interested in what he was teaching. He'd cover the reading material the way a history teacher covered a unit in grade school, but once the textbook part of the day was over he'd disappear and leave us to our own devices and tools and skills during the shop part of the day. I learned engines mostly from the other students. They let me help them disassemble engines, scrape carbon deposits out of cylinders, watch them grind valves.

The next teacher we rotated to was another good solid teacher. He was a short middle-aged guy, very relaxed and matter-of-fact but he knew his stuff. He taught us about the angles that are involved in how the wheel sits in relationship to car and road, and the different manufacturers' implementations and how you made the adjustments. Then disc and drum brakes and fluid mechanics and what happens to the brake fluid under pressure and how the component parts of brakes did their thing.

I was in his class when a couple of guys started harassing me. I'd noticed them nudging each other with an elbow and pointing my way and apparently talking about me. I'd wondered if it was going to become a problem. Then as I was coming into the classroom after lunch...

"*Besa la verga, joto, tu concha en mi verga, joto, chingate,* hey man, you know what that means huh?" I didn't, since I didn't understand Spanish, but it didn't sound good. "You suck my dick you fucking *joto* pansy I can smell you. *Uso cuyo conchito* like you, you pussy."

The one doing most of the talking was staring at me with amused contempt, while his short friend with the pockmarked face was intermittently laughing and saying something that sounded like "*chingatu hu wey*" and egging his companion on.

Something that sounded like "hoto" seemed to be my new nickname. They called me that several times a day for the rest of the week, interspersed with longer elaborate insults and threats when well out of earshot of the teacher. And they seemed to be upping the ante each day, leaning closer and slamming my toolbox closed on my fingers when I was reaching for a socket wrench or suddenly throwing a screwdriver into the workbench next to my arm.

I discussed it with Donald S. Skyler, that these guys were determined to get me into a fight and I didn't want to deal with that. He said they were probably just shooting off steam. But they intruded more and more and always seemed to be daring me to do something about it. Shoving into me. Kicking over my parts box. Saying things contemptuously to me in front of their friends from two feet away.

I had an idea. Once back in Los Alamos I'd been hassled by some kids on the late afternoon activity bus. I'd been exhausted at the time which had put me in an aggressive irritable mood. I'd confronted them and they'd backed down without a fight when I stood up to them. I told Donald S. I was going to try to get this over with. Their constant harassment had put me in a no-nonsense mood.

The first interaction took place when the pockmarked guy started his harassment and I walked over close to him and told him I was sick of this and he could damn well knock it off. It surprised him and although he talked back he was off-balanced by it and I got in the last word and spun away and felt satisfied.

An hour or so later I was in the parts room standing in line to request a set of brake drums and the taller guy came up and shoved me out of line to the side and took my place. I stared at him a second or two, feeling the adrenaline, and then stepped forward, grabbed him at waist level and moved him sideways the way you'd move a heavy trash can, and regained my position.

As he came at me, furious, fists cocked, I just walked into him, strode toward him at full hiking pace. I got whapped a couple times in the head but then I was practically on top of him and moving fast. He scrambled backwards, awkwardly, never regaining his balance as I kept striding toward him, and he fell backwards hard onto the cement. I hadn't even tried to hit him. By the time he had regained his feet, three or four guys were restraining me and another half-dozen were keeping him away from me.

He lunged at me a few times and I made a couple of reciprocal not-very-serious lunges in his direction that didn't really test the strength of the folks holding me back, but it looked like I wanted to go at it some more.

We both had to sit in an office and get berated by a school official for fighting and I hung my head just like the other guy did, and said yes I would abide by the rules and so on.

Seriously, I thought to myself, *boys can be so stupid and this is such a stupid game and it is a game. I know the boy-rules of fighting and can fake my way through the protocols of it, including sitting here in this office doing this pretending-to-be-sorry ritual, but it is pathetic to have so much geared toward fights and intimidation. The institutional response is so pro forma and not at all designed to stop the behavior. Everyone just expects it.*

I saw Donald S. at lunch and said to him, "So I got into a fight." I rolled my eyes. He said something noncommittal. An hour or so later he ran across me and said "Hey, you didn't say you kicked his ass! Everyone says you beat the shit out of him. I thought you meant you got beat up. Why didn't you tell me you'd kicked that greaser's ass?" I shrugged and said I didn't believe violence was a good way to solve problems and that fighting was stupid. "I don't understand you," he said.

Donald S. had brought some record albums from his storage locker, and played them on my record player. He had Edgar Winter Group and Alice Cooper and Black Sabbath, a dual album set of Melanie called *Starportrait Melanie* and a Bloodrock album titled *Bloodrock 3*, and Jethro Tull's *Aqualung* and a few others. He played DJ, putting on some of his favorite individual tracks like Black Sabbath's "Sweet Leaf" and Alice Cooper's "I'm Eighteen." I liked some of his music quite a bit. The Melanie album starts off with "Peace Will Come" and I fell in love with her sad plaintive voice.

In addition to going out to practice piano, I also stepped out and went walking around in search of social life. I missed the bonfire parties of Los Alamos. Albuquerque was much larger and logically ought to have more variety and more opportunities, but I had no idea how to find the kind of thing I was looking for. Albuquerque consists of large swaths of residential buildings intersected by large commercial streets.

The thing about wandering around in residential districts was that I wasn't at all an extroverted gregarious person of the sort who'd be likely to catch some person's eye as they're mowing the grass or talking with friends on the front lawn or getting out of their car with a bag of groceries, and end up chatting with them and making friends. I was a quiet person who'd hang out on the edge of things and get to know people as *they* chose to interact with *me*. Or if I'd been sitting or standing there long enough and some conversation was going on, perhaps I'd eventually participate. As a stranger looking for a social scene—looking for the existence of a relevant crowd on the verges of which to hang out—I viewed the residential areas as unlikely prospects.

I had this vision of myself appearing to some middle class family to be scouting the neighborhood for burglary opportunities, or to some belligerent guy my age as a peeping tom trying to glimpse his sister through the bedroom curtains or something. So I gravitated toward Central and began walking. Looking for something that might remind me of the liquor store parking lot in Los Alamos where kids gathered to find out where the party was and exchange information and score pot and so on.

I began to worry about whether or not I had an ethnicity issue, that I was prejudiced. I hadn't thought I was. But the "mood" coming off clusters of people roughly my age seemed a lot tougher and more aggressive and hostile when they were substantially Spanish. Chicano, as they say in New Mexico. In most of the US, folks would probably say Hispanic.

I don't mean they seemed to be bristling at me, an Anglo, walking by or standing around checking their group out; it was just the tone of their conversation already. It had been a barrier to making many friends at Vo-tech, too.

One night I walked east toward the Sandias and the tramway, and out past Juan Tabo Boulevard, I found some girls hanging out, talking, but not in a tight cluster all gabbing with each other like close friends out together, more sort of intermittently mingling. They seemed a lot more approachable that way than people do when they're all clustered up tight if you understand what I mean, and the way they seemed to be waiting around definitely reminded me of the Los Alamos parking lot scenario.

I walked over closer and listened in to get a sense of them and realized they were older than I'd initially thought but they seemed friendly and I was fascinated. And then one of the women took active notice of me and told me I needed to either make an offer or be off and on my way because my standing there was bad for business. I realized then that they were hookers. Sure enough, as I obeyed and crossed to the other side of the street to give them space, a car pulled up to the curb and the driver began negotiating through the open window.

The next time, I walked west instead, in the direction of UNM campus. Midway down, I came to what had been a movie theater but was now apparently the venue for Mastermind from March until April, and posters identified Mastermind as a rock band. And the shows were free.

I went in. On the left was a keyboardist playing a black electric organ that had "Zac" appliqued to it in bold white letters. There was a drummer in the middle of the stage with a very impressive array of drums, tom toms and snares and the big bass in the middle with "Mastermind" written on it. On the right was a guy playing electric guitar. The sound and the visual antics were all dominated by the keyboard player and the sound coming back from them was damn impressive.

I sat down and listened for the remainder of the show. It was movie theater style seating, of course, and only about ten other people were in the whole place, which made it feel invasive to go sit by anyone already there and start up a conversation. Had it been an outdoor venue with people standing around listening instead of in scattered seats that could have been different. I stayed to say hello to the musicians.

"Hey, thanks for coming. What did you think?"

"You sound great. I would buy your records and play them along with the best in my stack. How long have you been together? Is this all your own music that you're playing?"

"Wow, that means a lot to hear you say that. We actually do have a record that we cut as a demo, but it's not very good. I mean we sound better now than we did back when we made it. We've been playing together for about a year now. We'll be playing here all month. Bring your friends. Tell people about us."

I told them I'd definitely be back to hear them again.

Hearing the keyboard-centric Mastermind inspired me even more to take my own composing and piano playing seriously. I began spending more time down at the practice rooms.

I went tripping again with Donald S. and this time I had my composition book out on the table. I figured I'd jot down the interesting thoughts that came to mind as I tripped. What happened was that as it kicked in and I again started to understand things clearly (and it *did* seem that I was recapturing a lot of the same content that I'd gotten the first time, by the way), I found that trying to encode it into words (that's how it felt, encode) was limiting and frustrating.

I began to doodle instead and in the course of the next couple hours the doodling turned into this incredibly detailed and flamboyantly celebratory joyous expression of things with energy and interconnections. It wasn't precisely a diagram, not like "This symbol represents militarism" or something, and yet it stood in a representational sense for a way of seeing. It was more akin to an attitude than a series of concepts and premises, but the concepts and premises seemed to just sort of shake out easily from the attitude.

This was my clue that the kind of thinking I did while tripping was not verbal thinking where you have terms for things in your mind. To some extent I guess all thinking departs from that, but a much higher portion than usual seemed to involve manipulating symbols that sort of stood for ideas and relationships and associating those symbols to generate new ideas and yet more relationships. I was convinced the understanding was real but now I was seeing why it was difficult to hold onto when I came down. And yet I had made progress trying to put things into words from my first trip.

I had some colored construction paper and I'd made little homemade signs and taped them to the walls of my bedroom. One of them—taped to my *ceiling* instead of to one of the walls—captured a kind of court jester feeling, declaring that my role in life was to "freak you out," to never be what you defined me as because the moment you think you know, you cease to look and see. What had initially remained behind only as a silly catchphrase, "uncertainty is certainty," had yielded back to me an important concept that continued to make sense, continued at this point to *not* look like an empty byproduct of drug-induced euphoria.

I began writing poems too in my composition book. Not iambic pentameter but sentiments and raw gut feelings and potential lyrics for songs. Some of them ended up with music wrapped around them, became songs when I took the comp book with me to the UNM music practice rooms.

Sex and romance were not a part of my life and I was lonely and horny and feeling left out. In high school I had had my relationship with Olivia, flawed though it may have been, and by being in school and at weekend parties surrounded by girls my own age, I had always had a sense that something else *could* develop at any moment. On top of that there had been the optimistic expectation of more sex and romance to come when I was in college.

Now I was in a vocational school nearly exclusively attended by guys and had no parties or similar social occasions to go to in order to mingle and meet. At nineteen I felt as if somehow I'd missed my primary opportunity. I'd never really learned how to mix being friendly with being sexually flirtatious, and I didn't do either one well. Girls seemed wary of me as if I were always about to come on to them in some annoying way. Everything had seemed so promising just a couple years ago but now it seemed impossibly faraway and unlikely. Instead of everything getting better once I got older, it seemed to have worsened.

A neighbor, the mother of a pair of teenage girls, came to our apartment from time to time to buy a joint or two from Donald S. and sometimes smoked with us. Her name was Julie. The girls, Becky and Susannah, often came with her. Donald S. flirted with them a lot in a self-deprecating "I'm way too old an old fogey for cute young girls like you to take seriously" sort of way, which made them visibly uncomfortable, which in turn made me uncomfortable as well. It didn't seem like he was coming on to them in any serious sense, especially with their mom right there, but it also didn't seem necessary and the girls didn't seem to be liking it.

I was out walking around in the evening again, lonely and restless, and a car pulled alongside me and a guy in perhaps his thirties asked me if I wanted a lift. I said I wasn't really going anywhere, just bored and out walking around. He said he had nowhere to go either and would I keep him company; he had some good weed back at his apartment and it would be good to have someone to hang out with. I was amenable; I got in. He had wine too, and we sat around talking, him telling me about business trips and the hassles of airports and me talking about the band I'd heard.

His pot was strong and once I was stoned I felt uncomfortable. As if things were not as they seemed. Something about the guy...felt, I don't know, sardonically malevolent. Sly. After a while I indicated that I ought to head back, and he said I should sleep there overnight and then he could drive me to my home in the morning but he was too intoxicated to drive now. I kept reiterating that I walk really long distances and didn't need a ride, but he kept saying that it made no sense to go out so late when I could just sleep there and he'd take me home in the morning.

It got to the point that, short of being rude and argumentative, I didn't feel I could insist on heading home. I really didn't have any compelling reason I needed to be home that night. He showed me the guest bedroom and went back to his own room. I lay in bed briefly but I was profoundly uncomfortable and after about twenty minutes I very quietly dressed and put on my shoes and very quietly opened the door to slip out. The guy opened his bedroom door and leered out at me, "Already finished doing it, huh?"

I mumbled something and waved and he didn't argue anymore and I left and walked home.

It was fall and my parents were comparing their schedules with mine for Christmas. It had been decided that we would spend Christmas with my mom's parents in Athens Georgia. My folks were going to drive from New Mexico, and wanted to leave for Georgia a week earlier than my Vo-tech semester ended, which meant I would not be riding with them. They suggested that they would deposit enough money into my account for me to buy a plane ticket to fly to Atlanta and then get a bus ride or shuttle flight from Atlanta to Athens.

"Hey," said Donald S. Skyler, "we're currently spending nearly a hundred fifty bucks a month on pot between the two of us. Julie and the girls go through about the same amount. What say we take some of the airplane money and buy a pound? We'll give Julie a good rate on half of it, which will be more than enough to make up the difference on the plane tickets, plus we'll get our own smoke almost for free."

"I don't think that's such a hot idea. This is my parents' money, and they gave it to me explicitly for me to get to my grandparents in Georgia at Christmas time."

But he had Julie and Becky and Susannah over and they all promised me they'd guarantee me a plane ride to Georgia and eventually, reluctantly, I agreed.

I was yet again out walking and found some folks hanging out in an urban park listening to rock music on a portable cassette player and laughing and talking. This time when I edged up on their periphery, someone greeted me in a friendly way and I said hello and soon was sitting with them on the grass. We talked about music, cops and speeding tickets, other things at random. It felt good to be part of a group, however briefly, surrounded by friendly conversation. After a bit, the group split up with folks going in different directions. Three of the guys were going to one guy's house to watch a movie on TV and they asked me if I wanted to join them, so I did.

At the end of the movie, the two who did not live there got up to leave and the remaining guy asked me if I wanted to stay behind and share a bowl, and I was amenable. He was one of the friendlier of the guys and I was comfortable with him right up until he said, "So. Have you ever tried gay sex?"

My skin got all cold and sweaty and my stomach clenched. *Let's come right out in the open with it, shall we?* Although it was possible I read more into things than were really there, and took some things literally that had been intended just as hurtful insults, it still seemed incontrovertible that a hell of a lot of people thought I was gay. And things with girls...had somehow never gotten beyond a certain point and sex with girls seemed less and less accessible, not more so, as I got older.

Had I ever "tried gay sex"? Well *no*, aside from some, umm, experimental fumblings with Jeremy Michaels. And I'd known him for so long as a *friend* first, so who knows, maybe that made it sort of like incest. I knew I didn't like the way guys' bodies look the way I liked looking at girls. You know what felt *right* about it? The attention. I was being smiled at and someone wanted me.

"Try gay sex." Huh...interesting way of putting it. Like anyone can try gay sex; it isn't reserved for gay people only or something. He was *nice*. I don't mean I found him appetizing, but he was warm, benevolent, friendly, inviting, no flecks of hostility. I realized I had not *only* not had a girlfriend of any sort in a long time, I'd also not had any even peripherally friendly male companionship, and I was really lonely.

He asked me to sleep in the same bed with him and *not* have sex, just sleep there, and I thought maybe if I'm lying next to him like that and I am gay after all, I'll get turned on and then I'll know, at least. What could it hurt? So I did. Except I didn't sleep a wink the entire night, lying there with my head full of questions, feeling nervous and vulnerable. No arousal though. Or not until the morning hours when he very slowly slid his hand over to me and onto my midsection, around my navel, and moved slowly down. All the night's anticipation keyed with the sensation and yeah that worked. We were off to a good start.

Then...I don't know. Something gradually just changed. He was touching me there but he wasn't touching me there the way I touched myself there. He was *only* touching me there. I was too aware of him, male, a foreign

112

presence, not me, doing things down there; and at the same time I felt too disconnected, from him and then from myself, disembodied. He could stop now.

I felt boxed in. I hadn't stopped him while he was going so slowly and giving me every opportunity to say, "I don't want to." It seemed...like it would be *unfair* to say, "I don't like this," so I figured I'd just wait until he finished, but I got sort of in-between floppy, semi-erect, and he began working harder to make things happen, using his mouth on me, which was licky and full of his spit and made me think of food particles.

I felt myself shrink away and try to sink down into the mattress and disappear. I was embarrassed, I was appalled, and as he went on to try other things I was grossed out, and still just felt like I couldn't say anything until finally I came up with "Okay um I think that's all I can..." and he stopped and then he continued to be really *nice* to me and made me coffee and smiled at me a lot while I felt numb and weird and in shock.

I went out into the morning and the sky was bright blue and the sun was shining and it was a beautiful day and I felt like I belonged on a different stage, one with threatening dead branches and cold gray clouds and decaying bodies of dead animals and rust and sewage and screaming and broken bottles around me. Like I didn't belong under blue skies and should not be found in the sunlight. I was more like some kind of white multi-legged soft-bodied disgusting thing that belongs under a rock.

Seriously...I was...I was expecting...I don't *know* what I had been expecting really, not consciously, but maybe on some level I think yeah I was expecting to find out that, okay, this *is* how I am. It would answer so much. Instead, it had been so awful. I felt revulsion. It hadn't been anything he'd done wrong. It had been me. I'd taken something that was very personally me and casually flung it into a dirty toilet. That's how it felt. And now I was lonelier than ever.

After scuttling around for a week or so preoccupied with those kinds of thoughts and feelings, I woke up before sunrise one morning and stood at the bathroom mirror staring at my reflection.

"So...you had sex with a guy. You're worried that that makes you a fag, just like they've been saying. And at the same time, you're worried that since you didn't like it, it means you're not, and now you're going around saying, 'Oh shit now what, what am I?' You're a real piece of work. You can't have it both ways, you know. So, surprise surprise, you're heterosexual after all. You're just not any damn *good* at it so you can't get a girlfriend and can't get laid. Waaah, poor baby."

I shook my head at myself, amused; it helped to put it into words. "I should have gone to a college in California or something instead of Mississippi, and then maybe I would've found those hippie chicks."

There was one flaw in Donald S. Skyler's brilliant plan to buy cheap pot with my airline money and sell half of it to Julie to get my money back: Donald had trusted her with her half of the pound of weed and now she and the girls had fled, leaving their apartment completely empty. I, therefore, did not have the necessary money to purchase a plane ticket. Donald apologized over and over, raking his hands through his hair and bemoaning that he could have been tricked when they had been such nice girls and he had trusted them all.

He said he had a friend in Louisiana he had been planning to visit for his own Christmas vacation. He proposed that he would take me along with him, we'd combine our meager remaining money to pay for gasoline for his car, and once we made it to Louisiana he and his friend would pool their resources to buy me a bus ticket to get the rest of the way from Louisiana to Athens.

I finished the last days of Vo-tech coursework and packed up things to take with me to Georgia into a suitcase, and took a little leather briefcase that held my composition book and drawing and poems, and loaded them into Donald S.'s car. We took both of our tool kits that had been issued to us by the school, the argument being that with both sets of tools we'd be well equipped to handle anything that happened on the journey. We shared the driving. I understood better why he drove like a timid old grandpa once I had done a stint behind his wheel: the steering was awful with the power steering disconnected, and the car wanted to meander all over the road. But we were in motion at least.

Hours later, I was dozing in the passenger seat when there was a loud *bang*, which I felt as well as heard, and the car lurched to the right. "Oh fuck!" he screamed, wrestling with that tiny black steering wheel as the Duster veered toward the ditch. He jammed on the brakes and managed to bring the car to a standstill. "My car, my car!" he wailed. I opened the passenger side door and walked forward and verified that the front tire was flat, with a mangled hole in the middle of the tread. "You okay?" I asked him. He nodded in a dispirited way and opened his own door and hoisted himself out.

A couple minutes went by and he just kept standing there staring at his car. "Let's get the suitcases out so we can get to the jack," I suggested. He shook his head. "I have those big fifty series tires on the rear and regular tires in front, and I didn't want to carry two spares around, so I don't have a spare." *You have got to be kidding me*, I thought.

"Well, come on, then, help me get this thing off," I said, irritated. We dug through the mess in the back until I unearthed our toolboxes, and then I used the socket wrench to remove the flat. He sat back down in the car seat and put his head in his hands and went back to wailing, "My car, oh this sucks, son of a bitch. I can't believe this happened."

"I'm going to hitch back to that town we passed a while back, San Jon or something like that. I'll get this replaced on the rim with a used tire and then come back." He nodded bleakly. I began walking west along I-40.

Motorists going my direction at highway speeds were *swerving* into the left lane and I saw the passengers in two different cars *locking their doors* as they rolled by. Yeah, okay, so I had long hair and a beard. I was also very obviously hauling a flat tire along with me. And *what*, did they think I was going to lunge at their car and grab hold of the door handle as it zipped past and force my way in? I thought sooner or later a kind Samaritan or sympathetic farmer or someone would stop and take me into town. No one did. It took over four hours.

I was a good hiker but my feet hurt like hell by the time I got to a service station in San Jon. It must have been ten or twelve miles and I had to carry that damn flat tire the whole way. My arms hurt, and my hands were red and sore where the rim of the round metal hole had bitten into them. Fortunately, the gas station attendant offered to drive me and the replacement tire back to the car, so I didn't have to walk back.

After crossing through the eternally wide state of Texas, we dropped into Louisiana and made it to Lake of the Pines, where Donald S. Skyler's Army buddy lived.

"Hey there, fucking A! You made it. C'mon in, wow, long time."

Skyler and his army buddy embraced and slapped each other on the back. I expected to be introduced but the two of them ignored me completely. I sat on the edge of the guy's couch and waited, hungry and tired. "So whatever happened to Cowface, and Rupert? What? Shit no, they don't call me, I haven't heard from them since that time we rolled into East Buttfuck with the red trailer."

Eventually, finally, the Army buddy did turn to me. "You want a ride somewhere? Like to the exit ramp, get a ride on I-30? Get in, I'll take you there." I was not offered any food or a place to sleep for the night. No effort was made to come up with money for my bus fare.

"You got a piece of cardboard and a magic marker?" I asked. I wrote

ATLANTA in big dark block letters, then grabbed my luggage and got into his car.

It wasn't the first time I'd hitched, although it would be the first time to hitch over such a long distance. I worried for a while that the mindset or attitude of the motorists back around San Jon might be in evidence here as well, but I soon caught a ride to Memphis, and the driver was kind enough to offer me a meal as well. From there I caught another ride to just beyond Chattanooga, perfectly poised to make the hop down to Atlanta.

Aside from being rather sleep-deprived, I was doing all right. The rides though Tennessee had eaten up the rest of the night and now the sun was rising. I lashed my suitcase to the smaller briefcase with a piece of nylon cord and then propped them at a shallow angle so I could sit on top of the suitcase holding my "ATLANTA" sign, gesturing with my thumb as cars came past me on the entrance ramp.

A big conventional cab tractor-trailer truck stopped for me, and a tall balding trucker with a beer belly stepped down to open a side compartment to store my luggage while I rode. I had to untie the nylon cord so he could slide the suitcase and the briefcase in side by side because his storage compartment was too short for them to go in tied together like that.

I stepped up into a very spacious and luxuriously appointed cab. The area between the two seats was up higher, sort of a hump with cup holders and ash trays and a shallow storage box that had packs of cigarettes and toothpicks and pens and pencils. I sat on a small cushion up there, between the driver and his partner. We were way up high above regular traffic and the big truck felt like it was only moving twenty miles per hour when it was going fifty-five.

The cab interior was warm and cozy and I took off my coat. "Nice wheels," I told them. It was a Kenworth, which I was familiar with from my days working for Mac at North American. Kenworths and Peterbilts were considered the luxury cabs compared to White Freightliners and Macks and other common makes.

"Yeah, thanks, this sure is one sweet beast," the driver acknowledged.

I asked him, "Mind if I smoke?" The guy in the passenger's side offered me a light and pointed out the ashtray up next to where I was perched.

"You making good time hitching?"

"I didn't set out hitching, actually, I was riding with a guy who was supposed to get me into north Georgia but he didn't think he saw any sufficiently good reason to carry a spare, so when the tire blew, well he wouldn't have, wasn't going to drive me in all the way anyhow, but he was supposed to help. Well...anyway, I hadn't been out there all that long today but I've generally made good time the times when I have hitched, and the weather's decent for it." I babbled on a bit, exhausted and sleep-deprived and giddy from it.

"Well, we're going into Atlanta and stop there for breakfast and weigh in, but where was it you said you were headed?" I identified Athens as my destination.

"I know the place," the one in the passenger seat nodded. He had long light brown hair queued up in a ponytail and topped with a Caterpillar cap. "I think we could swing through there on our way out to South Carolina, don'tcha think we could?" he said to the one driving.

"Yeah, I believe we could do that. You don't mind waiting for us to take care of business in Atlanta, could drop you off in downtown Athens if you like." I couldn't have hoped for better; I could easily walk from there even with the suitcases. Or I could call and someone would come get me from that close range.

Then things subtly changed. We were all smoking cigarettes. The guy in the passenger's seat sort of bumped into my leg with his knuckles as he reached to tap ashes into the ashtray. I repositioned myself a little bit to be less in the way. A moment later the guy who was driving, a big burly dark-haired guy, brushed his hand against my thigh as he reached to tap his own ashes. Then the first guy reached over to snuff out his cigarette, and after he had done so, while withdrawing his hand from the ashtray, he brushed his fingers against my shirt at waist level.

I was on the receiving end of a lot of incidental momentary contact and any of it could be an accident. Maybe all of it could still be an accident. Was I just overtired and sleep-deprived and imagining weird things? Inside my head I berated myself for having become so sex-obsessed, especially about people thinking I was gay, that I was on edge about it and halluci—*he just did it again*. Would some other guy even notice? Is it meaningless unless you're a person who is all wound up about such things? What happened back there with that guy in Albuquerque that time was my own fault, I just let it happen, and that's why now I'm haunted by it all the time. Thinking everyone has me sized up as wanting gay sex.

I wondered if, assuming this was indeed actually happening (Was it? Was it really?), this was also my fault, like again I had just let something happen. Well let's see, I'm wearing this shirt, it's not a very masculine shirt really, a white cotton button up shirt with pretty blue print patterns on it. And I started chattering like a parakeet all cheerful and silly as soon as I got into the truck. Did I do things to make them think I wanted this kind of a good time? These guys are truckers; no one jokes about "Watch out for horny fag truckers who pick up guys hitchhiking." Nope, everyone knows truckers are the ones who treat hitchhikers decently and they're professional and they're on the road all the time, they work for companies. Assuming this is actually happening to me, it's not likely that the same thing would be happening to any other guy who had been out hitchhiking. What did I do wrong that made this happen?

I got more jittery and condensed my body into ever taller and less relaxed bundles and my voice and face felt increasingly delicate and shatterably fragile, trying to deny, trying to stay cordial and act like nothing was happening while inside was a bunch of screams.

They pulled into a huge truck stop in Atlanta as they said they would, and the driver explained that there was a line and each truck had to be weighed and recorded. They wanted to grab breakfast first, and then as soon as the truck had been processed they'd be driving through Athens and they would drop me off downtown. I shakily thanked them and explained that I was going to walk around, pee, smoke a cigarette and meet up with them later.

Inside my head I was still torn between believing these guys were actually playing feely feely with me and believing that I was just stressed out and imagining creepy but highly unlikely scenarios. And Athens was so close and yet so far and if it was all in my head or *even if it wasn't*, once they resumed we would be there so soon and it would be over with. And otherwise I would have to get my bags which were still in their truck, which could be awkward, and then catch a ride with someone else. I was tired, and a thousand times more frazzled and frenetic than I had been when they picked me up and it was hard to think clearly and every course of action seemed problematic when I considered it.

I finally decided on a plan: I would find them and tell them that I'd found another ride to Athens and would like to go with that rather than wait on them. Their truck wasn't even *in* the inspection line, I discovered, and so it didn't look like they were in any hurry, so I figured it sounded plausible.

The dark-haired husky guy who'd been driving was examining his truck's tires. I walked over. "Umm, hey, umm, listen. I ran into someone who is heading into Athens now, and I figured I'd go ahead and ride with them, seeing as it looks like you might be held here for some time. I really appreciate you stopping for me and thanks for offering to take me the rest of the way." His partner wasn't around. He shrugged and acted neither friendly nor unfriendly about it, more like uninterested for the most part. "I need to get my bags," I added.

He led me to the truck and opened the bottom storage compartment where he'd placed them when they picked me up. There was only the full-sized suitcase in there. The little briefcase which had my poems and music and LSD-inspired artwork and various other writings and notes was missing.

"I don't see the other one. Little brownish tan briefcase about this size."

"This is the only bag you had with you when we picked you up," the truck driver stated.

I knew for sure otherwise. "They were lashed together through the handles. Don't you remember? We had to untie them from each other to put them in; they were too tall to go in here on top of each other tied together like that."

"I don't know anything about any bag but this. It's the only one you had. You accusing me and my partner of stealing your stuff, now, is that it?"

"No, no, nothing like that, but you got less reason to pay attention since it ain't your bags. I'm sure you just don't remember it, but it must be in here somewhere."

"So now you're calling me a liar?"

The fragile glassy external part of me shattered and the screamy part came out and I said, "I don't know what happened and I don't *think* you and the other driver have any interest in my stuff but you seem to want *something* from me that I don't want any part of, and I don't want to ride with you any more. I just want my briefcase and I want to leave. Please, can I just have it?"

"You know," he said with disgust, "this is why I don't like to do favors for people anymore. We try to help out guys like you out here on the highway and you know something it's just not worth it, this kind of shit."

My heart was thudding and my breath was shallow and my stomach felt like it was full of steel wool. The driver strode to the cab door and yanked it open. He gestured toward the little ladder-steps that one climbs to get up into the cab. "The only other place anything can be besides that baggage rack is up there. Go on up and take a look."

There *was*, I knew, additional space up there aside from the seats and the middle hump area where I had sat as a passenger. A sleeper compartment sat back behind a curtain behind the seats. I was stepping forward toward the cab door when I had a premonition, a vision of myself climbing up those steps with the driver coming up right behind me while his partner was waiting behind the sleeping compartment curtain.

No. I declined the offer to search the cab. It didn't matter. They can't *not* know what they did with it unless it somehow fell *out* of the truck's storage compartment. I kept my feet on the ground and took the one suitcase and walked away from him, the truck, and probably my briefcase, while aching for all the personal creations inside it that I was leaving behind.

I was so scared and angry and shaken up I could scarcely talk. Not too long ago I'd been sitting on this suitcase confidently hitching the last leg of this expedition, feeling like I could take care of myself in the "real world" a little better than folks thought—better in many ways than the Army veteran Donald S. Skyler, for example. But now I felt like someone had shown me myself in a mirror and I'd seen something pathetic, some kind of malformed half-person who'd never ever be able to survive without some kind of keepers to feed me and keep me out of trouble. Something wasn't right about me and bad things were always going to happen to me and I was always not going to deal with them adequately. I was fragile and delicate and my life would never get better in any meaningful way. Something was wrong with me in a way that the laws of nature meant I'd always be the pecked-on chicken, the painted bird.

I huddled next to a pay phone and placed a collect call to my parents at my grandparents' house in Athens. I did not say to my dad that my roommate and I had decided to spend the airline ticket money on marijuana, which had subsequently been handed over to people we did not know, who took off with it, leaving me to hitchhike across country and that I'd made it this far but that now because of the way I was different from other people bad things had happened to me and I needed to be rescued and taken to a world that wasn't like this one.

I instead constructed the best lie I could think of, which was that I had had trouble at the airport finding a way to Athens and had met up with a truck driver heading that way but he was now holding onto a piece of my luggage. I was at a truck stop with no public or commercial transportation options for getting from there to Athens. I didn't want to lie. I wanted to explain how everything, everything, had gone all wrong and had been wrong for so long, and that I knew something was wrong with me, and please help, and make it all go away. I wanted to cry while someone held me. I asked if someone could come get me.

After about forty-five minutes I recognized my father's Pontiac pulling into the truck stop. The person who got out of the driver's seat to look around for me, however, was not my dad but was instead my sister's boyfriend Jeff Maloney, a somewhat beefy broad-shouldered seventeen-year-old guy with blond hair. It was unseasonably warm for December, and he was wearing cutoff jeans shorts. Somehow it completed my humiliation, as if there were some disinterested third party observer watching everything transpire to whom it would look like I had had my boyfriend come get me when the mean man in the truck wouldn't give me back my poems.

I was at Grandpa's and Grandma's house and everyone was being cheerful and folksy. Sister, parents, grandparents, all talking according to patterns and rhythms that had been worked into place like a riverbed, familiar flow patterns, a long long time ago. They weren't seeing me, not really. They did not see that I was over. Over is when it's been too long. When you're out of it. When it's time to quit trying to go on any further. When you know, down deep inside, that you're drained dead empty of all the somedays and all the tomorrows and suddenly your days blur together and become a life. I was over and right then I wanted to be oblivious.

Conveniently, while rummaging around in the bathroom, looking for something without knowing explicitly what, I found a bottle of prescription medication called Seconal with a warning about how taking it could make you drowsy and unable to operate machinery. I wanted to get really oblivious so I could quit feeling and thinking. I shook out about eight of the fat red capsules and swallowed them. Then I shrugged and shook out about that many a second time and swallowed them too.

My folks and grandfolks were sitting on the front porch having a quiet easy evening of it, of the sort that once would have bored me with its lack of challenge and excitement. Now I claimed an unused rocking chair and rocked slowly, slowly, and smiled numbly and peacefully as I rocked, looking out over the view from the hill that my grandparents' house sat on.

I had maybe had some decent moments in there for which I was grateful, days of promise and fun so you couldn't say I had never lived. I had been held with love by my grandparents and I had laughed at birthday parties and I had once on a special evening thrown rocks off the side of a cliff and been in love. I'd sung in a great choir and I'd stood around a bonfire and felt like I was a part of things. Not everyone gets to have as fulfilling a life as I had had, even if some people got to have a little more.

So it was okay, sitting on this porch with my parents and grandparents, and being so much older than any of them were as a consequence of the fact that they had some life in front of them whereas I was over. Everything was okay. Nothing mattered anymore. I smiled. In a little while I explained that I was tired from my long trip and would like to go to bed early, and did so.

I woke up in a hospital bed with an IV in my arm and a catheter up my works. I was quite cheerful and at the same time was sort of aware that I was cheerful in part because of the drug that was still in my system. Be that as it may, I was also cheerful in part because I was breathing air. Because I had woken up.

My head had lied to me, hidden some things from me, or rather since my head *is* me I had set myself up. I had said to myself I was going to get *real high* on those red pills. I had said to myself that I was going to get really oblivious and not have to think and feel any more. I had *not*, however, acknowledged to myself that I was trying to get dead. But I'd taken measures that had constituted a pretty damn decent attempt at becoming a dead person, considering the resources and situation I'd been in at the time.

This air I was breathing was a free bounty. By all rights I had no business being here anymore. So if I screwed this life up, the life I was living at this point was an unexpected extra anyhow. It was perhaps a strange way to look at it, but it felt liberating and I went with it. This life's a freebie and doesn't count so I can do anything I want. I had done the best I could with the serious one and ended it last night and somehow I got a bonus round.

The first thing to deal with in my new life was that I was in a hospital and had just taken some umpteen Seconal pills in order to get here, and that was going to create a problem. No way I was going to be able to make that look better by explaining that Part A of my head had fooled Part B of my head into not realizing that I was taking a deadly dose, so therefore it didn't count as a suicide attempt.

Okay so we don't tell them. Have to tell them something though. I could not come up with an explanation that would account for a bunch of red pills inside me without my having put them there, so I lied outrageously and said I had no clue whatsoever as to what had happened except that I had bummed a smoke from somebody downtown and smoked it later after supper and it had tasted really weird.

I didn't know if the hospital staff would fall for it but it was close to being the kind of thing my parents believed could happen in the dangerous world of evil drugs and hippies and whatnot. And maybe the hospital folks would believe I was lying my ass off but take from my story the notion that I knew what I'd done but was trying to hide it, that I'd accidentally OD'd rather than purposefully OD'd, and they'd release me and not try to lock me up for trying to commit suicide. It worked. I was released later the same day (subsequent to removal of tubes) and instructed not to beg any more cigarettes from strangers.

The Ongoing Project

It was 1979, I was alive, twenty, and still a Vo-tech student, and was back in my apartment in Albuquerque. Which was more than I could say for my erstwhile roommate, Donald S. Skyler. It was now the end of the first week of resumed classes and he was nowhere in sight.

We started the unit on automotive air conditioning. How decompressing Freon (refrigerant-12) causes it to plummet in temperature. The compressor, the condenser, the valves that controlled flow from high-pressure to low-pressure side, the cold coils inside the car that the forced air blows over, the hot ones out on the radiator to be air-cooled along with the radiator fluid.

My teacher from last fall's final unit, the front end alignment and brakes teacher, had talked up how strong I was, how I'd beaten the starch out of a guy to everyone's amazement. People left me mostly alone. I didn't correct the rumor.

Donald S. Skyler eventually got in touch with me by phone. "Hey, Derek, how's it going? Did you get to, where was it, Georgia, you get there okay? That's good. Hey listen, I've decided to withdraw from Vo-tech. I'm going to study somewhere else, and I called the VA on the phone and they say I can get a partial refund but they're only willing to send it to the address they got on file which is the apartment there. I still got your toolbox. We took them both with us in my car, you remember? If you'll forward that refund check to me when it arrives, I'll send you back your toolbox. How's that sound?"

I sent him his refund Veterans' Administration check. He did not send me my toolbox and I never heard from him again. I was glad he wasn't coming back. In his absence, I played his record albums from time to time. I became quite fond of the sad poignant Melanie and the dark dystopian Bloodrock and listened to them a lot.

I continued to practice the piano at UNM campus, and often stayed in that area well into the evening. I had finally, belatedly, discovered that the parklike front lawn tended to fill up in the late afternoon with an eclectic mixture of university students and nonstudents and was a place where one could buy pot and acid. People would chat about abstract ideas ranging from politics to theories of what is real and how you know it's real.

To my surprised delight, some people pronounced *me* wise and wanted to hear *my* insights. Along with the ego boost was the internal recognition that I didn't entirely disagree with them about that. Yes, I was keenly aware of the huge core of unanswered questions and unsatisfied yearnings for understanding I still carried around inside myself, and my shaky willingness to be alive didn't strongly recommend me as a person from whom to learn how to be happy. But my thirst for understanding things seemed to be accompanied by a capacity to comprehend large complex concepts, things I'd seen on my own, not just read in a book, things to which I had given my own descriptive names.

And I was finding that I could *explain* things to people and they could often follow what I was saying. I could make sense to them. And they often said that the things I laid out to them this way had implications for their real-life issues, even as I continued to struggle with such matters myself.

I still wanted to find more people who were doing this, people from whom I could learn, and I wanted to be a part of a group, a collective mindset, a community of such people. But I now envisioned myself joining them as a person who had not, as I once worried, merely shown up to collect on the wisdom and benefits of the social philosophers who had come of age before me, but instead as a person who had wrestled, struggled, and made meaningful contributions to understandings and illuminations, and was ready to continue to do so after having hooked up with my peers.

As soon as I was able to support myself as an auto mechanic, I'd be able to work in pretty much any community. Every town would need folks who can work on cars. Cars were everywhere. And in the evenings after a good hard day's satisfying work, with my tools in the oil making folks' vehicles run smoothly, I'd either have eclectic groups of thinking people over for a bowl and chat or I'd be at someone else's house for similar activity. I'd be a self-supporting viable hippie, integrating the everyday practical and utilitarian values with the idealistic visionary thinking that drove and inspired me.

I also continued to have sessions with the mental health workers at Albuquerque Crisis. I no longer went there only when I had those angst-ridden moments of feeling like something was so badly wrong with me that I was willing to be told what to do to fix it. I now went in more of an "ongoing project" sort of way, a person working on himself.

Officially they would have preferred that I go to outpatient services during the day at the outpatient center. Unofficially, the staff there said that I was both more in crisis and less impaired than the people those programs ministered to, and as long as I didn't take up time and resources that needed to go to other walk-in psychiatric emergency patients, and waited until they were having a slow evening, I was welcome to keep coming in.

Soon it was time to graduate. My parents came down and took me to dinner and we all went to the ceremony. My folks shook the hands of the various instructors and then came over to help me pack. Hours later, I was rolling back to Los Alamos, to live with my parents until I could get a job as an auto mechanic and move out to live on my own, independent.

"Sometimes you have to walk before you can fly," my mom told me. In my case, it looked like I would have to remain dependent on my parents as an employed auto mechanic at least to start with because the job I was able to land with my new skills paid only minimum wage. I was hired to work at Hilltop Conoco and would pump gas and manage the cash register during evening hours, clean the bathrooms at closing time, and then do flat tire repair, rotate folks' tires, flush antifreeze and recharge radiators for the coming winter, and put new tires on rims. It was a start.

It was the weekend and I was at another one of those outdoor bonfire parties, at St. Peter's Dome. I'd been horribly lonely in Albuquerque. I wanted sex, and/or a girlfriend, and in the aftermath of my recent experiences I was ready to try something different. Why didn't any of these girls fancy me at these parties? Why didn't sexual events eventually just kind of unfold, insofar as I was, or so I thought, decent company, reasonably nice looking, and easy to talk to? Girls knew my name and sometimes said hi and were friendly and talked to me but that's as far as things went. Honestly, did they think I wasn't interested?

Girls so often complain about boys only paying attention to them because they want sex. Pressuring them for sex. But do you see them clustering around boys who don't? Well maybe I ought to act more like other guys. I don't have to be nice. I can be pushy too, I'll show you. Act like I just want to score, see how you like it.

Tall flames danced and the sharp tang of wood smoke enticed my nose. I wandered over to Pam, a girl I'd seen at parties before, and greeted her. "Whatcha' doing?"

"Hey! Having a good time. Gettin' buzzed."

"I know how you could have a better time."

Pam raised her eyebrows. "Oh?"

"You should have sex with me and you'll feel really good."

Pam flounced indignantly, pouting. "That makes me feel bad, that you would say something like that to me."

I replied, "I don't want you to feel bad. I know how to make you feel better."

"Oh yeah, how?" She pushed her hair back from her shoulder.

"Come have sex with me."

She smiled but shook her head and said, "I'm not that kind of girl."

"What kind of girl aren't you?" I asked.

"What kind of girl do you *think* I am?"

"The kind of girl who likes to have fun." I tipped my beer toward her appreciatively while hooking my free thumb through my belt loop, rocking back on my heels.

"Well...I don't do that kind of thing"

"What, have fun?" I deadpanned, staring back.

"No!" Pam sighed, exasperated but still smiling. "I mean I feel bad that you think I would just go off with you to have sex."

"No, no, please don't feel bad. I don't want you to feel bad," I replied. "Let me make you feel good. I know how to make you feel good."

Pam lit a cigarette. "I don't think you should say things like that to girls; it's really disrespectful."

So I was right, it seems like stuff can happen if I act like this, like I don't care whether the girl wants sex or not, as long as I do. I could come up with a cute rejoinder to keep the volley going back and forth if I wanted to. "You're right, and I'm sorry," I said.

Pam sipped on her beer. She fiddled with her jacket button as she studied me for a moment, then said, "You should be ashamed, asking me to go off and have sex with you. You're a bad boy."

"Yeah, that wasn't very nice. You're a girl who doesn't do those kind of things. I apologize." I nodded politely to her and went to refill at the keg.

She was waiting when I returned. She said, "I'm really upset that you thought you could just have sex with me."

"I'm sorry I upset you. I got drunk and stoned and said some selfish things. I'm not like that usually."

Pam scuffed her sneakers in the pine needles and twigs, looked at me as if formulating what she was going to say, but then sighed and strolled off toward a nearby cluster of partiers without saying another word.

I thought about how intensely I missed Linda Sorrens and how things had been when we'd been together. I wanted that, not this stupid charade. I was *not* like the other boys and I wanted to be with someone who knew that and was glad about it. I wanted to feel special.

The job at Hilltop Conoco was essentially another "teenager caliber" job much like my job at Anderson's Pharmacy had been. If I gave up eating food, parked my car and walked everywhere, and didn't spend money on pot or music, I could probably pay the rent on an efficiency apartment on Gold Street uptown. But practically speaking I wasn't earning enough to push off and live on my own. Economic independence wasn't mine yet. It also wasn't really auto mechanic employment. I was using very few of the skills I had been taught and rarely had the chance to open my tool box (which, by the way, Albuquerque Vo-Tech had sold me to replace the one Donald S. Skyler had reneged on returning to me).

I was afraid that without practice I'd forget what I'd learned, so I pestered my boss fairly often to keep in mind, when dealing with customers, that he did have a fledgling mechanic who would do more involved things. He finally allowed that if I did my work after hours and people wanted to pay me to mess with their cars, I could use Conoco's bays, but I had to clean up after myself. So I bled a few brake lines for my friends for the experience (not charging them) and changed a customer's wheel bearings and bearing-race on all four wheels, and examined a customer's weak emergency brake.

Then for my own car I bought a B & M Shift Improver Kit which involved draining the automatic transmission fluid, removing the pan, and carefully drilling some new holes in the baffle plate that controlled when fluid would press on the valves that regulated shifting. There were also a couple check balls I had to remove. While I was at it, I installed an external automatic transmission fluid cooler that attached to the radiator and would keep the automatic transmission running cooler.

It took hours to get it done (I was being slow and very careful to not get foreign material anywhere or bump something and send tiny parts flying). Automatic transmission pans don't have drain plugs like oil pans do, and transmission fluid splashed beyond the drain funnel I'd set up and made a mess on the floor. I tossed a layer of kitty litter on top of the spilled transmission fluid to start soaking it up, and then locked up and went out for a test drive.

The transmission shifted much more quickly and crisply and did everything it was supposed to do. The new cooling system worked well and the engine temp stayed below 160°. Then I ran out of gas. My fuel gauge was defective. I was quite a distance from any open service station (including Conoco) and I couldn't afford a wrecker, so I had to walk and come back with a jug of gas.

When I finally got to Conoco, the owner had come in and was waiting in the front office with a final check for me. He was mad that I'd left the bay in such a mess and didn't want to hear that I'd planned on getting back and cleaning it up before he'd be in, so here was what he owed me for the week. He did not want me back Monday morning.

Losing the Conoco job was worrisome and I'd brought it upon myself by not cleaning up the bay completely before leaving the shop. I knew my boss was obsessed with keeping the bay area clean. Los Alamos was a pretty small town and although the operating idea behind choosing auto mechanics as a field was that I could go pretty much anywhere and get a job, I was for the moment limited to the surrounding area. I didn't have the resources to keep myself alive and fed while looking for a job elsewhere.

"Listen, son, I guess you know your mom and I never visualized you as an auto mechanic, and I suppose I'm still not entirely comfortable with that. But we've always said we'd respect whatever career choices you and Jan make for yourselves, and I want you to know we're proud of you for getting through that school and getting out there every morning to work at Conoco. I hope you don't mind but I spoke with the service manager at the Chevrolet dealership in Española where we looked at pickup trucks last year, and he says they're taking on some extra entry level mechanics. He said to have you stop by and talk to him."

My mood perked up. I drove down and introduced myself to the shop foreman, Armando Lujan. "You're Derek, right? So...here's the deal. We aren't putting anyone on actual payroll yet but we're interested in trying out some new hands, so if you come in and we've got enough work to hand off some tasks to you, you get paid the standard salary rate for those hours. You indicate on the sign-in sheet which hours you work. I don't know if that sounds like something you'd want to try or not. I know you have to come down from Los Alamos to get here."

I told him I wanted to take a crack at it. We shook hands and he welcomed me onboard and told me when to show up the next day. I was again employed, this time officially as an auto mechanic, even, although it was not a full-time permanent job, exactly.

There was an early 1970s Custom Deluxe pickup truck and the service ticket said it was difficult to start and ran choppy. I signed in and got the vehicle started and drove it into my bay. Yes, it stuttered and shook, and it would die if you added a lot of gas all at once. Very ragged. I stared down the neck of the carburetor. Sprayed the fuel jets by pulling the carb lever manually and watched the spray, symmetrical in both barrels. The butterfly valve seemed to be seating correctly.

The spark plugs, when pulled, were dry and the contact points were intact and the spark gaps were appropriate. Distributor rotor looked fine. Dwell on the condenser was a little off, and oddly when I tried to change it to factory specs the engine ran a bit worse. Firing order wasn't wrong (no one had hooked the wrong wires to the spark plugs). Ignition timing was pretty much correct but it...wandered. The sensor hooks to just one of the eight spark plug wires and therefore flashes the strobe for just that one cylinder, which ought to be firing at an exactly identical number of degrees before maximum compression position (top dead center). As I watched, it seemed to oscillate occasionally. Hmm. I wonder...

I turned off the engine and manually rolled the crankshaft around until the alignment notch on the crankshaft pulley was visible, then pulled paraphernalia out of the way until I could loosen a cover plate and see the corresponding notch on the big camshaft pulley. They looked like they weren't synched up right. I took a compression gauge and started the engine again and the engine compression was down sixty percent.

I told Mandy Lujan I thought the timing chain had skipped some notches and was maybe damaged, and he said go ahead, let's find out. I had to pull the alternator and the power steering pump and a spiderweb of electrical wires and hoses from the front of the engine first, but eventually I was able to remove the cover plate. Sure enough, the timing chain was shredded and twisted. I'd figured it out. I'd diagnosed it myself.

I did wheel balancing, front end alignments, removed brake drums and turned them, replaced wheel bearings, took my voltmeter into the passenger compartment to diagnose electical accessories that had stopped working. I got a reputation: I was slow but I did good work. Mandy said I'd speed up over time. A lot of the other mechanics were doing things that were routine for them.

Nothing was routine for me yet. Another pickup truck was hauled in by a wrecker. It had locked up at thirty-five miles per hour and could not be started. I told Mandy it looked like a transmission problem and put it on the lift for a look from below, at which point I realized a connecting rod was protruding through a hole blown out the side of the engine block. I went back to Mandy and revised my diagnosis.

It was Saturday night and this time the party was down inside the rim of the Rio Grande, at Pajarito Springs, where once upon a time I had been taken by Jay and Terri and Tina to swim in our underwear. Older, more confident and expansive, I went down the narrow trail, passing the pipe to others behind and in front of me, expounding on the meaning of the universe and the quality of weed compared to what we used to get when I was in high school and the superiority of Pontiacs to Chevrolets, just generally having a good time. I was decked out in cheerful ceremonial regalia, wearing that red and gold paisley shirt that I'd made myself, a festive burst of joy.

At a particular point, the trail hugged the side of a rather steep hill of crumbly sand, and it made for tricky walking, especially for a person decently buzzed and doing it by moonlight in the middle of the night, as we were. I was second in line among a handful of party-bound people negotiating this part of the trail when a couple other guys suddenly loomed over the rise coming from the other direction, facing us.

I guess the first guy from that group was startled or something—he brought up his fists. The guy directly in front of me in my own group, a tall blond guy I didn't recognize, said "Ho" or "Whoa" or something, and everyone relaxed. It struck me as funny—like Cheech Marin thinking the cops are busting the place and it's just Tommy Chong returning to the apartment or something like that.

I laughed and drawled lazily, in my best wasted stoner voice, "Like yeah, man, you totally wouldn't want to get into all that aggressive shit when we're already stoned and stumbling around in the dark on this fuckin' sand dune." And the blond dude turned around and punched me.

I mused to myself afterwards as I plucked out cactus needles. I'd once thought there was this kind of shared accept-everyone mentality among pot smokers. Love peace and brotherhood, just be cool, man, no heavy trips to be laid on other folks' heads...getting over distrust and just being mellow with each other, ditching all the uptight society rules and going with simple rules like do it if it feels good and if it doesn't hurt anybody there's nothing wrong with it and do your own thing.

I'd liked that attitude and gradually decided to join them, and I'd tried to leave behind my old uptight ways, but those people back there at the party hadn't been perceiving me as one of them. They'd seen me as a person to pick on and try to hurt just like those kids who used to pick on me years ago. I pulled another needle out. *I still believe in that stuff. Being non-judgmental. That if you aren't hurting anyone no one should interfere with what you're doing. That there should be goodwill and benevolent welcome extended to all people if they're willing to not be hurtful and not try to control other people.*

I peeled back the layer of denim overlaying the pocket lining and began working on the deeper needles rammed through the pocket fabric. *Smoking pot doesn't make all that just happen. This isn't the first time I've smoked pot with people and then discovered that they were not safe.*

It had been convenient to the other kids I'd gone to school with that I'd stopped telling on them to adults. On the other hand they really had been nice to me.

Well, maybe they accepted me, but that doesn't mean I am automatically accepted into some kind of all-encompassing cool kids' group just because I smoke pot. There were a lot of people at that party back there and I don't think that blond guy somehow got everyone else to go somewhere else while he filled that little area with his friends. And no one was saying, "Shit, dude, why don't you let the guy alone? I think he's had enough already." They weren't playing by their vaunted boy-rules of fair fight. A bunch of folks back there wanted to see me get hurt and they were laughing.

Back in school, I'd tried to start over, put aside my differences from other kids and make friends and be a part of things. I had been in Boy Scouts and in the high school choir, and I had become a partier who went to pot parties. But it never seemed to quite work out. I ended up on the outside, looking through the window at everyone else having fun. I heard the fun and I saw the fun but I was never really inside where it was happening.

I finished up, pulled my pants back up over my sore bleeding thighs and limped to where my car was parked. Someone had bashed a dent in the trunk of my car with some blunt object and scrawled FAGGOT in the paint with a sharp tool. Maybe someone who had been down there had come up from the party and passed me while I was ministering to my wounds, or maybe not. My car sort of stood out. A lot of people knew it was my car.

I'd thought I'd been accepted as a mellow countercultural guy of the peaceful Aquarian age, just as I'd thought the pot scene was going to be about free love without sexual hangups. That's how it was supposed to be. But the girls at pot parties seemed to go for the boys who played pushy with them while they protested, like Pam, instead of it being that we all like sex and enjoy being mellow and loving with each other. And meanwhile the peace thing didn't really mean no fighting and belligerence, either. This simply wasn't working. I didn't belong here.

At home the next morning I woke up, got out of bed (painfully) and glanced down at the previous evening's clothes, which were in a pile on my floor. There sat my red and gold paisley shirt, my homemade shirt. They had beaten up a guy in a bright red paisley shirt.

I don't like it when people think I'm queer but then I go to pot parties wearing something like that. They had seen me in that shirt and then I said something about when you shouldn't fight. So from their perspective, here was this guy everyone thought was gay and then he wore this shirt to a party. Maybe the shirt by itself doesn't mean much but if everyone already thinks you're gay it's not the kind of shirt you wear unless you're saying "Yeah and so what." So I guess they didn't like it when the faggy guy with the faggy shirt offered his opinion on where and when real boys should do their fighting.

It was just like when I was hitchhiking. *People think they know all about me because there's something about how I look or act or dress. I need to be careful about that kind of thing because if all the girls think I'm gay I'm not going to get a girlfriend, am I?*

After that I took to wearing jeans and a t-shirt as a standard uniform.

Back in Albuquerque I had gotten in the habit of talking with mental health counselors at Albuquerque Crisis, so here in Los Alamos I decided to do the same. There was a place called Family Counseling that I was eligible to go to, and a counselor was assigned to me, Pamela Teague. I didn't think she was as good as the people I'd spoken to in Albuquerque, at least not for the things I went in for, but it was still good to have a sort of sounding board. I talked about my frustrations trying to get involved with a girl.

"What kind of girl would you like to become involved with?"

"Someone I could talk to," I replied. And I spoke frankly about the more carnal aspect of the frustration: "I want to make out."

"Sometimes," she responded, "you just have to make do."

As I came into work a coworker said, "Hey did you hear? Mandy is dead." For some reason I thought he was joking, although it wasn't terribly funny. I headed back to work on the vehicle I'd started on the day before. But after a few hours enough gossip had floated within earshot that it sounded real. They called an official meeting at noon, and the CEO spoke to us and explained that Mandy Lujan had suffered a heart attack and died the previous evening. One of his junior associates, Ruben Padilla, would be taking over. I didn't feel good about that. I'd never gotten good vibes off Ruben and didn't think he liked me. I thought about Mandy being dead. Sad. I'd liked Mandy.

With the advent of Ruben Padilla, there ceased to be any work deemed appropriate for me to sign on for. I spent days *not* working, hanging out at my bay, in case something came in, but after a week and a half I got the idea. Ruben didn't want me there for whatever reason and this job was over. I wasn't going to get any more paid hours.

My parents wanted me to try college again. This plan of being an auto mechanic wasn't working, they said. I was not supporting myself and had no job prospects at the moment, and if pursuing a course as an auto mechanic wasn't going to give me economic independence, it no longer had anything to recommend itself over going to college. And in college I would be with people my own age and with interests more like my own, and would not be so cut off. They had a point there.

My counselor at Family Counseling agreed. Despite the University of Mississippi experience, college really was where I belonged. I needed to pick an appropriate college. I started to like the idea, imagining political and philosophical discussions in college dorm rooms and getting to know girls by being in the same classroom with them. I'd developed good feelings about the University of New Mexico while I was in Albuquerque and I'd already had some of those conversations out on the front lawn. I knew it would not be like University of Mississippi all over again. So I was amenable. But first I wanted a short little vacation first, a trip to Lexington, Massachusetts. I needed to see Linda Sorrens again.

REUNION

I had been invited. Linda and I had written back and forth a few times in the last eighteen months and her most recent letter began, "I owe you an invitation I believe. Derek Turner is hereby invited to vacation at the modest but lovable Sorrens abode. Located in the heart of exotic Lexington, Mass. Six rooms, a color TV and Linda at your service—all at the incredibly low price of transportation and a good conversation!" She added, farther down, "Three years? I remember it like yesterday. We sure don't have secluded cliffs like those around here. Sigh."

By this point I was almost desperately harkening back to how things had been between us in our brief fleeting encounter. In all the intervening time, in all the opportunities to talk, flirt, make out, or otherwise interact with girls, that tiny handful of days with Linda, culminating in that evening sitting on the side of the cliff, was the gold standard, the example of how I wanted it to be.

I was well aware of what a short fragment of time we'd had, and how long ago that was, but Linda's replies over all this time seemed to indicate that it stood out as something special for her too. I assumed she had other boyfriends, or at least at some point had had some, and she was well aware that I had tried dating and being involved with other girls. But if I could just see her again, be with her again, it would make up for so much even though I'd be returning to New Mexico afterwards.

Maybe we'd do the things we hadn't done back then; maybe we

wouldn't. Certainly we would talk for hours and catch up and share ourselves, and for a little while at least I would not feel alone in the world. I called her and we talked on the phone. I explained that I could actually really come if she'd really like to see me, if the invitation was serious. And she said that it was, and come, definitely.

My parents offered to buy me a round trip Greyhound bus ticket and I packed my bags. I sat in the back and made myself comfortable and alternated between reading books and looking out the window and daydreaming about Linda.

"Here's an extra blanket if you need, and towels are in the closet. Let me know if you need anything else. Oh, and here are some brochures and tourist guides in case you want to walk around Lexington some while you're up here." Linda briskly and efficiently led me on a tour of the house and then suggested I wash up and relax by myself for a while before supper, then departed down the hall. I wondered why she was being so distant and constrained. Had something upset her? Was someone in her family making her feel like she couldn't speak freely? That didn't seem likely, but there wasn't anyone else around so maybe there was something going on that I didn't know about.

I took a shower and put on fresh clothes and came down to the supper table, complimented Mrs. Sorrens on the food, chatted with Mr. and Mrs. Sorrens about my folks and answered their questions about my life in New Mexico and my plans for attending the university. All the while I was trying to exchange glances with Linda, the conspiratorial warmth of mutual recognition I remembered, but she didn't even seem free to do that much.

I helped her carry dishes to the kitchen and load the dishwasher and used the opportunity to ask, "Can we maybe go for a walk, get out of the house for a bit?" I was impatient for us to be somewhere we could talk freely and either dispel this weird awkward distance or find out what was amiss.

"How about going to a movie? Have you seen *Kramer vs Kramer*? It's playing in the shopping mall not too far from here."

"Oh, that sounds nice. I read the book and liked it and I've been meaning to see the movie. I hope they did a good job on it and didn't make it too oversimplified." Not that I particularly cared what movie we saw. She snagged the car keys from the wooden post in the hallway, called out a "see you in a couple hours" to her folks, and I followed her to the family car in the driveway.

I felt much better already. I smiled at her. She gave me that little quirky smile I remembered, blue eyes crinkling, the freckles on her nose dancing, then glanced behind her to back up. "My brother David practically lives in this car, and I usually get the Volvo. But I got her first for once." I nodded. "Did you and your sister fight over the cars in the Turner fleet before you got your own transportation?"

"Not really. We had a little Datsun and the big family car, but Jan and I learned on both of them and I don't think either of us had a strong preference."

Linda parked and beckoned me to follow her down the block. "I like to walk fast; I hope you don't mind," she said, adding "I hate going places with people who just poke along like they aren't trying to get where they're going."

"Yeah, I can relate to that. I've got a long stride and I walk faster than most people. It's kind of fun to walk with someone who likes to walk at my own pace." She wasn't kidding. We covered several blocks of Lexington smoothly and rapidly. I waited, giving her space to open up when she was ready, listening and just being there.

"Do you like to sit close up to the screen or in the back? Is this good? We can sit here on the aisle or go farther in if you'd rather be more centered..." I indicated these seats were fine and we situated ourselves in them. "I should let you know," she warned, "when I go to a movie, I go to see the movie." So we sat side by side and watched the movie. I was impatient to get back to talking but considered that she wasn't ready, so after a bit I managed to relax and get caught up in the story.

On our way back to the parking lot, I commented, "I thought it was well cast. But I thought they could have painted her side more sympathetically. I mean, the book had a strong theme of how unfair it is that fathers aren't regarded as equal parents, but the movie made her into a lot more of a villain than the book did."

"Oh, well, I like almost anything Meryl Streep is in. Have you seen a lot of her other movies?" We got into the car, and Linda backed out. "So that building up there is the old courthouse. There was a skirmish down there, used to be fields back then, back in the Revolutionary War." My mood was plummeting. I was feeling anxious and frustrated. We were rapidly headed back to her home and had hardly spoken. "Linda, are you...is anything wrong?"

"No, why? Sorry, was I not paying attention? I get that way sometimes and don't realize it. You were talking about Meryl Streep's character being more of a villain than in the book?" I floundered. No, I wasn't really interested in discussing the movie further, but I didn't know what to say, how to get started. We got out and as we entered the house, Linda informed me, "I have some business and projects to attend to for a while. You might want to check those brochures or take a walk around the neighborhood or something." And with that she disappeared down the hall.

I sat there immobile, sort of in shock. I wished someone would explain what was going on. Nothing made any sense. It was like she had a wall built around her. I lurked nervously in the hallway, feeling as if I was doing something socially inappropriate like being a peeping tom or investigating someone's medicine cabinet, worried that one of her parents would come up and ask me why I was loitering there. Finally Linda came out and I accosted her. "What's wrong? Why are...I was expecting that we would talk. I came here to be with you and you seem so far away. Can we talk?"

She indicated that we should go down into the family's basement. We would have privacy. Once down there, she said, matter-of-factly, "This is where I go with boys sometimes when I have them over. I like a lot of boys and I've had several here to visit. I'm not going steady with anyone. I like to date around."

"Sure. I figured you did. I mean I never expected otherwise."

"However," she added, "we can fool around if you want." Her face was casual, almost blank. Well, yes of course I did want to, but I didn't want it to be like this. I wanted it to be the way we'd once been. I didn't know what to do. Every answer seemed wrong. I decided I wanted to touch her, at least perhaps I could have some kind of effect on her. We sat on the couch and I moved my hands to her. She pulled back from affectionate touching and kissing and urged me to explore the erogenous zones, and I did, and felt her arousal and played with her until I felt her shuddery orgasm. I finally got a good, if somewhat sly and naughty, smile from her and she said we should go upstairs before her parents decided we'd disappeared on them, but we could come back later for some more.

The family watched TV and I sat along with them, and soon the evening was over and Linda was off to bed in her bedroom with a, "Sleep good, see you tomorrow." I sat up much of the night, miserable, confused. It was too...overstated. It wasn't like Linda was uninterested in me as a person; it was like she'd taken out a fifty-foot-tall billboard and proclaimed her lack of interest in huge letters.

There was a missing puzzle piece and I couldn't figure it out. She'd had plenty of opportunity to fade herself out of my life if she hadn't wanted to get sloppy romantically obsessed letters from the weird New Mexico guy she had met several summers ago. Could have just said, "You know, that was a long time ago when I was fourteen, and we've both changed a lot and I'd rather remember us with fondness than try to recreate that time." Could have said, "I have a boyfriend now and it wouldn't really be appropriate for you to come out." Could have just not answered my letters, or answered them without encouragement.

Yes, I supposed I had been the pushier and clingier of the two of us, the one to reach out after periods of letter-writing dormancy and silence even if I'd been the last one to write. But surely I wasn't so implacably pushy that she'd felt compelled to invite me here, not if she had the determination to hold herself aloof and unreachable once I arrived? I wanted to know what she felt. What she really felt. It was pretty obvious what she was trying to convey to me. That seemed loud and clear. But *why*?

I was emotionally fragile and incoherent to myself. I could not plan how to handle the situation because no matter what conclusion I reached, an hour later I had discarded that as a spectacularly bad approach. I did go somewhere on my own, to one of the tourist attractions from the brochures Linda had given me. Then when I got back I sat around in Linda's proximity, feeling like a kicked puppy, wishing and hoping she'd talk to me, be with me. My limited time to be up there was running out.

Linda was studiously ignoring me and immersing herself in a book. I came close enough to whisper and suggested that we go down into the basement for some fun, and I added, "You can bring your book with you if you want." So we did. We went down the steps and she stayed standing, reading her book and at least outwardly ignoring me while I slipped my hand down her pants and flicked her clitoris with my fingertips. I could feel her reactions with my fingers but she remained superficially unaffected until the end, when it took her knees out and she slumped against me.

It was the last evening before I'd be going back. I sat at a table across from Linda and as she listened to music on the headphones with her head bend forward, I got my fingers into her hair. I began stoking her hair, very delicately in case she hadn't actually noticed and would pull back when she did, but she neither pulled away nor acknowledged what I was doing. I started crying. I couldn't help it and I couldn't stop it, crying silently as I stroked her hair, tears running down my cheeks and down my shirt.

I'd lost her. I'd lost Linda, I didn't know what had happened and it didn't make any sense but everything I believed we'd had once, if it wasn't some horrid cheating illusion all along, was gone. Or maybe it was right here sitting across from me, even now, but if it was I couldn't get to it. It wasn't available to me.

PART THREE
BACK TO UNIVERSITY

A New Start

I was barreling down the road in my Bonneville, returning to Albuquerque, my car loaded with gear. I was going to be a college student again. *Not* majoring in astronomy and physics this time, but in *music*. I would learn to compose, to synthesize in the stylistic space between hard rock and classical. To compose rock for symphony orchestra and to write piano music and to become a better performer. And to have fun and be politically-socially active. I had the radio tuned to the college station, and Joan Baez was singing "Ain't gonna let nobody turn me around, gonna build a brand new world."

My residence hall was named Coronado, which in turn was divided into two buildings, Zia and Zuni. I was in Zia. My roommate was already moved in, and he had company. "Hey," he greeted me. "I'm Leland. I hope you don't mind, I selected the bed on this side, but I can move if you prefer this one."

"Hi, I'm Derek. No, this bed's fine. No, don't get up," I said, gesturing to the guy sitting on it.

"We were thinking about sparking up something to smoke, so it's good that you're here," continued Leland. "Are you okay with pot smoking?"

I had a moment's flashback to University of Mississippi and being told I was in the hands of the devil. Compare and contrast. I opened my box of homemade pot pipes with a flourish, and everyone gathered around admiringly.

"Whoa, that's bitchin'," proclaimed the guy who had been perched on what was to be my bed. He raised his palm for an emphatic high-five. "I'm Ralph."

"And I'm Larry," said a guy in wire-rim glasses. He flipped long bangs from his eyes and offered me a rolled baggie of marijuana. "This is Eddie."

"I was just asking the girls. Ellie and...Gia? Gina?" Leland said, gesturing to the two sitting on a cushion on the floor, "and Suzanne, if they had heard of Cheap Trick." He lowered the needle onto the album that was rotating on his turntable.

Over the next few days, I met several of our immediate neighbors from either side up and down the hall and saw a string of visitors, male and female, who came by to hang out. Leland was a party magnet.

I had two standard required music classes, one in music theory and one in ear training, both of them taught by Mr. Vasquez. I also had piano sessions one on one with a piano instructor. The rest of my courses were electives. I took a course on technical writing from the English department, an introductory biology course, and chorus, since all music students were supposed to be in an ensemble group.

There was a piano, although not a very good one, in the lounge of our dormitory. It was very difficult to get any real sound out of it. But it was public. Having a piano out in a public part of the dorm meant that being a piano player could be as social a thing as having a guitar, a way of meeting people, whether they be musicians, fans of music, or girls who liked musicians.

Sure enough, later that evening someone came over to the piano, having heard me playing. "Hey," she said. "You play real nice. I'm Yolanda. What's your name?"

"Derek. And hi. Do you sing, by any chance?"

"Oh hell yeah, I'm always into singing."

"Well, I like to write songs. I could write some songs and maybe we meet up and you sing them for me?" Yolanda liked that idea, so we set up a Friday evening date for doing that.

The next evening, I was playing something and another girl, Melva, came over to hear and we got to talking and I tried the same approach. "Thanks for that, I'm glad you like my playing. Do you sing? You do? Cool. Would you have any interest in singing some pieces I wrote? Yeah, I write songs. How about Saturday evening, here?" And, just that easily, I had two dates lined up.

This seemed like a good start. I'd decided that I'd been taking the romantic and sexual side of life way too seriously and that I needed to pursue it as fun. Keep it light.

On Friday, I went down to the lounge early and warmed up. After a while Yolanda came into the lounge and said "Hello, Derek." I smiled and waved at her and we chatted for a couple moments and then another girl came into the room and called out, "Hi Derek." I said hi back and then realized it was Melva.

They stood next to each other and looked back at me with obvious amusement. From their behavior I got a sense of what I must look like to them: some kind of cynical wannabe pick-up artist using recycled lines to get girls. Highly embarrassing. Not that either of them had any appropriate proprietary claims on my exclusive attention but it did sort of look like I thought of them as interchangeable and therefore that my interest in them didn't have much to do with them in any genuinely personal way.

It was Tuesday. Mr. Vasquez came into the ear training classroom, gave us his customary supercilious smile and addressed us: "Good morning class. I realize I'm running a little late myself, but if we could have our pencils out and stop talking with one another, that will facilitate us getting started without any additional waste of time. Shall we begin?"

He sat down at the piano. "I'm going to play four notes, one at a time—an arpeggio chord for the benefit of those of you who studied your terminology from our theory class. I will play from bottom to top—bass, tenor, alto and soprano. I'll play it twice. What I want you to do is write down for each of the four parts whether it has the *root*...the *fifth*...or the *third* and...whether it is *major*...or *minor*. Bass, tenor, alto, soprano. Okay, here we go." After playing the chord slowly twice, he glanced around and picked someone. "Debbie? Give us your interpretation of that chord."

Debbie answered with an uncertain rising question in her response. "Major? and...the bass has...the fifth? Tenor has...the root? Alto...the alto has...the third? And the soprano...has the root?"

Mr. Vasquez corrected, "It is major, so you got that right, possibly because there were only two choices to choose from. Listen again. The bass has the third, but you can't know that yet because the rest of the chord hasn't been played. Don't just guess. Tenor does have the root. The *alto* has the fifth and the soprano repeats the bass...*how* many octaves above? Class? Anybody?"

"Two," I said. This stuff came easily to me.

"*Verr*-ry good," Mr. Vasquez cooed. "Try this one," he told me, and began playing more notes.

After he played three of the four notes, I rattled off, "Minor, bass has the fifth, tenor the root, alto the third..." I paused until he played the final note. "...repeating the root for the soprano." With the options limited to simple major and minor, I could nearly always identify the chord after the first three notes had been played, without needing to hear the fourth voice, and never needed to hear it played more than once. I was admittedly showing off. I had a hard time not bristling at Vasquez. Everything he said sounded condescending and snide and sarcastic and I didn't like being talked down to.

"You do have a very good ear," he acknowledged, somewhat sourly.

I had followed him to his office after music theory class the previous Thursday after a session in which he had drawn chord diagram on the blackboard and lectured us about which chords were allowed to follow which. "Mr. Vasquez," I'd said, "one of the chord structures I like to use is based on a minor chord in the higher voices, but superimposing the fourth in the bass, like an E minor chord played in the right hand with octave A's below in the left. I don't know if there's a specific name for that..."

"No, there wouldn't be. That would just be an E minor chord with a passing note of A."

"Well, I wanted to ask you about the chord progression chart. Am I correct in assuming it's a framework of transitions but not a set of rules that we can't depart from when we compose for class assignments? I mean, I do a lot of chord shifts that don't obey those, and I understand wanting us to learn those rules, but it would be nice to know that we have the freedom to step away from them when the assignment is on some other aspect." I was worried that the music curriculum here at UNM was going to be a lot stodgier and focused on older modes of composition than what I'd come here to do, and I wanted some reassurance otherwise.

"If your music compositions don't obey those rules, that's not surprising, since you're only learning the rules now, and now you'll know better, won't you? That's why we come to school, to better ourselves and improve our skills. I hope you'll excuse me, but I have some schoolwork of my own that I have to attend to. I don't know if you realize it but I'm a graduate student in music and I have my own studies as well as the activities involved in teaching intro courses to incoming freshmen to occupy my time. I have regular office hours if you need to continue this conversation, posted on your syllabus. You received a syllabus? Good." And he entered his office and closed the door gently behind him.

Given the opportunity, I would have been having sex with lots of hot beautiful women and hanging out with lots of appreciative accepting friends, or at least I thought that's what I'd be doing. I wanted fun and easy thrills. The problem was, that kind of fun didn't come easily for me. I found I didn't really want to put any effort into it either and was left on my own to be lonely and horny quite a bit when Leland and his entourage were out.

I had discovered masturbation by myself when quite young, and it had always been my harmless private perversion. I put on some shimmery floaty music and turned off some of the lights. Oh, this advertising flier with the girl in the tight jeans will be nice, it's good to have a visual aid.

I was immersed in sensation and fantasy when the sound of the key in the door intruded, and I was suddenly scrambling awkwardly to cover up as five or six people followed Leland into our room.

People talked. Word got around and I guess people were rather amused by it.

Ralph, with his easy insolent mocking joking, began dropping hints that maybe it wasn't an accident. "Peeling that chili, baby. You hear Leland out in the hallway, you get it ready for him, hey?" He brought it up often enough that I finally got sensitive and worried about what people might think of me.

One evening when we were passing the pipe around, just the two of us, I said to Leland, "Ralph's been getting on my nerves. He keeps making innuendos that I was arranging to have my pants down when you came in the other day. Listen, it was embarrassing enough as is without that added to it, so I hope you're not thinking the same thing. I'm not into guys."

He shrugged and said "I've always thought the most sexually liberated person is the person who can see anyone as a possibility."

Mr. Vasquez was passing back our music theory exams. He had been drilling us on what was meant by the I chord, IV chord, iii chord, and so on. The correct answers had to be given in the terminologies in which they were taught, which meant memorizing and drilling, not just understanding the idea.

For instance I had defined a chord as one where the tonic note was a certain number of half-steps above the starting pitch, and he wanted it expressed as this many whole steps plus this many additional half-steps. It wasn't ordinary math, such as converting all half-steps to wholes except for any odd leftover, either; the right answer might be "four whole steps and three half steps." There was some historical reason but as far as I could tell the reason amounted to "because that was considered to be the right answer a long time ago."

Mr. Vasquez was a person who exhibited a lot of the behaviors and nuances and mannerisms associated with gay men. I figured people were likely to believe him to be gay, which gave us something in common, whether he actually was or not. I didn't like being categorized without being consulted, so I didn't consider that I knew his orientation one way or the other, and I had no reason to care.

Whatever else the situation, he certainly wasn't warming to me as if we were kindred spirits or anything. He was every bit as hostile as the boys and men in my life who had called me names and harassed and ridiculed me, thinking I was gay. From Vasquez, it was a less belligerently violent kind of contempt, but it was still contempt. Not that it was directed personally at me, as far as I could tell. He didn't seem to like any of us. I wondered if he acted any nicer toward other grad students.

I wished someone else was teaching my courses. It was a drag having my relationship with my primary music professor so flavored with mutual dislike.

Our dorm floors were single sex. While there was plenty of partying going on in the dorm, that mostly meant one dorm room or another was the temporary locus of alcohol and marijuana consumption, with people up and down the hall, and friends and colleagues from elsewhere, coming in to partake. If Leland was the center-point, as he often was, there would be girls, girls he knew, but Leland's shadow wasn't proving to be a good environment for me to meet girls in. And many of the other parties on our floor were single-sex. So I made more of an effort to get out of the dorm and meet other people and get into conversations and get out of the dorm ghetto.

"Did you catch what pages he gave for our assignment?" the blonde girl in orange asked the dark-haired one in jeans and t-shirt. "I think he said chapters five and six but something about a loose-leaf notebook?"

I was sitting in a desk one row behind them, gathering my items as class was letting out, and I came closer and responded, "That part wasn't a reading assignment. We're supposed to write up a short description of how to operate a three-ring notebook, for someone who'd never seen one before." Which made sense because this technical writing class was aimed at honing our skills for writing technical manuals and describing processes, so the professor was apparently having us describe stuff we all already knew.

"I think if you don't know how to use a notebook, maybe you don't know how to read yet either," said the one in orange as she gathered her books and donned her purse.

"Well, yeah, but he probably wants to see if we can describe things that are simple to us in really clear ways for people who don't already know," answered the other, echoing my own guess.

"Well, she does have a valid point," I interjected. "You always have to assume some level of familiarity as a starting point. I mean, you can't assume your audience doesn't understand *anything*. 'Pick up the notebook with your right hand. To do this, contract the muscles in the palm of your hands, drawing the fingers toward the thumb, see Diagram A'..."

They both laughed, which made me feel clever and funny.

The dark-haired one sighed. "I think sometimes I need things broken down to me almost that basic. I've been away from school for a few years."

"Well, see you next week," the blonde girl said, departing.

"So, you're not right out of high school either, huh?" I continued, chatting. "Me either. I tried something else before college but it didn't work out."

"Yeah, same here. I thought I had my life figured out and neatly tied up, but then a few things unraveled." she shook her head and made a waving-away motion with her hand and then shrugged. I nodded in recognition and gestured for her to continue. She looked at me, considering for a moment, then said, "Hey, you want to come up to my dorm room and smoke a bowl? I need to unwind. My name's Julie by the way."

This was working out rather nicely. I gave my name, then followed her across the lawns to one of the residence halls. In her hallway, she beckoned another couple of girls to join us, so it wasn't going to be a one on one moment, which seemed wise since she'd only just met me, but it punctured some fantasy pictures that had been forming in my brain. Soon we were arranged on cushions on her bed or on puffy pillows on the floor. Julie sat cross-legged on an Indian rug and prepped the bong.

"I just got divorced last spring," Julie said, returning to our earlier conversation. "I got married while I was still in high school. We both were... we were way too young and didn't know what we were doing. So this is a brand new start for me."

One of the girls on the bed chimed in, "I don't think anyone really knows what they want until they get out into the world."

Julie paused to take a hit on the pipe. I was on the verge of relating some bit about my own new start when she continued. "I do regret that we didn't wait; we might have done okay. It wasn't all bad. I miss things like spending a rainy afternoon indoors and just having sex all day in bed, you know?"

No, I didn't. I nodded along with the other listeners anyway, trying to act sophisticated but I felt like a little kid masquerading as a grownup. I had a flashback to conversations I'd once had with Gail Clinton back when I was in high school in Los Alamos, but back then I'd been fifteen and not so unusual in my lack of sexual experience, whereas Gail had been precocious in being experienced far beyond her age. Now here I was, twenty years old and self-conscious about still being a virgin. It seemed like no one else was, except for a few people who were virgins on purpose, saving it for marriage. That certainly wasn't me.

I tried to think of something I should be saying or doing if maybe Julie had invited me up here to consider me as a potential sex partner. Nothing clever or witty came to mind and the things that did were gross and klunky or edging into confessionally personal and serious. *How do people learn these things?*

Instead of opening me up and relaxing me, the pot was making me feel isolated. Zombie-like, I nodded and listened while my useless worried thoughts bounced around inside, invisible unless she could read minds and could tell how awkward and clueless I was, sitting here not knowing what to say or do next. When one of the other girls looked at her watch and said she had to head off, there was a general shuffling and I joined it. Julie and I exchanged, "See you around" and I did a "Nice to meet you" toward the other two, making my escape.

PLACES TO DO AND THINGS TO BE

I was writing to Linda Sorrens again, in desperation and pain. Everything was wrong. In the wake of our rather disastrous reunion in Massachusetts, I'd come into this college situation wanting to lighten up and go for casual sex, quit obsessing about Linda and that damn cliffside so long ago, affirm the goodness of carnal lust, become flirtatious and playful, not take it all so serious and finally get laid and get on with my life.

But somehow everything that lay in that direction was twisted up with stuff that made me uncomfortable. I felt fake and phony all the time, an impostor. Now I was lonely, painfully achingly lonely. And the truth was that I still *did* want to be involved with a girl I could really talk to and feel tender toward and fall in love with. And it hurt that the visit with Linda had happened as it had, and I just couldn't live with that, couldn't accept it.

I wrote of my misery and tried to describe what I had been hoping for, and how horrible it felt to not have the connection with her that I wanted. I begged and pleaded with her to write back to me and tell me that she still loved me, and to just tell me what was wrong, because whatever it was, we could fix it, could cope with it. It wasn't a reason to run away from what we had.

At least in one respect, I wasn't the most inexperienced person in college. Larry Busher and his best friend Eddie had spent the prior year with Eddie's family in Hong Kong, and they'd done a lot of pretty wild things, but they'd never tripped acid. I'd talked up how fantastic acid was for self-knowledge and insights. Eddie in particular became strongly interested based on the description. He was Buddhist and was a serious student of the connectedness of everything and the importance of comprehensions.

I scored a hit apiece for the three of us. Larry put on some Jimi Hendrix and as we soared higher and higher we talked up a storm about society and politics and how to treat humans and what knowledge is and so forth. As was by now my tradition, I took out my colored pencils and did some more of my abstract drawings. My sketch looked vaguely floral, with lots of energy and action so that the flowers appeared to be almost dancing.

Leland told me he had made arrangements to switch dorm rooms with Larry Busher. Larry would become my roommate and I'd remain in the room and would not have to relocate. Leland was a very popular guy and I knew I'd miss the constant dormitory room party and the people he attracted to our space. On the other hand, I didn't really have much of a rapport with him and the people who constantly came over to our room weren't coming there to see *me*, so I often felt rather fifth-wheelish. And I liked Larry for the most part. *So this should be okay*, I thought.

One day shortly after moving in, Larry looked back over his shoulder at me and said, "The thing you're doing, wearing the kind of underwear that you wear, that's cool. I do the same thing by wearing my jeans tight and kind of low, so the top of my crack shows above the waistband." The latter of which was true, but I hadn't really thought of it as something he was doing purposefully. Now I just sort of looked back at him blankly, wondering if I was correctly understanding his allusion to "the thing I was doing."

I had by now taped up several of my acid-trip drawings to the wall, along with odd little written bits like a sign that proclaimed, "YOU ARE ENTERING THE REALM OF FUZZY HEADED LUNATICS." Ralph was in the room hanging out and began making comments about some of the artwork. "Ho ho, I like this one, I see what you were trying to draw here," he winked and made pumping motions in front of his pants. He pointed to the dancing flowers one and held his arms up and to the sides and minced and pranced around in little dance steps. "Right?"

I saw Julie in the technical writing class and we talked for a few minutes about the assignment, about getting into a study routine, and about the teacher, but there were no subsequent invitations to hang out. From either direction. I realized I was embarrassed about the possibility of getting into a situation where I would not know what to say or do.

I still hung out with Leland and his guests some of the time, as did most of the guys in our hall on our floor. It was where the party was, after all. I was sitting cross-legged on the floor and music was playing and someone glanced in my direction and I overheard him say something to the person next to him about gay people and everyone being comfortable with different kinds of people. I didn't catch it all so much as I caught the gist of it. So I ended up saying to Leland as I was leaving later on, "I may be imagining things but lately it seems everyone wants to express an opinion about my sexuality. Do they want to put it to a vote or something?"

He said, almost exactly as he had once before, "I always tell people, the sexiest person I can imagine is someone who doesn't rule anyone out as an erotic opportunity." He added, "You know, it's important to accept yourself. You'll find that other people are a lot more ready to accept you than you might think."

I was in one of the practice rooms in the music building and a girl my age caught my eye as she wandered the hall looking into the various practice rooms. After a bit of that I opened the door and asked if she was waiting to get in to practice. She said she was not actually a music student. I explained that I was, but not working on music homework, just practicing my own compositions. She indicated I should play something, which I was happy to do, and she made approving comments and said she'd like to sing some of the things I'd written. She told me her name was Annette. We practiced together for a while and then she looked at me and asked me what I was thinking, and added, "I don't believe in wasting time, do you?"

I didn't know how to reply, not entirely sure I was understanding correctly. Was she saying she'd like to get laid, that we should go somewhere and get our clothes off? Or that she thought we had good chemistry and that she found me fascinating? Or was I imagining it all because I'd become sex-obsessed? Maybe it was just intended as a question about the music? "I think it's coming along nicely," I compromised. Annette shrugged and said it was nice meeting me and maybe we'd see each other down here again some time, but she had to get back.

I found myself writing to Linda again. She hadn't written back. My tone this time was angrier than in the previous letter. I felt discarded. She had meant so much to me; hadn't I once meant something special to her? Maybe, for reasons still unexplained, I didn't mean much of anything to her now, but I once had, hadn't I? Hadn't she given me adequate and sufficient reason to *think* she still felt the same way up until I got out there? Didn't she think she owed me some kind of explanation, some kindness and consideration here? I felt badly treated and I told her so.

There were notices from the Rape Crisis Center reminding students that sex without consent is rape. That "no" means "no." But for consent—or "no"—to make sense there had to already be a proposition. Something to consent to or say "no" to. People had been talking about equality for years but when folks talked about rape they spoke of "consent" and "no." A girl's consent, a girl's "no." I wondered if the Rape Crisis Center ever sponsored social events for people who didn't want to approach this like a contest of wills to begin with.

In the school library, killing time more than doing any actual research, I saw a front page article about sexuality in an issue of *Popular Psychology*. I picked it up and read it. It was about the mating behavior of some kind of tropical fish.

They had found some way of inducing anger and aggression in these fishes, and also of intimidating them. Their study had shown that the male of the species could be in a state of sexual arousal when angry and aggressive, or when neither stimulus was being applied, but not when frightened. The female of the species on the other hand could be in a state of sexual responsiveness when neither stimulus was being applied or when scared, but not when provoked into aggressive anger. Then a bunch of conclusions were drawn with sidebar comments about how certain arguments favoring gender-blind egalitarianism were misplaced. About how the sexes really are *different*.

I was in the sub-basement of the dormitory building, in the dark. I had found a door that was probably intended to stay locked and closed but the metal door was bent in such a way that the latch could not catch properly. The stairway on the other side of the door led to the basement and from there down into this sub-basement. This was where the heating system pipes converged and where the boiler was, and it was warm, and from the big blower fans inside the system that blew the warm air came a deep bass thrumm of vibration and sound.

It was dark and cozy down here and I felt like being alone, so I stayed for over an hour. Maybe I could stay down here forever and no one would find me. I could just disappear and after a while people would forget all about me. From then on I returned to this secret place from time to time.

Mr. Vasquez gave us the assignment of composing a short piece of music containing a transition between a specific pair of chords. He didn't explicitly impose many other restrictions and I wrote one composition that superimposed the chords, making a nice complex harmonic. It was a short nine-to-ten bar piece when I finished it, and it built fast to a dramatic close. But the teacher's snide sarcastic approach to teaching music hadn't been accompanied by enthusiasm for unusual or innovative approaches. After writing it down and playing it a few times, I sighed and cranked out a second piece that did a much more traditional and much more boring transition between chords and that's what I turned in.

I picked up a book at the school bookstore about self-discovery. It was a workbook, not a text. There were lots of exercises to do and questions you were supposed to answer about yourself. I flipped through it and read enough of it to feel an affinity for how it was written, so I bought it. Back in my dorm room I began doing some of the exercises. Writing a poem from myself as I was now to the person I had been at certain earlier ages. Picking my favorite colors from color swatches and then answering follow-up questions about what I liked about those colors. The booklet wasn't designed to give you back any conclusions, really, so much as to prompt you to think about yourself in new and different ways.

I met a girl who seemed as lonely and nearly as socially excluded as I was. Her name was Sharon Rivers and she lived in the Zuni wing of Coronado on the girls' floor. She was overweight and sensitive about that. She described herself as having some mental health issues. She had had some kind of breakdown after her last year in high school. The drugs they had initially put her on had made her gain a lot of weight.

There's a sort of stigma about hanging out with other misfits when you are a misfit yourself, a bit of an attitude that that's pathetic, that the only thing you'll have in common is that no one else will have you or want to be around you. But actually I had had good friendships in junior high and high school with some other people who had been treated as misfits, so that didn't bother me. Maybe we'd like each other and maybe the things she had been through as a social outcast would have made her a sensitive and compassionate person with a head full of her own thoughts about things. We started hanging out together.

The self-help book I'd bought had a pretty extensive section on sexual and gender identity. There were a lot of questions about how you had viewed yourself back when you were a kid, and about your own sex and about the opposite sex and so forth. As I answered the questions and jotted down things from my remembered experiences and circled the statements that seemed most true, it really hit me that it was significant that I had been extremely girl-identified as a child.

I don't mean I had never noticed it before. More the opposite: I'd always known this about myself and took it for granted. Now, all of a sudden, it seemed *huge*. It wasn't a difference the way that being left-handed was a difference. It wasn't even a difference the way that having eyes of two different colors was a difference. For years and years I had wanted to be like the *girls*, to be perceived as being like them, to be accepted by them, to compete with them as an equal. It wasn't just some interesting but innocuous bit of personal history. It had to have shaped how I grew up, inside my head. I'd sort of tried to set that aside when I thought I would fit in as one of the long-haired pot-smoking countercultural guys, but that hadn't really worked; I had still been too much like a girl to fit in and be accepted there. I must have been different *to start with*, to have had that inclination, to have wanted to be like the girls in the first place. Wow, I wondered, what does this make me *now*? *What am I?*

I still occasionally went across Lomas Boulevard to speak with the counselors at Albuquerque Crisis. I headed over there and ended up with a new person. She listened as I described my concerns that being like a girl instead of a boy made me fundamentally different in a way that might mean I'd never fit in or feel accepted, and how lonely and overwhelmed I often felt.

She said, "We know what causes that now." She said I had something in my head that worked differently, and they had a pill that would address that difference. With my brain working under the same chemistry as everyone else, I'd soon find these problems going away. She dispensed a fourteen-day supply of a medication called Stelazine and I said I'd try it.

Sharon Rivers and I had some things in common. She too was still a virgin. And her breakdown had in large part been precipitated by a breakUP. Her boyfriend of several years had split up with her and it had really torn her apart. She, too, had been told that she suffered from some kind of chemical imbalance in her brain, which was the real cause of her suffering, and had been prescribed medication which she'd been taking for the last year and a half. We found that we had a lot to talk about and we decided to make a go of it—not to peel clothes off and have immediate sex but to move in that direction at our own rate, to take care of each other, and be girlfriend and boyfriend.

I didn't like the pills. It was nothing particularly dramatic at first but after a few days I felt *dull* somehow. Emotionally in a sort of whatever zone, where none of the concerns that had been bothering me were reconciled but I was feeling numb, less bothered by it all. And imagination-impaired. I decided to stop taking them.

Two days later, I was looking over the little fragmentary music theory assignment I'd done for Vasquez, the one with the chord transition. The original, not the wimped-out version I'd turned in. I played it on the piano a couple times and it brought to mind a dawn sunrise coming after some kind of horribly traumatic and dramatic night, like a critical night battle in a war. I sat down and wrote a forty-minute piano suite I called *The Forbidden Forest of Keida*. The music surged with lots of passion and excitement in some bits, and with shimmery delicate parts elsewhere. It immediately came to symbolize to me what the pills had taken away from me when I had been on them.

Next time I popped in at Albuquerque Crisis, I brought bits of my new composition and explained to the woman why I had decided not to take the medication. She didn't argue with me about it but said she had no other help to offer. Just like all counseling services, sympathy but no answer.

Larry had a friend visiting and explained that he would be sleeping on a bed roll on our dorm floor. He had a dog with him. The dog was friendly enough. I wasn't much of a dog person (our family had always had cats) but I let the dog sniff my hand and I petted its head. Larry's friend kept behaving as if he was making a funny joke or a clever comment, but I didn't get what the point or punchline was. At the end of his sentences he would stick the tip of his tongue out at me. We all shared a joint or two, then after a while switched the lights out and went to bed.

Ten minutes later I was hearing a rather slobbery licking sound. "What's that sound?" I asked.

I heard what sounded like muffled giggling and then Larry said "It's the dog."

I said oh and tried to ignore it but the licking sound came back and it was really gross and disturbing and I had the weird idea that the entire situation had been lifted straight out of some dirty joke skit. I finally got up, slipped on my clothes went out for a walk.

I would often go on late night walks when I could not sleep. I'd apologize in advance to Larry for the inevitability of coming in way late and then I'd choose a random direction in Albuquerque. Albuquerque was no 24-hour town; and when I went out walking after midnight the storefronts were dark, the streets deserted.

This time I ended up in an industrial section of town. Coils of razor wire and strands of barbed wire ran along fences in front of hunched old buildings, and broken glass and crumpled paper trash rattled under my shoes as I walked. Guard dogs barked and snarled and snapped. A bleached white moon skull rose up over this terrain and glared down from the sky.

It matched my mood. It was 1979 and the idealistic countercultural world I'd been running after and trying to find and join up with since high school seemed to have been pushed off the stage. The love generation was gone. The world was becoming dark and hard and authoritarian.

I had a handful of new books to read that I had checked out from the library. *Conundrum: From James to Jan.* And one about Christine Jorgensen. Books about transsexuals, people who had been born in the wrong body, a body of the wrong sex.

That self-exploration workbook sat in front of me, and the things I had written about myself had really driven home to me that I had this particular difference, of having wanted to essentially be one of the girls for years and years as a kid. Wanting the respect of girls. Wanting to be seen by others the way they thought of girls. Not merely indifferent about whether people accepted me as one of the boys, oh no, I'd actively sought to avoid being thought of that way, did not *want* to be dumped in categorically with the rest of the boys. Yeah.

And as I'd continued to think about all this I'd written down more observations. It wasn't just childhood. I could also think about how and who I was *now*. I had made a list of ways in which I was really more like a girl than a boy. Once I posed the question that way, it had not taken very long at all to write a pretty extensive list.

I included observations that other people had made about me. I didn't put down things that other folks said that I did not agree with, but really the only thing people kept throwing out that I didn't agree about was the idea that I was sexually attracted to guys.

Which if you think about it *is* just another way of being like one of the girls. It's what they thought the *rest* of the stuff on the list meant. When folks weren't saying so belligerently and right up front, they were dropping little hints and implying it and often being oh so very tolerant and open-minded about it, but it was being said a lot. But the reason for them thinking so was the other stuff on the list, wasn't it?

So now I was reading up on transsexualism, wondering if this was how I was. The things I'd written sat there in that workbook, an explosive secret. I was excited and nervous even to have the book open to that page, as if to let anyone glance at it would instantly change my life forever. Shocking. But not all entirely in a bad way. It was oddly thrilling too. The possibility of my life changing forever was more than a little bit enticing.

The people in the books said things like "I always knew...my body was male but that wasn't who I was. I knew who I really was. I was one of the girls." Maybe this *was* who I was. How I was different. The big explanation. I thought about how I could be in this world if I were female. I wouldn't *have* to go to bed with guys. I could be a lesbian. How would it feel to be a girl, a woman, to be perceived and treated as one? I smiled. You know, that sure would fit me a whole lot better.

Sharon wanted to go steady. It's what boyfriends and girlfriends did if they were going to make out. They promised themselves to the other person alone. We could still look at other people but nothing more than looking, and even the looking should be kept to a limited amount to avoid flirtatious temptations: "One peek per week." So we made out on the dorm room bed, and I was reencountering a familiar theme.

As had been the case with Olivia Vondersee back in high school, Sharon didn't reciprocate. Too shy? Didn't she feel that sense of mischief and teasing where you crave fooling with the other person's appetite and making them feel things?

I could feel her arousal, and her body became pliant and draped against me and I eased her onto her back and kept touching her. I wanted to give her sensations that would be closer to what it would feel like if we ever went all the way, so I pushed myself against her even as I worked against her with my thumb and fingers. It startled her and she sat up, flustered and worried that I was trying to make it all happen right then and there. I apologized and comforted and reassured her that I would not do that until we were both ready, and explained what I had been trying to do. I said that we did not have to be in a hurry, to please not feel like I was impatient or would get annoyed just because she wasn't ready.

But it felt like an unequal relationship. Especially if I was a girl just like her. Unfair.

I was not doing well at all in music theory class, but I had been thriving in the companion ear training class despite Mr. Vasquez's hostility. Then he passed out a book called *Melodia* and the focus of the class shifted to tone syllables: *do re mi fa sol la ti do.*

Before this, it had all been about intervals and chords and the distances between pitches. I could do that as easily as I could distinguish red from blue or green. But now we were supposed to identify notes and intervals by their syllables. I didn't see what this added. I had to translate in my head: *Okay that's a major sixth up, I was on the second note of the key, that's 're', plus six so let's see, 're mi fa sol la ti', that makes it 'ti'..."*

I saw no advantage to aliasing the actual note to some meaningless syllable and I had to sing "doe a deer a female deer" in my head to remember the stupid syllables in their stupid order. Then it got worse: there was a second tier of syllables I'd never heard at all before to make it fully chromatic—"*do di re ri mi fa fi..."*—and we were expected to learn and use the entire set.

Essentially I knew the right answers musically, tonally, but had to backwards engineer the syllable convention, and often got it wrong. By the trailing final weeks of the semester, I was flunking *both* of my music courses. Admittedly, though, my attention wasn't tightly focused on my coursework these days.

"Do you want to come up to my room for a little bit?" I asked Sharon.

"Well, not if you're going to start talking about that weird shit again."

"You mean what I was telling you about being more like a girl than a boy, and all that?"

"Yeah, exactly. I don't know why you want to be deliberately strange and different. I'm already plenty different enough, and I'm tired of it. I want to be normal and live a normal life. People talk behind my back all the time because I had a breakdown, because I'm *fat*." She raised her palms against her belly and made a disgusted face. "I don't think that's fun, being the one people whisper about. I like to pretend sometimes that my name is really Sharelle...and I'm skinny and slinky and sexy and everyone admires me and doesn't make fun of me, they all wish they could be like me. And I should have a popular boyfriend who thinks I'm cute and sexy. And he should want to be normal like that, too, not trying to be as weird as possible."

"Well, I think we don't aspire to the same things. I don't mind being different. I just want to understand what I am. And I wasn't expecting you to decide that what I am is weird and shouldn't be talked about."

"You make way too big a deal over things that don't matter. Any boy could have done the things you talked about and it doesn't make him a sex deviant or trans...trans*sexual*. There are ballet dancers who are men, and men who work selling flowers in flower shops. You should forget that stuff and quit talking about it."

I shook my head. "I don't agree with you, but there doesn't seem to be much point in talking to *you* about it at any rate. I'm going to go play the piano for a while in the lounge. They finally got it tuned and it sounds pretty good. You're welcome to come along and keep me company if you want." *If you don't mind being seen with someone so weird.*

"I have to put my stuff in my room, but I'll come down in a bit."

After Sharon padded up the stairs, I turned and entered the lounge and sat on the piano stool. I played a couple riffs and chords and then launched into the overture of *Forbidden Forest*. When I let the final chord fade at the end, a couple people applauded. "Play some more." So I happily obliged them, doing an array of chord transformations to shift into the lament.

Whoever had been in to tune it had done some work on the action as well, and the keys were responding and giving me what I asked of them, delicate auditory lace and then angry chords of hot steel spiking the air. I shifted the key again and switched to the lead-in to *Red Line*. This time when I let the sound die out, there were a dozen people, including Ralph and Leland, standing around listening. Sharon was here now and gave me a little wave.

"Hey, Derek, I never knew you could play like that. Damn, you sound good. Did you write that? Yeah? Play something else."

A guy stuck his head around the corner. "Where's that music coming from? What, seriously? All that sound from just a piano? Unbelievable."

People began calling out requests. I had been in a mood to play my own music, but I was enjoying the moment. What the hell. I played for nearly an hour and my crowd continued to grow. I could forget for the moment that the admiring girlfriend wasn't really my lover and that we'd just had an argument. And I could forget for a while that the musician at the piano was flunking his music courses. Here was a taste of what could be if I could manage to untangle the threads and get on with my life.

I was not at peace. My mind was scurrying around like a squirrel in a cage, repeating the same little thought-loops and basically getting nowhere. The gender and sexual identity questions were compelling, and I couldn't leave them alone, going back to them perpetually like a tongue seeking out a sore tooth. But at the same time I was uncomfortable thinking about it for long. Being like a girl inside instead of like other boys made me just as different as being gay would have.

The experiences described by the transsexual authors were eerily similar to my own in so many ways, and yet ultimately the path for them had been to decide that the male body they were born with was wrong for them. Did I want a sex change operation? Seriously? If I were female, if I were a girl, a woman...well, it was hardly as if, at *that* point, people would cease to assume I probably wanted to have sex with guys, if you see what I mean. I wouldn't *have* to, no matter what everyone thought. I could be...well, a lesbian.

So I would be getting a sex change operation in order to have sex with females as a lesbian? Yeah, now there's a course of action I'm sure everyone would recognize as eminently logical. It would be horribly lonely. I'd not just be a lesbian; I'd be a lesbian with no past. I'd have to disown who I had been all my life up until then, unless I was lucky enough to find a lesbian partner who could love me as a transsexual person and not be freaked out knowing that I'd been male, not be weirded out knowing that my female parts were surgically created. And if there were such a lesbian person out there, with that much openness and acceptance of weirdness and difference, would she really reject the same me if I were still male?

With my luck, if I did this I would then meet a woman who really liked me and would want to share and talk and love...and she'd be attracted to male bodies and there I would be, in a surgically modified body and wishing I had the old one back. And...would I miss it anyway? Did my male body seem all wrong to me? Did I hate being male? What *did* I think of my body itself, really?

A memory came back to me, of striding across the junior high campus lawn on my way home. The sun had been shining and my shadow was cast upon the ground and I'd glanced at my shadow-shape and felt good. Felt... *pretty*.

Look at me. I look the perfect way for a guy to look. I have nice shapes and I move nicely.

It was still true. I really did still like my appearance. I did not want to look like some other guy, some movie star, some athlete. I have a skinny upper body with a shallow chest Good, I want it that way. I really like my face. Small taut waist. Tiny taut ass. Damn right. I was so glad my body had not broadened and become like so many adult bodies. It was almost like a child's body at waist and hips. I liked it that way. Then curvy muscular legs. My legs as curvy as any girl's. All that hiking and walking. So yes, I was... vain. Really. I do like my body.

Okay, but what about the male bits? Is that all wrong? .I dunno. Penis. Silly part. I do like the way it feels but I don't...feel cute for having one, or think mine is...nice looking, I dunno it's just kind of there, you know? To be female instead...? I think I'd hate having big breasts. Maybe tiny cute perky ones.

I thought about female bodies as if I were shopping for one to be inside of. Hmm...freckles, I want freckles and dark hair and a nice smile, small tits, medium tall, definitely not short...curvy down below but not too wide...and girls parts of course, a cunt, my own perky V shape with a nice mons. WOW hmm bloody hell I'd never bother leaving the room. Okay ignoring that, umm, I would try being female if I ever got the chance, yes I would, and you know something: I think I would be good at it. I would be a good female person, and yeah actually I really really wish I had the chance to try that out. It would be fun and people would see me a lot more the way I see myself, I think. But seriously, my existing body is not the problem.

I asked Larry and Eddie what they were doing for Christmas break and learned that Eddie had nowhere to go and was just going to stay in the dorms over Christmas break. I liked Eddie and was more comfortable with him than Larry or Leland or the other people I'd become acquainted with this semester, and after checking with my parents to make sure it would be okay, I invited him to come home with me over break.

I was following Sharon down the first floor hallway of the Zuni building to the stairs leading to the girls' floor, and some guy who knew her said something brief from a dorm room doorway as we passed by, something I didn't catch. Sharon replied over her shoulder as we kept walking, "You should have, as far as I'm concerned. And yes I know he's gay, okay, and I don't care." I'd missed what he'd said but I got the distinct impression that I was the "he" to whom she referred. But how would I know that for sure? Was I starting to read implications where they did not exist? To think that everyone was spending all their time contemplating my sexual orientation and sexuality?

I really did wonder about my growing penchant for thinking I was such a fascinating subject for speculation, but at the same time it really did seem to be taking place. So now, added to the pile was the strong possibility that my current girlfriend thought she was dating a gay guy.

"Hey, Derek" said Larry, "Eddie and I have a friend who needs to move to another apartment and he needs help moving his stuff. He said anyone we can find to pitch in, he'll treat to some good acid afterwards. We can come back here afterwards and listen to the newest Pink Floyd album;

it's called *The Wall*. It just came out. You like Pink Floyd, don't you?" Well yeah, in fact they're my favorite group. Listen to a brand new Pink Floyd album while tripping? Sure, count me in.

My experience with North American Van Lines in Los Alamos had made me proficient. I helped folks get big pieces around corners, helped them wrap things in moving blankets and strap them down in the van, moved refrigerators on four-wheel dollies and turned heavy items in narrow spaces by putting them on a blanket and then rotating it. Larry's friend was pleased that everything got where it was going without getting all scratched up. I swallowed the little microdot and we went back to Eddie's dorm room to trip to Pink Floyd.

Eddie pulled off his shoes and sprawled loosely on a giant mint-green beanbag chair directly below an imperial Japan "rising sun" poster that he had mounted on the wall. "Aah." I patted out a hollow next to him and sat facing him with my feet comfortably propped up on his battered wooden side table.

Leland came in accompanied by two new girls. "This is Stephanie and this is Suzanne. Say hello to Eddie, Derek; that's Jerome; you've met Larry..." We nodded and said hi back to them. Suzanne punched out another socket in the big beanbag and flopped back next to me on the other side.

I sat back. Eddie dropped the needle into the grooves and the music started to play. I felt the usual anticipatory butterflies in my stomach and started to tingle and float. Across from me on Eddie's couch, Stephanie started bouncing and swaying. Time for liftoff.

Something wasn't quite right. Normally by now I'd be aloft, my mind deliriously ecstatic with new understandings and insights, forty thousand feet above everyday reality. Instead, everything felt...muddy. Murky. On the record album, an aching, almost panicky lonely voice asked about filling empty space, then described an inexperienced boy seeking good times with a dirty woman who could make him feel like a real man.

Ralph snorted. "Come on, yeah. Show me around." Leland was peering attentively at the artwork on the inside of the record album. Why was I feeling squirmy, panicky? What was wrong with me? I tried to smile at Suzanne sitting next to me but it felt weak on my lips.

The band seemed to be singing about *me*, trying to fill the emptiness of a post-Linda Sorrens world, cheerfully setting forth to ditch my virginity, have some fun, to lighten up about sex and try to get a girlfriend and all that. *Making fun of me.*

I turned to Eddie in confusion. "Is this real?" I blurted. Inadequate. He won't know what I'm talking about. Unless he knows the song is about me. Is that possible?

"What is real?" Eddie responded, wide-eyed, his pupils giant black dimes. "Is there a single real?"

There was an interlude between the album tracks and a girl's voice came in oohing and aahing about all the guitars, said she was going for a drink of water then asked, flirtatiously, "Want some? Huh?"

Ralph grunted. "I want some, uh huh baby." He belched and grinned.

I tried again. "It feels like they're singing this to me personally."

Jerome nodded. "Yeah, I know what you mean."

Eddie nodded as well and gave me a thumbs-up. "Good acid."

Damn.

I'd been obsessing all semester long about this stuff. Tonight I had just wanted escape from my concerns and instead my favorite rock band was rubbing my nose in it.

The vocalist was singing about seeing the writing on the wall and realizing he was never going to have anybody. He followed up on that with one about committing suicide. I was aware that I was trembling. I was having a no-kidding bad acid trip. I was cold and terrified. *How can they know what it's been like to be me and taunt me with it like this?*

I remembered years ago when I'd first started smoking pot, getting high in Bob Diaz's living room with Kraftwerk's *Autobahn* playing while a motorcycle race was showing on TV and how disconcertingly weird it had seemed that the music from the record album was being illustrated by the television show. This was like that except far more personal. Pink Floyd was singing the most intimate worries and apprehensions that had been haunting me worse and worse all season long.

Ralph nudged Larry, and when Larry looked over at him, nodded in my direction. Larry's eyes tracked over to me. Ralph leaned over to him and whispered.

Eddie got up to put on the second part of the album. In the momentary quiet, Leland called out to me. "Derek. Hey, you okay, man?" I started to speak but I didn't know what I wanted to say, so I shrugged and shook my head. Negative.

Suzanne was saying something inaudible to Stephanie, then more loudly, "I think the best trips are when your mind gets really blown." The music started up again with a sad lonely guitar.

And now they quit playing gently with me and came in for the kill. A loud voice yelled out from the stereo speakers: "You! Faggot!" After a few dreary draggy intro bars the singer explained that this wasn't really Pink Floyd but some other band and that they had suspicions about the kind of people who came to Pink Floyd concerts. "Are there any queers in the theater tonight? Get them up against the wall. There's one there in the spotlight. He don't look right to me. Get him up against the wall."

Everyone was looking at me. I felt totally exposed in front of everyone. I tried a third time: "So is this *real*? Is this *happening*? Did you know this would be?"

I was shaking all over. I could hardly breathe.

Eddie gripped my shoulder. "You know you'll be okay." Immediately everyone else was talking to me, advising me.

"Take deep breaths. Try to relax."

"I think we should go for a ride, get out of this dorm room."

"I think you should lie down."

I shook Eddie's hand off and stared at them all, glancing rapidly from Leland's face to Ralph's, Suzanne's to Stephanie's, Jerome's, Eddie's. "There should have been somebody out there," I insisted. "There was supposed to be. I tried. Everyone else found their place."

I stood, nodded my sweaty shaking face to them, and stepped past everyone to the bathroom door.

I'd been stripped naked in front of everyone. Outed. Okay, I get it. I am "like this." I am "that way" whatever that may mean. When they can put your life on a record album and sing to you what you're like, you don't have much denial space in which to squirm. And anyone looking at my face would know it had all hit home.

Identifying / Coming Out

Pink Floyd's *The Wall* is darkly obsessed with maleness and masculinity. It wasn't just the LSD, although that was causing me to respond to the music far more personally and intensely than I otherwise might have. And now my attention had been forcibly directed to something I'd managed for so long to avoid thinking directly about.

It's got nothing to do with what I want, does it? It's got nothing to do with whether I find males sexy or attractive, or if instead I find females sexy and attractive. It's not about what *I* want, is it? Everything is divided up into fuckers and those who get fucked. It's like those fish in the fish tank in that popular science article. Hard-wired sexual behavior, different for males and females. And I'm like this, internally constructed like one of the girls.

I'm not heterosexual because I'm not heterosexually eligible. I'm not normal. I'm not a regular man, a guy. I emit the wrong signals to attract women and I don't have the right behaviors to make things happen even when I do. How I am, how I think and behave and feel and all that stuff. I always thought of sexual flirting and courting as being between basically identical people, but I guess it's really a biological courtship dance where the male does one thing and the female does something else. Girls don't respond to me because of what they expect and want and need in order to experience it as sexy and romantic. The male moves don't come naturally to me. So it doesn't really matter if I don't get horny for males, because that's all that's available for guys like me. That's it in a nutshell, isn't it? That's all that's left. And everyone else knows, whether they feel sorry for me or they're contemptuous of me. As usual I'm the last one to figure it out and accept it.

The others in the room gradually realized that I was shuddering there in the middle of the room and they became solicitous. They insisted on taking me for a ride in a car to get me some coffee. They talked gently to me. I finally reassured them that they could leave me alone. They were tired too, so eventually they did. By now it was late night, dark on an early December night, and I was out by myself walking around, stalking around aimlessly, briskly, my mind careening, ambushed by Pink Floyd, forced to finally spin around and deal with it once and for all. Everything had been building toward this moment all semester long—perhaps for my entire life— and now it was reckoning time.

Inside my head I was screaming. God. It has been a long long time since I tried to pray to God. The realness of God had been in undetermined limbo for years. Well. Hey, God. Do you exist? Are you out there? Well if you're not then you ought to be. *Someone ought to be answerable for all this.* And it all ought to mean something, somehow. If you exist, you've got some explaining to do.

How about tenderness? If the way things are is that everyone is either a fucker or a person who gets fucked and it's all about power and one up, one down, like the fishes, then why do we get all misty-eyed about love and empathy and caring and stuff like that? If human sexuality is such a nasty oppositional thing, how'd we end up craving sensitive compassionate tender gentle loving feelings and their expression?

Okay...so I'm like a girl. So? What's wrong with that? What part of being like a girl is a bad human characteristic? And don't tell me I'm acting all sulky about how I'm such a nice guy but girls don't prefer me. I don't necessarily believe anymore that I'm a better person than normal guys, but am I really not even as good? No girl would ever want me because I'm too much like a girl? Why am I like this? I'm attracted to them and I want to be with them; there must be a way out of this mess.

I want an answer. I want to understand.

This continued for hours. Then...abruptly I was exhausted and suddenly it did feel like I could go back to bed and actually get some sleep. That my mind would quit racing in little hamster-wheel circles. I crawled in and closed my eyes and fell asleep. Maybe tomorrow would bring answers or maybe it would bring an empty horrid life with no options I wanted to exercise, but I'd see what it looked like when I woke up.

I actually woke up feeling...okay. None of the questions had any more answers but I felt cautiously hopeful that somehow there would be a resolution to all of this. There was even a feeling of relief at finally having the issue out in the open instead of skittering around the edge of it.

Within days, I'd be going home to my parents' house for Christmas. I was a little nervous at this point about having Eddie around because I thought that maybe Larry and Eddie had been a couple. Larry had dropped some hints. I realized that maybe if over the next couple weeks I ended up feeling boxed in on the sexual preference issue, I might not be at my most comfortable with a possibly gay guy there.

Still, I was tired of avoidance. I didn't feel like running away. And I liked Eddie. He didn't make me feel creepy like he was taunting me or making innuendos about my sexuality the way so many people seemed to.

In Los Alamos, over Christmas break, Eddie and I soon fell into the habit of stepping out of the house and smoking a bowl after supper, and I started using that time to think out loud, to process things.

"One difference between being fourteen and being twenty is that virginity is different," I began.

Eddie nodded. "Not so many people are virgins by the time they're twenty. Could be you start to worry that you'll be virgin forever, that it will be permanent."

"Yeah, and becoming increasingly obsessed about it and feeling more and more left out while everyone around you is having sex. But I mean the virginity thing keeps you blocked if you aren't like other boys, like me." I sat back against the cast iron porch railing and faced him. "Way back in third grade I had girls who liked me, and they liked me as one of them."

He nodded again. "It's easier for girls and boys to be friends before sex and sexual appetite get in the way."

"Well, most of them *were* just friends, you know, but I also had a girlfriend back then, and we were in love. We held hands and kissed and wrote love letters in class. We were two of the same. And that's how I like it. But the virginity thing gradually gets in the way of that. If you want to be heterosexual, sooner or later you have to go there. It's like a gate, you know—THIS IS SEX—and it's set up so it only works, it only happens, if someone is the boy, doing the boy thing. Not two of the same. I mean, maybe it isn't sexy for girls unless the other person is doing that, pressuring, making sex happen. Or they just don't have to, as long as the boys will. Either way, it's how it's set up. So it's a gate with a gatekeeper. Keeping boys like me out."

"Or maybe it's just how we're taught to think it's set up, and when you are virgin you don't know if it is true or not."

"Well, if nothing happens and nothing happens...and you start to think the reason is that you aren't doing the boy part...and then you try it, you find out that for you it *is* true because you just *made* it true." I knocked the ashes out of the pot pipe and put it back in my coat pocket. "Anyway, it's always there, and it gets in the way, I mean it looms bigger and bigger the older you get. You're the BOY; you have to make things happen. And it seems so absolute when you're a virgin: You've never had sex with a girl because you've never made it happen, and you never will until you do."

"Maybe it doesn't seem so much a big thing after you do that. And then you can find ways to be with girls more like what you're looking for. Just get it out of the way and move on."

"Well, the problem there is that it's not just set up so that the boy has to take the initiative. That's bad enough but that's not all there is to it. While he's getting ready to try that, he's hearing girls say all boys are like this and only care about sex, and boys are selfish, and it means the boy isn't interested in her as a person. All that stuff is already written on the wall. So it's not like he can just walk over to a girl he likes and say, 'I like you; sure, what the hell, let's have sex' and that's it. She wants sex but she wants it to be meaningful and special, or at least she's supposed to pretend she does or she'll be called names like 'slut' and all that. And she's been taught she has to slow the boy down and make him get to know her better first if she wants a relationship."

I leaned back against the porch railing. "See, he's supposed to keep trying. So it's not just 'do this one thing once that's specifically a boy thing, then you can be equals.' The whole process is like that. And it keeps out boys like me."

I sighed. "I want to feel special and valued before I share sex with

163

someone *too*. I want to feel like...well, wanted, not like I'm pushing myself on someone. And I *want* a girlfriend, I want to be in love and have a relationship. That's just as important to me as it is to them."

Eddie nodded again. *Was I making sense? Did he understand what I was trying to say?*

Eddie stared out across the snowbanks covering our front lawn. After a moment he said, "You're saying it's like a Catch-22. You can't qualify to be in the relationship you want except by starting a relationship that is *not* the way you want *instead*, with someone who won't see you for how you are."

Make that a yes. Someone on this planet thinks I make sense. So I should make sense to others as well.

The next thing that fell into place for me was the women's liberation movement. Feminism. I was standing there on the front porch talking with Eddie and it hit me, this vivid image of an intense woman at the podium, her voice snapping like a whip, talking about the unfairness of sex role expectations, that when men do it it's assertive, taking charge, showing initiative, oh but when women do it, oh, now it's pushy, she's being domineering, she's a bitch. "Well fuck that shit," she says, and the audience of feminist women cheer and raise their clenched fists in a salute.

Oh yeah, *feminists*. Sure, *they* had talked about the double standard. How, if it was okay for men to be sexually assertive and be admired for their sexual activities and proficiencies, then it should be okay for women to be sexually assertive about their interests and appetites. If sexually active men were admirable, sexually active women should be similarly admired instead of demeaned as "sluts," and so forth.

And I realized that the very existence of such women punched holes in the notion that only males who did the man-role thing could be heterosexual. Because since women apparently existed who weren't playing by those rules, I could interact with them and things could happen differently.

Excited, I outlined all this to Eddie. "See? This is important. This changes things. The gatekeeper can be bypassed." Eddie grinned and patted my shoulder and said this was a good thing.

At first, it felt like solving an equation, or a technicality, almost like a legal point or recognizing a good argument to use in a debate. But a few days later I thought about it from a different angle. The feminist movement had provided a home for a certain kind of woman: tomboyish non-feminine females who were more like boys in a lot of ways than they were like the other girls. Some people liked to claim that all feminist women were like that, which wasn't at all true, but there were such women and the women's liberation movement, with its attack on the unfairness of different expectations according to sex, obviously would have a direct and personal appeal to them. Some of them were lesbians, of course, but not all of them.

Maybe I would find that I liked feminist women not just because I could interact with them outside of the regular rules but because of their, well, tomboyishness, you know, butch characteristics. I might like that a lot. Meanwhile, yeah, it also meant I had natural allies of a sort. I needed to meet some feminist women.

A couple nights later I stood on my front porch feeling militantly angry, ecstatically joyous, triumphant, determined, furiously vindictive, and free. Standing at my *own* damn podium. Yeah, fuck this shit.

So...I stand here a virgin because I don't want to be the boy and take sexual initiative? Then by god, I will damn well *die* a virgin before I'll take responsibility for any more than forty-nine percent of it. I've never known any girl who wanted to feel like *she* was pushing sex onto someone who didn't properly appreciate it. Why the hell should I?

I'm supposed to let the world paint me as only interested in sex, like I don't fall in love or get emotionally invested and vulnerable to hurt when I'm in relationships? So it's somehow okay for girls to only want me for sex in a way that it would not be okay the other way around? It's that same damn double standard.

When girls are uncertain and ambivalent about their sexual feelings and appetites, people understand, it's portrayed that way in movies and songs. But males are just supposed to be enthusiastically ready, like there's no risk or reason to be hesitant? Fuck that shit too.

Girls have to put up with being seen as sex objects, and yeah I can see it's no good being treated like that's all you're there for, but dammit I never get to feel desirable, cute, attractive in any kind of reciprocal way, that's part of it too, and fuck that.

There are so many ways of thinking and behaving associated with girls that people don't comprehend the same way if you're a boy. I have been yelled at for being smilingly cheerful, ridiculed and despised for trying to play within the rules and get some protection, considered weak and cowardly for not valuing fighting and violence. Well, I'm claiming all of that back as my own and I'll be damned if I'll be shunted shamed or ridiculed away from it ever again.

I was...out. The door was open and I was out of the closet now.

Hey, not my fault that when I come out it's different from what everyone expected. Not straight. Not gay. Not transsexual, even. Something entirely other. It's something else. What shall I call it? I'll think of something.

There had been something wary and guarded and furtive inside me that wasn't there anymore. I no longer worried that someone would tease or harass me for being too much like a girl or not right for a guy. Now I didn't care if they noticed.

This is who I am, how I am. Get used to it! I will never again tolerate people being mean and nasty to me and acting like I deserve it because I don't act like a guy. From now on being all worried about that is gonna be *their* problem.

I smiled.

Before I left Los Alamos to resume classes, I dropped in on Pamela Teague at the Family Counseling Center in Los Alamos, where I'd last been told to "make do." I explained some of my new insights, concluding with my new ban on expressing more than my share of overt sexual interest. "You can't expect to get something out that exceeds what you're willing to put in. That's not possible," she told me.

I crossed my arms. "Wait...you're not seriously going to try to tell me my new dating policy would violate the second law of thermodynamics or something, are you?" She started to reply but rethought it, whatever it was. I continued: "Tell me—would you be giving the same feedback to a girl?"

She sighed. "Well, that's simply not how the world works."

"So, were you able to get in to see Pam Teague?" my mom asked.

I nodded as I finished off the last of my iced tea. "Yeah...she fit me in. It wasn't a regular session. I just wanted to toss an idea at her and see her reaction. I won't be going back."

"Sometimes I think people go to counseling or therapy hoping someone will tell them nothing's wrong with them. And then when they get tired of waiting for that, they storm out and realize that sure enough, there was nothing wrong with them."

I chuckled. "Pretty much, yeah."

My dad was stacking our dinner plates in the dishwasher. "I know some things have been rough for you. I hope things are better now that you're in college. You've got your friend Eddie. He seems nice." He gave me a wink. "More better now?"

"More better," I agreed. I turned to leave the room, but the wink and the teasing tone lodged in my head, bothering me. I turned back around and rested my hands on the back of the dining room chair where I'd been seated. "There are some nice people at college. They accept lots of people who probably didn't fit in when they were younger. I think they want to make me feel welcome, and it seems like a lot of those nice folks think I'm gay. That's 'more better' than getting beaten up and called names I guess."

My parents glanced at each other. I tried to read what passed between and couldn't.

"You always made me feel that you thought I was normal and okay and that you love me the way I am. Maybe you think the same thing as my college friends. I think probably you'd still love me if I was gay. I'm not. It's something else."

My dad spoke first. "What? Why would you wonder about such a thing? You went out with Olivia in high school, and you always liked girls. We never thought you were gay."

My mom's lips were compressed thin. She blinked. "I...I wasn't brought up that that's healthy and I don't suppose it would be easy if you... told me something like that. I love you though and you would always be my son. You aren't...I mean, you're saying you're *not* gay...right?"

"Yeah. I just...so many people have wondered or thought so for sure, it just suddenly occurred to me that you might have thought so too. I'm not like other boys. I wouldn't be upset if you'd thought that."

We stood in close awkward proximity in the edge of the kitchen for a moment. I started to say something then stopped. My dad stepped closer and then we were hugging, all three of us.

It was 1980. Ronald Reagan was expected to seek the Republican nomination. Patriotism and a sort of post-sideburns machismo were in style, and women in *Vogue* sported Joan Crawford shoulder pads. Feminism had come of age and was being taken more seriously. The gay rights movement was emerging in a big outspoken way. Dan White had recently avoided a murder conviction in his trial for killing Harvey Milk in San Francisco, prompting more gay people to get politically involved. The hippie ideals, the visionary ideas about things like living on communes and getting rid of laws and money, on the other hand, were mostly forgotten, except for a few that had done a better job of taking root, such as environmentalism, getting back to nature, vegetarianism, favoring a simpler and less plastic life. I was about to turn twenty-one.

I switched rooms with Eddie's roommate and moved in with Eddie.

Larry Busher and I were not the ideal combo, and when I had mentioned that I was thinking of asking the residential authority to find me a new roommate, Eddie and Larry had suggested doing this.

That night on my parents' front porch had felt fantastic, liberating, joyous, to channel the radical feminists shouting "fuck this shit" and to be all zealously righteous. But although there really was an angry component to my sense of having been deprived, it wasn't *power* that I was seizing, it wasn't *power* that had been denied to me all this time, but rather an array of softer and more delicately important things, some of which might be more complicated than anything easily condensed down to a slogan.

For example, I had declared a personal moratorium on being the sexual initiator in charge of making sex happen, but in practice I was already realizing that it was more intricate than that. It didn't mean I should be entirely passive and simply wait for things to happen. That wasn't likely to be a good strategy for anyone, female or male. But I could seek an environment where I'd be more likely to encounter women who would be interested in someone like me. Women with whom I could negotiate some different expectations and understandings. I realized now that I had so often sought and valued a girl I could talk to openly and honestly—as with Linda—because I knew on some level I needed to work out another way, a different idea of how to be sexual.

Meanwhile, without being fully passive, I could flirt less overtly and I could just see where things might go. I'd seen how many women did it: Maybe they'd make the initial overture or maybe they'd be responding to an overture from the guy, but they would then wait for the guy to respond, like a volley in tennis or volleyball, you know, your turn or else you must not be interested.

I could do that. I could ban from my mind the notion that I should be doing more lest the opportunity pass by. This was a toxic notion that had even crept into *my* head, since even though I didn't make overt sexual overtures often, or do them with any sense of comfort, I'd definitely been haunted by the idea that *not* doing so constituted a problem. I had come to worry that it was making me sexually uninteresting, probably to the point that I was blind to other possibilities. This felt amazing, like getting a permanent reprieve from a scheduled daily torture session or something, to say "never again" and toss that aside.

I enrolled in a creative writing poetry class for the spring semester, and a human sexuality class offered jointly by the biology and social sciences departments. I was in music theory and ear training once again but with a different instructor, and I continued with choir.

Poetry class was a small class with only eight or nine people. "What I'd like you to do as your first assignment...think back to a time when you contemplated how people would remember you after you were gone. Try to recall some of what was going on with you that caused you to be thinking about it and capture some of that in a poem."

It was the first time I'd written poetry since my briefcase was stolen that day in Atlanta. I wrote about hiding in the dark sub-basement of the college and I let my poem wallow in the sad sniffly feelings of being inadequate to be out with other people, of something being secretly horribly wrong with me. I concluded it with a request that when I died I wanted to be buried by myself, no marker / no record / no one would know that I was there.

I titled it "Things to Be and Places to Do" and when I read it out loud in class there was a moment's silence and then a very satisfactory chorus of "Wow." It felt good to write. I was in a different place emotionally and I felt proprietary about my own history and what I'd been through, as if it were a source of power, not just bad memories of bad times.

In music, I was rehashing a lot of the same material covered under Vasquez with the new teacher, Iris Morales, a much less sour person. It was still dull and mechanical and formulaic—very much in contrast to the poetry writing class—but I dutifully turned in my work and did my own music compositions on my own time.

After choir class one evening, I was putting on my winter coat after rehearsal and preparing to walk across campus when a small soprano with a short bouncy haircut asked if I would walk her back to the dorms. I was happy for the company and she was attractive and seemed nice. Her name was Jen. We chatted for a while as we walked. She had a quick mind and a fast speaking style, rattling off amusing observations and sudden insights as the conversation turned to different things. Oh, and it definitely *was* freeing to not feel like I had to do something in order to avoid being marked down as sexually uninterested. I didn't even feel like I had to *know* whether I was interested in her that way or not.

I was happy about it when Jen invited herself to come up with me to my dorm room and continue the conversation. She said, quite frankly, that she'd picked me because she could tell I was safe to walk back with, and that as a small woman, she didn't feel safe alone on the campus at night. As for me, she said, I was one of the "pretty" boys, she could tell, and that meant I would not be a mistake. She explained that she knew I was "pretty" because she was in an equivalent position herself. She was a tomboy, unlikely as it might seem for a small blonde person. She had had her close adult connections with girls. She wasn't ruling out boys but she had a lot in common with other dykes.

Since she had brought the subject up, I told her a little bit about being one of the "pretty" boys and my own particular variation on it, and I described some of my history and the barriers that had made it difficult for me to get a girlfriend.

"Maybe you try too hard," she suggested. "Guys who really want to be in a relationship sometimes come across as desperate."

"Well, yeah, I guess I've been kind of girl-crazy. But it's also a double standard. Girls are expected to want to be in a relationship. It's like the equivalent of how girls can get tagged as 'too easy' for wanting sex. I guess that makes me a relationship-slut or something."

"I suppose," she conceded. "It's really not fair, is it?" She paused, looking at me. "It's really kind of amazing. It makes sense but it's unexpected. So...you actually like girls, huh? How about boys?" she asked me. "Do you think you ever would?"

"Well, I've tried it...or it has tried me, you might say. It's not for me. I've been accused of it all my life so if I ever did want to, I've already paid the social penalties on it, but...no, I don't seem to be wired that way."

Later, I was replaying the conversation with Jen in my head. Yes, the "relationship-slut" thing really was a double-standard issue. Imagine a girl saying "I want to get to know you better first. I do want sex, but I want it to be with someone who likes me for who I am." Now a boy with the same attitude, wanting the same thing. He isn't necessarily being approached or pressured for sex the way she is, but he broadcasts "I want sex but I want someone to like me for who I am" and it gets seen simply as "I want someone to like me" and he's perceived as needy and pathetic.

My human sexuality class was a big class, over 150 people, and we met in an auditorium. I was very much interested in exploring how my new sense of sexual identity meshed, or didn't mesh, with what was being taught on the subject, so I was happy to find that our first unit would be on variety and variation in human sexualities. The professor, Dr. Martinson, told the class on the first day that we would be discussing pornography, homosexuality, sexual kinks, and other subjects that might be upsetting to some from religious or conservative backgrounds, and that he'd sign their drop sheets if they didn't want to stay in.

By the end of the second week of classes, we were covering the Kinsey scale, where an exclusively heterosexual person was a zero and an exclusively homosexual person was a six, and many identities and experiences all along the continuum in between. The classroom was restlessly active with whispers and students were raising their hands all around the room.

"I always heard, like, that if a guy is really into guys, that when he gets with a girl he has to fantasize that she's another guy, and that's why some guys want girls to take it up the butt. Is that true?"

"I'm Eric and I'm bi. I hate how if you like sex with both, but anyone finds out you do it with other men, then you're a fag, like the only way you can possibly like sex with girls is if that's the only way you like it."

"Why do so many lesbians hate men? I mean you don't hear about gay guys going around acting like, 'I hate girls. You're all evil and out to get us,' but lesbians are like, 'Die, filthy man' and stuff."

"Hi, I'm Toni, and I want to answer that question that someone over there asked about roommates. My roommate last year was a lesbian and at first I was all 'Eww, I can't get dressed until she leaves'..." *lots of laughter* "...you know, but after a while it was fine. She said if she were into me that way she'd have told me and I feel like I learned a lot."

I went up to the professor after class. "Dr. Martinson? I don't know if we're going to cover it or not, but my situation is a little different from gay and lesbian, straight, and bisexual. I'm kind of different too but not like anything I've read in the book. I'm basically a girl inside, in terms of who I am, but I'm attracted to female people. But not specifically to feminine girls."

"You mean like transsexual?"

"No, I don't want to change my body."

He nodded slowly and pursed his lips. "Well, we're going into masculinity and femininity and androgyny next week and I'll ask for any volunteers to share their experience, and I'll be sure to look for you to call on if you'd like."

I nodded. I didn't like "androgynous" as a word for what I was. It sounded like a watered-down description for girls who weren't into lace and Barbie dolls or boys who liked to eat salads and put conditioner in their hair or something, but it sounded like the right general topic area for me to come out in public, in class.

Across Central Avenue from the university buildings were several esoteric and trendy businesses catering to the college crowd. There was a head shop selling marijuana pipes and rolling papers, a restaurant called the Frontier, another eatery called The Purple Cow, and a feminist coffeehouse, the Siren Coffeehouse. I began hanging out in the latter, bringing something to read, figuring I was putting myself in the vicinity of interesting people and someone might say hello and so forth. I knew some feminist women might not be friendly to males. Separatists. But hopefully as long as I wasn't being intrusive, they wouldn't object to my just being in there.

I woke up in the middle of the night and grabbed a pen and some scrap paper and wandered out into the lounge where I could turn on the light without disturbing Eddie. In my Human Sexuality class while we were discussing the Kinsey scale. Dr. Martinson had included a "spectrum" graph, a continuum for men from straight to gay, and, under it, a similar continuum for women from lesbian to straight. He didn't say all lesbians were masculine or anything, but because of the way the graph had been drawn, the left end of the spectrums was used for straight men and lesbian women, and the right end for gay men and straight women. To me this sort of implied that lesbians' characteristics were shared by straight men and that gay men were like straight women.

I redid the spectrum graph just for heterosexuality by itself. I created my own labels: a "Dominant/Aggressive" at one end and "Diminutive/ Docile" at the other. Then I drew a line between the male and female spectrum rainbows, connecting the Dominant/Aggressive end of the male spectrum to the Diminutive/Docile end of the female spectrum. This represented the traditional assumptions about heterosexuality and, moreover, it somehow represented the *past*. Then I drew the same spectrums again but this time drew connecting lines all across the spectrums from each point to its opposite. This was somehow the future. *There was something radical about uncoupling personality characteristics from sexual orientation.*

I couldn't put my finger on it yet but it had something to do with the species surviving and entrenching itself on the face of the earth and there was also something about the species being well established now, no longer under duress, that made the second diagram not just possible but inevitable. I felt excited and nervous, much the way I had the previous fall when I was reading about transsexuality and filling out my self-discovery workbook. I didn't understand it all yet but I labeled my papers anyway and taped them to the outside door of our dorm room. The next morning I asked Eddie how he felt about that being on our door and he said he was fine with it.

Was this real, this sense of having found The Answer that made everything click into place and make sense? Or was I inventing things in my head out of a desperate desire to have an answer? The life I'd lived up to this point had had lots of worrisome problematic components, and now as I tried on this new sense of identity, those parts of my life formed a pattern that made sense for the first time. The pieces of the puzzle made a lot more sense if I examined them from the starting point of thinking of myself as one of the girls. It all seemed to fit.

A New Color in the Spectrum

I wanted to do something to make more of a public statement about who I was, that I was aware of my difference and out of the closet, that I was proud, not ashamed, of who and how I was. I was out walking and went past a Salvation Army thrift store and on impulse turned around and went in.

After ten minutes of walking slowly around the racks of used clothing, I found a denim wraparound skirt. It tied on like an apron. I tried it on for size and it came down to midway between my knees and my ankles, and because it was a wraparound skirt it accommodated a wide range of waist sizes. Including mine. I took it to the cash register, ready to defend my purchase choice if need be, but the bored woman at the counter rang me up without comment.

When I got back to my room, I discarded my jeans in favor of the new skirt and went back out. I felt furtive and self-conscious in the dormitory hallways, as if I were a pervert waiting in ambush, but more at ease once I was out on the sidewalks. I could see some people glancing then glancing back again, others nudging people they were with and calling their companions' attention to me. Others either didn't notice or didn't react. After the first hour, I stopped wondering what other people were thinking and I was just me, out and about in a skirt on an early spring day. It felt great.

I had been made to feel self-conscious several times about the way I dressed. I knew now that it was actually an entire range of behaviors and expressions that people had been reacting to. But clothing—like my homemade paisley shirt, which probably now lay crumpled in a back corner of my closet back home—was a symbol for the rest of it, and my skirt was a symbolic gesture in response to it all. No one was ever going to make me ashamed of being like this again.

The Siren Coffeehouse had a bookshelf. I stopped bringing my own books and started picking up books from their bookshelf instead. There were several books of short essays—*Sisterhood is Powerful* edited by Robin Morgan, *Woman in Sexist Society* edited by Vivian Gornick and Barbara Moran, and *Notes from the Second Year* edited by Shulamith Firestone and Anne Koedt. I read at random, skipping around a lot, and Siren Coffeehouse became an extra classroom.

I was shy in there but not trying to overcome it. Instead I was letting it work for me if it would.

"It's good to see a man reading that book. How do you find it? Do you feel threatened?" The speaker was an older woman, perhaps in her seventies, with long gray hair, carrying a colorfully bejeweled purse or briefcase.

I grinned. "Not at all. It's making me think, but also a lot of it fits in with a lot of what I was thinking already, and I keep wanting to say 'right on' and pump my fist in the air."

"Which piece are you reading, if you don't mind me asking?"

"Umm, Kate Millett. 'Sexual Politics in Literature'."

"Interesting." She paused, and I thought for a moment she might sit down at my table, then she added, "You should read the book it came from. That's an excerpt from a full-sized book she wrote." I promised I would. Then she called out a question to someone behind the counter about finding parking and went over to her. I returned to my reading.

Professor Martinson stepped to the lectern and raised his hands to the class, palms out, and the babble died down. "Okay, that was interesting, wasn't it? I want to thank the students who came up here this morning and presented their experiences." He turned in our direction and motioned for us to stand, and then he began applauding. The rows of students in their tiers of auditorium seats did likewise before rising to file out of the room.

I turned to face Joel on my right. Joel had earlier described how he'd finally come out on campus after so many years of being in the closet. How he no longer felt as if he had to constantly fake a masculine persona in order to pass, and what a relief it was. I wanted to say something.

I'd been seated between two gay guys during our presentation. Rafael, now standing to my left, had introduced himself as a "militant faggot" who was as masculine as any straight guy. He had really taken on the audience, challenging them and practically inviting anyone who had a problem with gay people to say so to his face. I wanted to say something to him too.

This was my first time feeling like I was among allies when I was with gay guys. I'd never tried to talk with them about this stuff and now I wanted to. I felt awkward.

"I think what you talked about, coming out to your friends and all, that's what many of my friends thought I was going to do," I started.

Joel glanced back. "Huh? What's that now?"

"I mean they could tell I was going through something like that, and I think they figured sooner or later I was going to come out as gay. I'm pretty sure several people were trying to tell me it was okay and that they were supportive."

He smiled and looked at me, appraisingly, it seemed. "Oh, I definitely had people who were, like, 'Oh honey, you don't think you're telling me anything I don't already know.' I had to get to the point where I was ready first."

Rafael had apparently been tuning us in; he spoke from behind me. "So what's your whole thing now? You just want to make sure everyone knows you're not gay; that's it, right?"

"It's a little different than that. I'm a lot like a girl. Effectively that's who I am, and people tend to think that what that means, if you're like that, is that you're gay."

"Oh right, god forbid anyone should think that. So you have to tell everyone you're horribly mistreated and it's not fair, people assuming you're gay." Rafael stuck his hands in his pockets and stared at me, not very warmly. "People sometimes assume I'm straight. You think that's never uncomfortable? What's the big deal? Why do you feel you gotta get up in front of everyone and correct them like that?"

Joel interposed himself. "Hey, go easy; it takes courage to tell your personal stuff in public. I thought he had some interesting points about masculinity and femininity and sexual orientation."

I gave him a grateful glance and smile but addressed Rafael. "Well, what're *your* reasons for wanting to speak out?"

"It's not an equal situation. I could go out those doors and find six guys waiting to beat the shit out of me. And the police would say it was my fault."

"I've been beaten up several times for being a sissy, for acting too much like a girl. They thought I was you. Apparently homophobia is more of an equal opportunity experience than you realize. And while we're at it, I know what you mean about being blamed for it and treated like I brought it on myself. I get that too."

Joel said, "I don't think we need to be all 'us versus them' here. That's what's wrong with the world, everyone going around hating people who aren't the same. We're all affected by the hate, not just those it's mainly aimed at."

Rafael nodded, conceding. "I'm just busting your chops a little. If you've been gay-bashed you understand why we've got to stop that and it happens all the time, all over. I'm just saying you don't need to be denying that you're gay. It sounds to people like that's the main point you're making, that you're not us. Straight people don't need to come out as straight. It's the default. You never hear of anyone coming out to their family, 'Hey Mom, hey Dad, I have to tell you something. I'm straight.'"

"Well, *you* were denying being a *sissy,*" I retorted. "Seems to me that masculine is the default if you're male." I saw that I'd caught him from an unexpected angle. I continued, more softly, "And I *did* come out to my parents. It got into my head that maybe they'd assumed I was gay. I mean they never gave me a lot of shit about being a sissy boy, and we'd never talked about it."

"For real? How'd that go over?"

I thought back to that conversation, that day after dinner. "Well, they seemed a little relieved, but also really uncomfortable, like they wanted to change the subject. I told them it was 'something else,'" I said, doing air quotes, "but they didn't ask any questions. For all they knew, I might have decided I needed a sex change operation, you know? But they were just, 'Oh no, son, we didn't think you were gay,' and they ignored the rest. And I still couldn't tell if it was totally something they'd never thought about or if they'd wondered about it sometimes."

"Hmm, interesting. Hey, there's someone I think maybe you should meet." Rafael glanced at Joel and favored him with a raised eyebrow. "Joel, you've met Michelle, right?"

Hell, I didn't even realize these guys already knew each other.

Joel's face dawned into amusement. "That's...oh yeah."

"Michelle would want to meet you," Rafael stated, still eyeball-conferencing with Joel about it.

They're finding something very entertaining. Care to clue me in? Rafael seemed to be enjoying my exasperation. "Michelle's mom still says 'Mitchell'," he finally told me, relenting.

"Oh. He's a transsexual, then? Oh, cool."

"Don't say 'he.' It's 'she'," Rafael corrected. "I'll talk to you after class Thursday. I need to ask her, but I think you should meet."

"Hi," I said, "I saw your sign in the window, that you do custom jewelry. I'm interested in a silver pendant that I could wear on a chain." The jeweler nodded. I sketched out the design I had in mind. I drew the traditional male and female interlocked signs, except inverted vertically: the crosspiece of the female sign, the part that looks like a plus sign, was above the circle instead of below it—the arrow from the male sign was at the bottom instead of at the top. He said he could do that easily enough and I left him a deposit to create the piece.

I woke up in the middle of the night again and wrote more stuff. This was 1980. Students majoring in English or journalism might have typewriters but as a music major I did not, so I wrote everything by hand with ink pen. I wrote about society, totalitarian regimes and military authoritarian control, and tied that back to personality and behavior, and especially to the conventionally dominant-aggressive *masculine* behavior in males, which in turn was socially tied to heterosexual eligibility. I included my spectrum graphs. My paper straddled politics, biology, anthropology, and sexuality. I saw human sexuality on the large scale like this, where it could be *set up* across the board under various permutations and constraints by attitudes and social structures, as a sort of *machine*.

So I titled the paper "Four Ways to Run the Machine" and described what would happen or was already happening in a society with different possible attitudes (and social enforcements) defining heterosexual "sexiness" for each sex in different ways. It felt...powerful. Somehow what had started off being all about my personal sexuality had become more and more political. Now I was positing it as *the* core of politics, the central driving axiom of what made societies the way they were, peaceful or militaristic, cooperative or competitive, free or coercion-based.

The sexual identity that yesterday had felt daring now seemed to be radical. I also realized, as I read and reread what I'd written, that from the female side the radical feminists had already been saying exactly that, themselves, that this *was* the ground zero central core of all politics. But I had a piece of the puzzle that they didn't have, and I could bring that to the table and help complete the puzzle. It felt incendiary, explosive.

If it made as much sense to other people as it was making to me, it would almost instantly polarize people. It would mesh with some folks' political and social agenda and it would challenge and threaten that of others. It would be seriously controversial. I needed to show this to some people, get some feedback, see if I had just put dynamite onto paper or if it only had this compelling power for me and me alone.

"Do you mind telling me why you're here? I see you sitting here pretty often and I want to know." The question was phrased politely but delivered flatly and peremptorily, a demand. I looked up to see the dark-haired woman from behind the Siren Coffeehouse counter. Part of the collective running the place.

"I'm interested in feminist ideas and I have some notions about society and sexual identity and sexism, myself."

"Okay. I've never seen you bothering any of the customers but I just wanted to ask. We've had a few men causing trouble." Level gaze from pale gray eyes.

"I can believe that. I think a lot of dominant-aggressive men get angry when women step out of the diminutive-docile zone."

"I like those terms. That's just it; that's it indeed. So...you aren't intimidated by some anti-male sentiments, I take it." Not quite a smile.

"I haven't run into anything that's anti-male," I said truthfully, waving *Woman in Sexist Society* in the air. "These articles are angry but it's honest anger, and they're mad at how things are and they're angry at men but I'm not seeing anything where they hate men or where they're anti-male." I smiled, feeling my eyes crinkle. "I was sort of expecting to—that's the reputation y'all have, you know. I'm still waiting to see it."

I discovered to my surprise that I did know how to flirt. I wasn't really doing anything—and yet I was. I was...letting things happen. *She's cute.* Momentary daydream: us sitting apart from each other talking for hours, sharing, her smiling at me. *What would it feel like to be holding both hands and leaning forward, kissing each other?* And when I caught myself fantasizing—*It probably shows on my face*—as my awareness of that made me feel shy, I didn't fight my self-consciousness, just went with it, let that show as well. It wasn't anything deliberate and I wasn't trying to make anything happen, nor did I expect anything to, but this felt right. This is how you leave room for possibilities.

She raised an eyebrow. "Oh, it exists. With that much anger and so many angry women with a chance to finally speak out, there's going to be some hate. Wait here." She went into a back room and brought out a skinny little pamphlet. "I'd like this back when you're done with it. I'm LaRetta, by the way."

The title on it was *SCUM Manifesto*. In smaller letters under SCUM it said *Society for Cutting Up Men*. By Valerie Solanas.

"Oh, I saw this mentioned in someone's article," I said, "but this is the first time I've seen a copy. I'm Derek."

"I'm curious to know what you think."

"Actually..." I dared. "I've written a little bit myself, just trying to get some of my thoughts on paper, about patriarchy and how certain personalities are tied to sexual attraction as part of the social system." I realized that my right hand was preoccupied with the hair behind my ear. *Where do you suppose I picked that up? Probably doesn't really convey anything in my situation, but you never know.*

"I'd like to read it if it's short."

Yes! "Okay, I'll bring a copy next time I come in," I promised.

178

I wanted feedback. There were three other students who had also stood up to say interesting things about gender identity in the human sexuality course: a young guy who, using somewhat different words than the ones I used, had self-identified as effeminate but was unsure about sexual preference; an older woman "returning student" who was in her thirties or early forties who impressed me as thoughtful and as a person who liked ideas; and a girl who had said she'd always wanted to be a boy when she was a young girl and still felt like a boy inside.

I had made photocopies of my little treatise "Four Ways to Run the Machine," and gave copies to Joel and to Rafael and asked them if they would read it and let me know what they thought. And I left one with LaRetta at Siren Coffeehouse, as promised.

There was also a Women's Center on campus. I had found it while wandering around, and they had feminist theory books in a little library and offered feminist counseling to female students. I had gone in and spoken with one of the counselors for a session or two, although she said their funding really set them up to target female students so I hadn't made a habit of it. But I sought her out and asked if she'd be willing to read my paper and then if she felt like talking about it later, I'd like to, and if she didn't that would be fine.

I placed a personal ad in the *Albuquerque Journal*, giving it the heading STRAIGHTBACKWARDS PEOPLE, asking that any male who was either like a gay male or like a woman in personality but who was heterosexual, or any female who was either like a lesbian female or like a man in personality but, again, was heterosexual, to please get in touch with me for a project I was doing.

I met Michelle at the Frontier Restaurant, following in Rafael's wake to the checkered booth seat across from her at her table. I actually had a hard time believing Rafael was *not* mistaken; that yes this person was technically, from a biologically essentialist perspective, born male. I guess I had been expecting a sultry vampy overly-made-up sex vixen, with heavy lipstick and high heels and fishnet hose and pointy bra cups and fluttery false eyelashes. The person I was introduced to was compact, wore no discernable makeup, had short pageboy hair, was wearing a pair of pants that, although probably marketed as women's pants, were not overtly sexy, and a top with a harlequin-diamond-patchwork vest and no prominent boobs. And sneakers.

Not flirtatious. Straight head-on meet-your-eyes matter-of-fact kind of person.

Yeah. I believe you. I don't have to remind myself to think of you as she. You just are.

"This is Derek," Rafael said, indicating me with a tilt of his head. "I told you about him. From my college sex studies class. You two got some things in common and he hasn't met anyone he thinks of as being like him."

Michelle glanced at me casually, momentarily. Reserved, hard to read.

"So," Rafael continued, "I'm going to head off for now and leave you two to discuss pantyhose or whatever turns you on. See you later." He abandoned us to any awkwardness or ease we might establish.

I wanted conversation. To hell with awkwardness. "I only read about being transsexual for the first time last fall. I mean I vaguely remember hearing about it before that, but I checked out books written by transsexual authors and read them."

Michelle gave me a direct blue-eyed gaze then did a nose-to-toes glance. "Well, you're nice and slender and you have a good face. You're tall but that won't hurt anything. But I think people would probably notice the facial hair." She scrunched up her nose in a wrinkle of distaste but I sensed amusement and the implicit question mark there.

"I don't think of myself as female. I'm not. I'm a girl; that's my gender. But I'm male; that's my sex. Neither one is wrong."

"You may have a hard time convincing other people of that."

"No shit."

Michelle furrowed her brows. Looked down at the laminated table. Back. "I wanted a figure. Curves. I couldn't look in a mirror and see the sex I was born, not without hating it for telling a lie. It was lying to everyone about who I am. It was lying to them; it was lying to me. That body was a lie. I'm telling the truth now about who I am. Do *you* believe that?"

"About you? Absolutely. Or do you mean me, and my body? Hmmm..." My turn to contemplate the western-motif designs in the tabletop. Am I falsely advertising as a boy-person? No, not my fault. I really am a male person. People read that wrong as meaning I'm a boy-person.

I returned my eyes to Michelle's. "I didn't choose this body but it's authentically the one I came with. It doesn't say I'm a boy, but people make that assumption. That's their error though, not my lie."

"Who would you want to touch it? Don't you crave someone's hands on you sometimes? Will the person with those hands want to touch you in that body?"

"I'm not sure. I haven't had enough experience and I wonder about that too. She might like male bodies or she might like female bodies. If I changed to have a female body I might meet one who prefers male bodies."

"*She*. I see. That does complicate things."

"Yeah, tell me about it. I'm male. I'm a girl. I'm attracted to female people. What does that make me? A lesbian in a male body?"

"Ugh, don't say that. Seriously. Lesbian women have heard that before and they'll tell you it's offensive. You aren't going to win them over with that line." Pause. "You like them? Lesbians I mean?"

"I like the ones I've met. And I think I'd like...would maybe like seriously butch lesbian feminists if, I don't know, maybe some of them like male bodies but don't like men, you know?"

"They don't like people like me. 'You aren't a real woman, you're a spy for the patriarchy, get away, get out of here.' I don't know why you think they'd like you any better. Why would you want to be with them anyway? They're a hateful bunch of bitches."

"I don't know for sure. I'm just saying there may be some chemistry. I like radical feminism. I grew up with it and it's always said to me that I wasn't wrong or crazy. Now that I've figured a lot of stuff out for myself, it seems to fit right in. Anyway, yeah they're angry. I can see why. But some of them might like someone like me."

"Good luck with that," Michelle said, waving the idea away with her left hand. Then she looked at me again. "I don't know," she added more thoughtfully, "maybe some would."

I lifted the ringing phone from its cradle. "Hello?"

"Hey, I saw your ad. I've got this huge cock. Eleven inches. I'm sitting here in my living room and I can't put on my underwear because I can't get it on over my big dick, and I was wondering if you could help me."

"Hmm. Sounds like what you need is something built sort of like a giant pencil sharpener, but I don't know where you'd get such a thing. But a potato peeler might work. Have you thought of trying a potato peeler?"

Click

"Sorry, Eddie. I should have anticipated there would be a lot of crank calls from that ad. Has it been bad today?"

"No, don't worry. It doesn't bother me. I try not to be upset by the behavior of foolish people who just make noise."

Among the deluge of foolish people making noise, there had been a few responses of more interest: "Hello?"

"Hi. I'm calling in response to your ad in the paper. My name is Sierra Longfield. Yeah, like the mountains. Can we set up a time when I can meet with you?"

"Sure. Is this afternoon or tomorrow afternoon, either one, a possibility?"

"Let's make it tomorrow afternoon. Four? Okay. And where should we meet?"

. "There's a little restaurant on Central across from the university, the Frontier, do you know it? Yeah, that's the one. I'll meet you there. I'm a fairly tall guy with long hair, and glasses."

We met up at the appointed time and she followed me to my dorm room.

"I saw your ad and I discussed it with some of my friends. I'm an escort, a call girl. Anyway, I'm definitely interested in this project you're proposing. My friends didn't understand it the way I did. I don't think they got what it meant, but they might be interested once they do."

Now I was the one wondering if I was getting it or not. I remembered the street walkers on Central and how it had actually seemed like they could be good company. But I also thought maybe she had a somewhat more specific and kinkier interpretation for it, somehow, and was seeing this as a customer opportunity. I couldn't think of any way to ask the question without maybe badly offending her if she wasn't thinking of me in customer terms.

I sketched out some of my ideas. "I think sex and the whole courting and dating and flirting thing could be very different with the roles...not just the roles but the assumptions, how men and women think of each other...not just suspended but actually flipped. Like if you try to be neutral, you're still going to err on the side of the sex expectations that usually apply to you, but if you deliberately flip those, invert them, it can become an entirely different thing."

She seemed genuinely interested. "Well, I need to get back, but it was very nice meeting you. I feel it, and I enjoy your company. Here's my phone number. Call me, Okay?"

Shortly after that, I got a call from a woman named Luciana d'Urbanes who also came over to the dorm to meet me. She said she tended to see herself in many odd descriptions, and that the "straightbackwards people" ad had intrigued her quite a bit.

"I've always thought there must be *some* explanation for why I never felt like a normal person. Normal people were all around me but I never aspired to join them in their endeavors, never wanted to. But at some point I began to wonder, what is there about me that makes me be the one who doesn't crave that. I saw the other girls trying so hard to be normal, to fit in, and to get boys to like them, and I would say to them, 'Whatever for? Why would you want boys to like you, anyway? They're icky.' And they would pat me on the head and say that boys are fun for sex once you get married, but of course first you have to get them to marry you. And at first I said, 'Well I don't want to ever have sex with boys, that's gross and disgusting.'

"But then later I found out they were right about sex. Who knew? That something so...*odd*...could feel so good. But then the other girls were saying 'You can't just let them have sex with you; you have to make them wait so you can make them marry you,' and I said, 'Why not? I don't want to have one of them married to me; they're still boys, and they'll want me to clean the house or something. I just want them for sex.' And they were *shocked* and put their hands to their faces like this and said 'Ooooh, Lucy, you are a bad girl.'

"So," she continued, "when I read your ad, I thought, 'Wow, maybe that's it.' I mean, I never thought about it that way, you know? But it does sort of make sense. It could be, it could explain a lot. So I thought, well, it doesn't hurt to find out, so I came over to learn more about your project."

Her mannerisms were not butchy/tomboyish nor slutty-bawdy, but more like those of a fascinated dilettante trying out new ideas. But it felt like the challenge was on me to provide truly different and interesting ideas and I sort of liked that.

"Here's my telephone number and my address," she said, giving me a slip of paper. "I do hope you'll contact me. This could be a really good thing you're doing."

I managed to speak with some of the students and other people I'd shared the first batch of writings with. The prevailing mood of all the people who spoke with me was...wariness. Cautious and careful praise for some of the things in my writings.

The older woman returning student talked about the Vietnam war and how the angry men of her parents' generation had yelled about the young men growing their hair long and opposing the war and praising gentle values like love and brotherhood and peace. LaRetta from Siren Coffeehouse talked about the directions that feminism as a movement might take, and what it would mean, if a male movement also against patriarchy made an appearance.

Above and beyond what they were inclined to discuss, the folks whom I talked with seemed...well, they spoke in subdued tones, and slowly, like they were mulling over exactly what to say, and with quite serious facial expressions. I definitely got the impression that it had hit them between the eyes, that as primitive as my writing was at this point it was having quite an impact.

My poetry professor, Dr. Martinson, informed us of a poetry reading to take place that evening at Siren Coffeehouse. I'd seen the fliers the last couple times I was over there, so I decided to go.

Paula Gunn Allen, Native American feminist poet, was the main presenter. The other presenter, Sandie Asherah Megansdaughter, was a Native American woman also. She was the director of the UNM Rape Crisis Center. Their poetry was powerful and evocative, about women's experience and women's oppression, seen through the additional lens of being Native American.

I wanted to communicate with them. I took a copy of the combined set of my writings and paper-clipped it and took it with me to the Rape Crisis Center the following evening after choir. Ms. Megansdaughter was not in at the time; there was just a woman at the reception desk. I asked if they had personal faculty-office-style mailboxes there, and it turned out that they did, so I asked to borrow an empty manila folder, slipped my writings into it, and addressed it to Sandie Asherah Megansdaughter. I put my name on the "from" line and asked the receptionist to put it in her mailbox for me.

Another target audience came to mind: the folks at Albuquerque Crisis where I'd been going off and on since back when I was at Albuquerque Vo-Tech. I thought about all the years of uncertainty, worry, loneliness and confusion and how my new sexual-identity understandings had rescued me from all that. Surely these ideas represented profound mental health solutions for lots of other people whose sexual identities were akin to mine or who would otherwise benefit from these perspectives.

I made copies of my writings and took them over. I actually had other things to do that day and didn't feel like waiting to be seen, so I addressed another manila folder to a couple of the people I knew on a first name basis who worked with the program and asked at the reception desk if they'd hand it to one of them when they came in, and they said they would.

My resident advisor at Zuni Hall wanted to talk to me, said the note on the door. That door was now festooned with concise little snippets of my ideas and concepts. I wondered if that was what I was being called in for. I went to the RA suite and knocked.

"You're Derek Turner? There have been some concerns about you, about your behavior. People are wondering if you're okay, and frankly you've disturbed some people. Is there anything going on that I should know about?"

"Only the sort of things that I think everyone should know about. I have some ideas, political thoughts I guess you could call them, and I've been sharing them with some people. I've done so peacefully but someone might have found it disturbing. I don't know. And in my everyday behavior, I may have done something that someone might find disturbing. Do you have any specific complaint I should know about?"

"Well, for everyone's peace of mind, if would be a good thing if you'd be willing to go over to Albuquerque Crisis across the street and talk with the counselors and let them evaluate you. That will clear up any questions or misunderstandings."

I was amenable. I'd been going over there for years, and in fact I'd just dropped off a copy of "Four Ways" for the counseling services folks.

I was aware that one likely response, if you're bouncing around and getting really fervent about some sexually tinged ideas, was that people might think you were neurotically trying to block what was *really* bothering you. Like someone who goes around claiming that everyone around them is making sexual double entendres and is trying to touch them when what's really going on is that they've having strong sexual feelings themselves, feelings that they aren't comfortable acknowledging. All that Freudian shit, you know. So, yeah, let's get that stuff dismissed. I don't mind getting evaluated. At this point I'm confident I'm okay in the head.

I was directed past the Albuquerque Crisis offices and into a more clinical emergency room and into to an exam room. I sat in the chair indicated, across the desk from the doctor. A couple of other staff members sat at the adjoining table, either to watch or to participate; I wasn't sure of their role.

"Thank you for coming in, Mr. Turner. How are you feeling today?" the doctor asked.

"I'm doing quite well," I answered, then seized the initiative. "I was told by the RA that there were some concerns about me and I thought I'd see if I could clear things up."

He nodded and jotted something on the paper on his clipboard, then asked if I were getting along okay with my teachers; if I were getting along okay with other students; if I had any issues or disagreements with any of the student service offices on campus. I gave my answers: I wasn't currently having any problems with any of these categories of people.

"So you haven't been making any threats or writing any hate mail to anyone on campus?" he continued. He sounded dubious.

"Definitely not. I have been circulating some material that I've written, and it may contain ideas that some people could find threatening, I suppose, but I would never threaten anyone with violence and I'm not angry or resentful toward anyone. The things I've written about, the social situation, is something I am angry about but it's not something I consider to be anyone's personal fault."

The doctor drew out some papers from a manila folder and I recognized them as pages from "Four Ways to Run the Machine." I could not tell if they were from the copy I had left at this office previously or the one I had provided to Megansdaughter. "Yes, those are the writings I'm referring to."

"Have you ever been inside the office of the Rape Crisis Center?" he asked.

"Yes," I nodded, "I left off a copy for the Crisis Center's Director, Sandie Asherah Megansdaughter. I was at a poetry reading where she read and I thought she'd be a good person to get an opinion from."

Is that what's going on here? They think I have an issue with the Rape Crisis Center Director? How could anyone read through what I wrote and think it was hostile to her?

"It's not a threat," I reiterated. "I'm a feminist and we should logically be allies. I was expecting her to react in a positive way. And like I said, I've been circulating this to other students and other people, not just Ms. Megansdaughter."

"So can you explain what this says?" He tapped the papers.

I noticed that they were no longer in order and sorted through them and put them in proper sequence, then became aware that I was being stared at with clinical fascination. "Hmm," I observed to myself, "they think I'm a little obsessed with my writings being arrayed just so, aren't they? But seriously, who could be expected to read through and make sense of a batch of esoteric writings if page two was followed by page five and then page one?"

I began trying to give an overview but they waved it off and said it would save time to just run through it all just once, for the psychiatrist.

For the psychiatrist? I thought I was already talking to a psychiatrist!

Oh, and they said I had to sign a form, a consent to treatment, before the doctor could see me. When you go to see a surgeon you sign a consent to treatment that says you agree and understand that the doctor is going to perform surgery on you. Or if you go to a dentist or a podiatrist or whatever, *I do hereby consent to receive a root canal using the described medical procedures* and so forth. Psychiatrists *talk* to you but yeah apparently you need to consent to that, too, just like it was a procedure. It seemed pretty straightforward so I dated it and signed it.

Oddly, they then indicated that the doctor would not be seeing me here at this facility but instead wished to speak with me at a nearby affiliated institution, the Mountain View Psychiatric Hospital. And they had transportation to take me over there. I got into the van and was driven across town.

Upon my arrival, a dull-eyed female attendant handed me some forms on a clipboard. "Fill these out and bring them back to this desk." I filled in the blanks for name and address and contact person and social security number and returned them to her.

"Okay, you can go on out there," she said, waving her hand toward an open doorway into a large open area.

It didn't have the feel of a waiting room—too large, with people sitting in clusters at two different TVs and other folks pacing the painted concrete floor. Banks of fluorescents overhead. Additional open doorways all along the walls, portals to other uncertain spaces. "Don't want to get lost in here," I warned myself. "I'm just here for an evaluation."

I sat down in an orange plastic chair very close to the desk where I'd turned in my forms.

I wonder if the psychiatrist's going to ask me about my childhood potty training traumas or make like all these ideas of mine are compensation for not getting enough nipple time before I was weaned and stuff like that? I'm ready. Bring it on, I'll consider anything, but I know this stuff is real. And important.

An orderly came by shortly and asked me to remove my shoelaces and my belt, rules of the ward. People were known to use shoelaces or their belt to commit suicide. I waved him away. I wasn't here for any kind of permanent visit. I was just here to sit down with the doctor and answer whatever questions the doctor might have in order to alleviate concerns about my behaviors. He went into the intake office where I'd filled out my forms.

A moment later, the attendant came over to my chair. "Sir, the doctor has gone home. This is Friday. The doctor will not be able to see you until Monday."

"Well," I said. "I have things to be doing back at my dorm room, I have homework. I get that you folks think you have to rule out the possibility that I'm crazy, but seriously, you're not planning on holding me here over the whole weekend? I think I should go back to my dorm for now and come back Monday and we can finish this up then."

"You would have to talk to the ward administrator about that. I'll take you to his office when we're done here if you'd like, but first let me show you around."

She nodded toward a room partitioned off from us with thick acrylic walls, where three people in medical whites were sitting, talking on the phone or typing. It was set up sort of like the teller's window at a bank, with a narrow slot to allow sound and small objects through. "That's the nursing station. If you need to speak to staff, you stand by that window and someone will come to speak to you."

I could see through to the far side of the nursing station to another thick transparent wall, beyond which other people in street clothes were visible. "Who are those people over there? Is that the actual psychiatric ward where people go if you decide to admit them?"

"That's...those are the patients who have been determined not to pose a risk of hurting themselves or being dangerous. After an evaluation period, the doctor may decide that a patient is ready for that environment, and they get transferred over to that side."

"So over here on this side...?"

"Are the people who have not reached that stage, yes."

And also people who haven't been evaluated yet at all, apparently. So while a person is waiting to be cleared by the doctor as not crazy, our waiting room doubles as the ward for the seriously deranged? Gee, I can't imagine that that would be stressful for anyone or anything.

The attendant hailed some people: "Hi, Carolyn. Derek, this is Carolyn. And this is Denise, and this is Tommy. They're patients on this ward. I have to take care of something in the office but I'll be back in a moment." And with that, she departed, leaving me among the dangerous deranged crazies.

Carolyn looked to be in her thirties, a tall woman with an intelligent face. Tommy and Denise were teenagers, standing together in a way that suggested they were a couple. "So welcome to the loony bin, huh?" Carolyn greeted me. "What did you do to get to this place?"

"Apparently something I said or did upset some folks on campus, and I was told to come in and get my head checked out, so they don't have to worry that I'm an axe murderer."

"Naah, you don't look like one of the axe murderers. You're more like the guy who dynamites the bridge if the city doesn't agree to your evil demands."

I was a bit startled. Somehow I hadn't expected banter. "Uhh...I haven't thought of any evil demands yet though."

Carolyn explained that her Air Force husband had put her in here and had done so before. "I hate being in here. He says it's for my own good but really he does it to punish me."

The young couple explained that their parents had been trying to break them up, and they had responded by branding each other's names in their forearms with lit cigarette tips, which was the behavior that had landed them in this place.

"Wait...so they were trying to split you up and then when you branded yourselves with the cigarettes they threw you in together into this place? That doesn't seem like a good way to split a couple up."

They took each other's hands and said they weren't going to let anyone split them, but that it wasn't their parents who had brought them here; the police had. "If you've got insurance, you get put here for mental health assessments. People without insurance get put somewhere else. There's a state institution somewhere."

More people wandered over from other corners of the big room. A guy about my age with a wry sense of humor said he was being held because of alleged substance abuse problems but, he said, he just liked a little weed and some booze now and then. A frightened-looking younger guy talked rapidly about Jesus and whether God was going to punish him for being sinful or not, and a middle-aged woman who also looked frightened and worried and could not sit still, came over, muttering and pacing, not making eye contact with any of the rest of us.

The female attendant who had been guiding me came back with a couple male staff members, and asked us all to join her. "Let's show Derek the outdoor recreation area." So we all trooped out the side door. Outside, in a narrow grassy passage next to the ward corridor, I was once again asked to remove my shoelaces and belt. Again I declined. This was ridiculous. I hadn't been evaluated yet, and yet I was being treated like some kind of psycho killer.

They tackled me, and held me down until they were able to pry my shoes off and pull off my belt, and then they released me.

Well, two can play that game, I thought, and, upon being released, selected one of the orderlies who had participated and tackled him and told him with good-natured humor but serious intent that I didn't accept their authority to impose silly rules on me. I hadn't been evaluated yet, and if it was considered appropriate behavior around here to go around taking away folks' shoes, we were going to have some parity. With that I removed his shoes and proceeded to toss them up onto the rooftop above us. Of course they quickly had me pinned again.

They didn't let me up. A stretcher was brought out and I was tied to it face down. Then they injected me with something and lifted the stretcher and transferred me to a padded seclusion room where I was moved from stretcher to bed and tied at all four limbs to the bed, and left there alone. Every hour or so someone came in and injected me again. Whatever was in the needle made my brain go all murky and cloudy, and I felt despondent and cranky. Eventually they stopped shooting me up and after another couple hours someone came in and extracted from me a promise that I would not fight them physically any more, and then they released me from the restraints.

VIEW FROM THE MOUNTAINS

Well, I'd been looking for a reality check. Now I had one. Okay...first and foremost: I had *not* been taken here in order for them to rule out the possibility that I might be crazy. I was here because they had already decided that I definitely *was* crazy.

I smiled, amused. For all those years I had felt so desperately lonely and deeply worried that something was profoundly wrong with me and in need of fixing, and had come in to counselors and mental health service providers, and they had essentially patted me gently on the head and sent me on my way again, unable to help, unable to tell me anything useful. But *now*, when for the first time since I was a little kid I was confidently certain I was okay and was feeling good about myself, *now* I get locked up as a crazy person.

I had been assuming that the folks on campus had been understanding what I'd written. I'd thought they had been reacting cautiously because it was so polarizing and controversial and could have enough impact to change the world. But now I realized their wariness was probably just a response to a very intense very excited guy who was handing them handwritten material that didn't entirely make sense to them, a guy who was then asking them what they thought of it. Here I was thinking I was shaking the world with my compellingly powerful ideas and understandings, and instead I was now bundled away to a back ward for the violently insane.

I had been locked up because I came out and wrote about my peculiar sense of sexual identity. But probably not because they were out to get me or people like me, or people daring to speak of such things. Oh, that kind of thing might happen—I could believe that—but right now it looked more like I got locked up because the things I was saying and doing didn't easily fit into their world and they couldn't make sense of them. And when they couldn't make sense of them, they concluded that it was because I wasn't making sense.

Well, let's just start over, I decided. I'm pretty sure I'm not crazy. And my ideas and concepts still make sense to me. I can question them and suspend belief in them, but when I stare at them head-on they still seem to explain things. I am therefore going to act on the premise that they really are valid and important and relevant ideas.

Many of the people on the organizational staff—in particular the head nurse on the daytime shift, Fenton Richards—seemed *scared of* us. Hostile, treating us as discipline problems, trying to keep us away from each other, not wanting to get close to us themselves, always ready to call in the orderlies and have us restrained or shot up or tossed into a seclusion room for any provocation. I saw how ordinary behavior that made perfect sense in context, from any of us "disturbed and violently dangerous" folks, became in their eyes a symptom of mental illness.

The other patients didn't seem like something was inherently wrong with them so much as they seemed traumatized by stuff that had happened to them. Much as I had been emotionally and psychologically frazzled by all the sexual identity stress in *my* life all last semester.

Would my ideas help the other patients here? I wondered. Would they make sense to them? Even if they didn't, it seemed to me that these people could use someone to listen to them and treat them like they were people and care about whatever was upsetting them, instead of locking them up and pushing them around coercively and yelling at them and threatening them at every turn with those horrible psychiatric drugs.

To be fair, not all of the staff were like that. Some were solicitous and kind. They listened to the things we said as if we had minds that were producing thoughts that made sense. As if we were real people. They reminded me of the counseling services people I usually saw at Albuquerque Crisis. But they weren't the ones running things.

"Hey, spacecase lady, I just mopped that floor. Don't be putting your dirty shoes down on it. I'm not telling you twice."

Carolyn made an exasperated huff and scowled at the orderly. "I've got to get something out of my room. What am I supposed to do, fucking levitate?"

"I don't care how you get there but you ain't walking down this hallway, got it?"

She spun on her heels and stalked around the long way, motioning me to follow. One of the aides whistled from the nurses' station as we barreled past. "Pumpin' it, go mama, strut it baby."

"Oh fuck off."

"Whoa, are you off your medication or just on the rag?"

Carolyn stopped, put her fists down next to her hips and turned to face him, grinning insolently. "I don't *use* them."

"What?"

"I don't use rags. I like it when it runs down my legs."

"You're fucking crazy, you bitch!" he pronounced, turning away from the window as everyone watching laughed.

I began talking more deliberately with the other patients. The young couple were angry, stormy and short tempered, but as I got them talking with me they did calm down. I got them discussing their feelings about each other. None of their issues seemed to dovetail with my sexual identity theories, but a lot of them had to do with authority and authoritarian forces in their lives. I talked with them about beliefs about social order and authority. I talked with them about approaches to dealing with coercive authority figures, how not to fall into patterns of reacting with anger and unfocused misbehavior. I urged them to lay out what they wanted and what they were willing to do and so forth and simply stand up to authoritarian people without being goaded into hot-headed destructive acting out, which was only fueling the authoritarians' conviction that they needed to be coercively controlled.

The guy who was so terrified that God was going to punish him for his sins came from a fundamentalist family. I wasn't really religious but I'd gone to church and read the Bible. We talked about God and the nature of God, of forgiveness and not judging people and I talked about the incompatibility of the ideals promoted in the Sermon on the Mount and the Sermon on the Plains with these images he had of a tyrannical punitive God. He began crying and thanked me for talking with him.

Fenton Richards, the head nurse, yelled at us often for sitting too close to one another and reiterated over and over that "PC"—personal contact— was forbidden on the ward.

"So...you don't think I'm batshit insane, huh?" Carolyn queried me. Indeed, I didn't, and I shook my head. "I don't think so either, most of the time, but it's hard to know in this place. My husband says I don't realize how deranged I've been behaving and how hard it is for him. I mean, either I'm crazy and don't realize it or else he's being really and truly horrible to have put me here. And the place, this *place*...how can they just *keep* anybody here, keep us locked up unless we're mentally ill, I mean, how paranoid is that? If I went around telling my friends 'Oh watch out, you could be next; they'll lock you up too if your husbands say you've been acting weird,' they'd say

I was crazy for saying it. So either I'm crazy or else I'm crazy for thinking I'm not crazy."

"Yeah, if I'd been put here any time before a couple months ago, I would have been easy to convince that I was nuts," I replied. "I remember reading that book *I Never Promised You a Rose Garden* and some of it kind of reminded me of myself. But I've never been more sure that I was okay than I am now. Listen, this place doesn't look like it would be beneficial to anyone with problems. I mean, it could drive you nuts, just to be treated as a mindless drooling idiot and they're so nasty and insensitive, the way they talk to us. If a person was really upset and having problems, that would be a horrible way to treat them."

Carolyn nodded. "It's the way my husband betrayed me that I find so hard to believe. I mean, things aren't good between us, they haven't been for a while now, but he used to love me. How could he *do* this to me?"

"How are things...in what way are things not good between you? If you want to talk about it, I mean."

"Oh, he wants me to be..." She closed her eyes for a moment, then opened them wide and put on a big smile and looked upward adoringly, tilted her head, and clasped her hands in front of her chest. "Oh, you got the policy approved by the senior brass, you're *so* smart and clever." She pouted and moved her hands to cover her breasts reproachfully. "No, don't *do* that, you make me feel dizzy. Please don't touch me there, I can't think when you do that."

Carolyn dropped her hands and grinned at me, shaking her head. "I made the mistake about three years ago of telling him he couldn't count on me doing faithful wife anymore. I wasn't going to leave him but I wanted more out of life, and if he wanted to leave me because of it, I could understand that.

"Well ever since then, he tries to make me take it back and never say it again. When I say anything like that or he doesn't like the way I act, he says I'm going out of control. He brought me here the first time and he'd called ahead and told them I was sleeping around at random, fucking asshole! And that he had to pick me up and drive me home from passing out in a bar. None of that ever happened. I don't mean like you should hear my side of the story, I mean nothing remotely like that ever happened. And I'd like to have an affair, I think, but like an idiot I told him so instead of just going out and doing it. Anyway, they held me for evaluation. And now whenever he decides I'm not being a proper Air Force wife, he brings me back in and *now* of course they've got a case file on me, so obviously I belong here, since I've been here before, you know?"

By now I had finally met my designated shrink. I would only be seeing him for half an hour once a week. At long last, I got the opportunity to summarize my writings, and explained that I knew I had disturbed and upset some people with the way I'd distributed them and then interrogated them about what they thought of them. None of it should have been experienced as a threat, though. It was all just a miscommunication.

He indicated in our first session that he did not see anything overtly nutty in my ideas especially given my casual acknowledgement that they were new ideas of mine that I wasn't sure were viable and valid, that I was not insisting that everyone in the world should consider them gospel truth or anything. He asked me if I wanted to be put on any psychiatric medication and I said I would strongly prefer not, and he said he didn't think I needed any either, as long as I didn't cause disturbances by resisting staff physically the way I had when fighting to keep my shoelaces.

As I kept talking with my fellow patients, we all began sitting together, except for the unhappy mumbling woman who continued to pace around, apart from us. I talked about how we were treated in this place and I spoke of an article I had read recently about a revolutionary political movement, the Mental Patients' Liberation Front, and said we should join. I didn't see anything wrong with us that we couldn't address by listening to each other and caring about each other and helping each other deal with what life had dealt out to us.

I was finding myself quite drawn to Carolyn. She *was* frazzled and angry and scared, no doubt about that, but there was nothing at all irrational about her. She was entirely coherent, and her behaviors made sense in context. She still had sympathy for and understanding of her husband, as angry as she was with him. She had a plan of action, once she got out of this place, to obtain her own psychiatrist independent of this institution or of anyone or anything affiliated with her husband. Then she would be able to rely on his authority as her regular shrink to fend off any other psychiatrist's attempts to participate in committing her again.

"Hi, I'm Elaine, and I'm the occupational therapist. I'm curious. What are you guys doing?"

I indicated the ring of people, sitting in chairs just far enough apart to keep Head Nurse Fenton Richards from yelling at us to avoid PC. "We're talking about our biggest problems and comparing notes and trying to help each other with our issues. Since they aren't providing us with any real therapy, we're doing it ourselves. We call ourselves The Patient People because it takes a lot of patience to cope with some of the factors in our lives, including being locked up in here and treated the way some of the staff treats us."

"Oh, well I hope I haven't done anything to cause you to include me in your list of people who try your patience," she said—very earnestly I thought.

"No, not you, Elaine, you're okay," said Tommy, the guy with the cigarette brands on his forearm. Other patients agreed. She was one of the good ones.

"I think what you guys are doing is terrific. Can staff join? I have some stuff I could use some advice about."

I wasn't sure how I felt about that, but Carolyn and Tommy both gestured toward an empty seat. But Elaine smiled and shook her head, "I can't really, not right now. I wish I could. But I want you to know I think it's a great idea."

"What are you folks up to over here?" asked one of the staff nurses. I think his name was Marvin or Martin.

Carolyn answered him. "We're just talking about our shit and listening to each other. Crazy people's social hour. You want a seat?"

"You're not supposed to do that. You could interfere in each other's therapy. Go watch TV or work a puzzle or something. C'mon, break it up."

"Seriously? We're not supposed to fucking *talk* to each other?"

He stared sourly at her. "Okay, do whatever you want, but I'm writing you up, all of you, and you can see what Dr. Wenford thinks about it."

Carolyn really was interested in me. I was emotionally accessible to her, and although she acted wise and tough she was lonely and frightened in this place. She said I was kind and listened to her and cared about her and she felt like I understood her.

Her doctor had, unfortunately, put her on a psychiatric medication and the night nurse was determined that she was going to take it or she'd be held down and injected involuntarily. Carolyn hated the stuff; she said it robbed her of her own mind. I said I'd support her in her opposition to taking it, even if necessary standing between her and anyone coming to forcibly shoot her up. That probably wouldn't stop them from doing so but, who knows, it might send a message to the staff that we were willing to stick with each other.

She thanked me and said my courage and loyalty gave her the courage to just take the damn stuff as much as she hated it, and work on getting out of here and doing what she needed to do to get her life in order and prevent being stuck back in again at any future point.

It was lights out on the psych ward. In addition to having no shoelaces or belts, we had no doors, lest we get up to some kind of self-destructive antics in our rooms where the staff could not observe us. Our lights were all shut off, as were the lights in the day room beyond, but light from the nurses' station cast a dim glow that kept full dark from being present anywhere.

"Derek," came a whisper from the door. A Carolyn whisper. "Can I come in?"

"Yes, come on in."

She crept around the doorframe and padded quietly over to my bed.

The night staff were a mixture of lazy people plus a few perverts who often came into our rooms ostensibly to do routine checkups but made lewd comments and suggestions to us while we lay in our beds. Patients weren't supposed to be in each other's rooms after lights out, but the night staff either weren't paying attention, didn't care, or were permitting the visitation in a spirit of cynical and prurient amusement.

"You don't know how much it means to me to have your support and compassion in the midst of all this mess. You are a lovely person, and you're very intelligent, and you're gorgeous. I think you're aware you're a good person but I don't know if you realize how hot you are. I love your hair. And you...have...very nice lips," she stated, kissing them, taking my hands in hers. Curvy warm woman-skins moved against mine. The thin hospital gowns we used as pajamas were sliding and rubbing in between, helping rather than hindering what she was doing, making me want more.

"It's been so long... Oh God you feel so good... Let me..." Carolyn kissed me more slowly and emphatically, pushing me back against my pillow and swinging a leg over, and I was mere inches and moments away from being able to tell people for the rest of my life that I had lost my virginity on the violent and dangerous locked ward of a psychiatric hospital.

"Oh, wait, you're a virgin. I forgot. Listen, don't hate me for this but your first time really shouldn't be with a married woman who isn't free to stay part of your life. And I'm not yet. I'm working on it, thanks to you. I will get free, but I have some work to do first. I want you to know I do love you." She hugged me fiercely. "See you tomorrow." Then she slipped back toward her own room.

I got transferred later that week. I had now been in Mountain View Psychiatric Hospital for three weeks and apparently they had decided that I did not properly belong in the land of the dangerous and violent mentally ill. I was being moved to the mainstream population ward.

I didn't get much opportunity to say goodbye to the rest of the ward's patient people, which I wasn't happy about. On the other hand, being out of violent and dangerous meant I could get a day pass and leave the locked environment, so I did so immediately. I definitely craved conversation with someone outside of the nuthouse environment.

I called Luciana d'Urbanes and she greeted me warmly over the phone. I explained that I'd been asked to talk to the nice doctors to make sure my head was screwed on okay and then found that the consent-to-treatment form was a voluntary commitment and that they'd essentially tricked me into committing myself. But I was coping. She was sympathetic and at the same time not fazed to find herself talking to an alleged psychotic on a day pass from a mental ward. She invited me to drop by and I did so.

We chatted for several hours and ate lunch together. We talked about the whole sexual identity thing and recounted our respective sexual histories and so forth. As evening approached, I reluctantly rose to go back to my cage; maybe now that I'd been moved to general population, I could get some of the staff people to actually discuss the materials that had gotten me locked up, and to consider that I might actually be onto something.

Luciana gave me a rather nice caress and said she would like to see me again.

When I got back to Mountain View, I found all my possessions had been dumped into a pile in the middle of the floor. "You are not mentally ill," I was informed laconically. "You have to leave. You need to take all this with you." I explained that my folks had withdrawn me from UNM so I no longer had a dorm room, and they'd also taken my car back to Los Alamos, leaving me ill-equipped to remove all my stuff on such short notice. "That's not our concern," I was told. "If this stuff is still here tomorrow morning, it will be thrown out."

Faced with this well-tailored discharge and aftercare treatment plan, I thanked them for their hospitality and said I'd come back shortly for my stuff. I left Mountain View and walked through the streets of Albuquerque to the nearest interstate on-ramp and hitched. After half an hour or so I caught a ride to Santa Fe and then, after hiking across town, caught another ride onward to Los Alamos and walked to my folks' house. They were surprised to see me. I said hello and goodbye, explaining that I had to go right back to Albuquerque to get my stuff or they'd throw it in the dumpster, then got in my car and did precisely that.

While I was unpacking my gear in my old room in Los Alamos, I reviewed the week's events. I had been transferred to the mainstream population and then very abruptly out of Mountain View altogether. *Bye, dude, don't let the door hit your ass on the way out; don't bother to write.* My doctor hadn't discussed either transfer with me beforehand. One would *think* the shrinky people would do that under most circumstances, would talk to the patient about their transfer or their discharge and imbue it with whatever meaning they wanted it to have for the patient. Of course admittedly no one at Mountain View had seemed very concerned about making us feel disoriented. They'd been appallingly uninterested in how their actions made us feel.

Still, it had a very impromptu ad hoc kind of a feel to it. In particular, it seemed weird that they'd transferred me to the lower-risk general population ward, then just hours later dumped me out on the streets before making me attend crafts or occupational therapy or even orientation. What had been happening just *before* the transfer to general pop?

I thought back and realized that the organizational staff on my original ward had become pretty polarized. I had overheard staff members arguing with each other about our homegrown "patient people" support group. We had been making something happen, and it had felt powerful; we had been taking responsibility for our own therapy. Yeah. Then they'd transferred me, and just hours later put me out completely.

Yes...I think I've just been evicted from a locked mental institution! I had been scooped up and placed in there because the university thought I was freaking *nuts*, and a month later the hospital evicted me because they apparently thought I was some kind of activist who'd faked an episode in order to get inside and cause trouble. Ha! I pumped my fist in the air. Okay, what's up next?

I was free. I had a head full of concepts and thoughts and no clear idea of what my next step was going to be. But I was ready for the next adventure. I would find a way to communicate what was in my head. I would live my life and have love and find happiness. I was sure of it. I knew who I was. The world was going to find out who I was too. I'd see to that.

My parents glanced at each other and my dad cleared his throat. We'd just finished dinner. "You know we would be supportive of whatever path you decide to pursue, but your mother and I are concerned that you don't seem able to finish anything you start."

Mama added, "I'm afraid that by taking so many drugs you've made yourself mentally ill and won't be able to function as an adult or support yourself. You can live with us permanently I guess, as long as you agree to obey the rules of the house..." but by then I wasn't really listening.

They obviously hadn't really been listening to me either. I felt sad that they didn't understand that something *good* had happened for me. But mostly I felt a lot less vulnerable to their opinion, just as I was less vulnerable to anyone else's. It wasn't difficult to forgive my parents. They'd been supportive of me when I'd needed it the most and they would understand me better later, eventually.

"Hi, is this Luciana? Yeah, it's Derek. I'm out of the loony bin."

"Oh, I'm so glad to hear it. I never thought you belonged in there, I've had many conversations with you and you seem perfectly rational to me. Of course, that may not be saying much, or it may say more about me than about you." She chuckled. "It's so good to hear your voice. So, do they want you to come back for group therapy or counseling and whatnot?"

"No, that's the weird thing about it. When I got back from visiting you on a day pass, they stopped me at the nurse's station and said I had to leave, and get my shit out of there immediately. They acted like they were going to call the police if I didn't go away."

"But I thought you were being held there because the college said so. Didn't you say you tried to change your mind the first day and they wouldn't let you leave?"

"Yes, exactly. And then they end up treating me like I got caught trespassing. They even threatened to throw away all my clothes and books and stuff if I didn't take them with me, can you believe it? I had to go all the way to Los Alamos and get my car and then drive back, and they stood there while I packed it up and wouldn't let me talk to any of the other patients. You know what I think? I think they decided I was some kind of patients' rights radical and that they'd been tricked into letting me in or something."

"Well, if I ever get locked up myself, I shall have to try the same approach. Do you feel a bit like B'rer Rabbit? 'Oh no, please don't throw me in the briar patch'... On the other hand, I do worry sometimes about wearing out my welcome to the point that no one will want me around. I assume you're glad to be out, but are you worried that the mental ward apparently thinks you're too crazy for them to deal with?"

I laughed. "Oh, I'm very glad to be out. I don't like being kept in a place with locks on the doors and bars in the windows and treated like my brain is out of order."

"So what will you do now? Will you go back to your classes at school?"

"No, my parents withdrew me and even if they let me get readmitted I've missed too much of the semester. Besides, my folks wouldn't support me to go back, at this point. They think that since I got put into that place, it means I'm all messed up and they're talking about me spending my life living with them and getting a weekly allowance and a curfew and stuff."

"That sounds awful. What will you do?"

"I know who I am now, and I want to make a career as an activist, like a male feminist or a public education person about all this stuff I've been talking about. I'm convinced it's important, and that there are people like me everywhere, who are like the opposite sex on the inside but they're not gay or lesbian, and they aren't transsexual where they want to change their bodies either. People need to be aware that there are people like us, and that it isn't unhealthy or wrong. No one should have to go through what I've been through to figure this out."

"But how will you live?"

"I don't know. I could go back to trying to be an auto mechanic, but I think first I want to try to see if I'm good enough on the piano to earn money at it. Los Alamos is way too small, I need to try the big cities. I thought maybe I'd head for the west coast."

"Well, I don't know if Albuquerque is big enough, but you're welcome to visit me as you're passing through. I can ask my friend Isobel if she knows any bars or nightclubs. Do you wanna?"

Luciana's friend Isobel Lopez said she didn't think Albuquerque had good prospects for someone doing original compositions. "I asked my friend who used to be in a band, and he said the nearest good places to go are Las Vegas and Los Angeles." She said it was nice to meet me, gave Luciana a smirk with raised eyebrow, and left.

I regarded Luciana, seated next to me on the sofa. "You think your friend assumes we're getting it on?"

"Oh, yes, she definitely thinks I've found some boy candy to play with." She straightened up and faced me more directly. "Don't get me wrong, you're cute and delicious. You have this wonderful skinny body, like a tube, and if I got started touching I would surely enjoy it. But I'm just not comfortable being the courtesan who deflowered you. I'm enough older that it would make me feel like I'd molested a boy scout."

It didn't seem like a particularly good time to confess that I had in fact been a boy scout. I was meeting several fascinating women lately who seemed quite interested in consuming me as a sexual experience, which was quite nice for my sexual self-esteem and confirmed a lot of my insights about my sexual nature, but they shared a solicitous concern about despoiling me, and I was wondering if a virginity would eventually spoil on its own, like a carton of milk in the refrigerator long after its due date.

Luciana took me to the shoulder of the interstate the next morning and gave me a warm hug, and I began hitchhiking once again.

A week or so later I was washing a load of clothes in a launderette outside Los Angeles. A couple came in and put their own clothes in to wash. I offered them the remaining soap from my machine-vended box of detergent and we got to talking.

"I guess I came out looking for flower children and hippie communes and free love idealists. People keep laughing and saying I'm about a decade late. I'd also like to find, I don't know, maybe a feminist collective or something."

"Well, we're headed to a vegetarian commune we heard about. Anyone can stay a while if you don't mind doing some gardening and stuff. You want to come with us and check it out?" Of course I did.

The main house was cozy and comfortable, very lived-in, a bit worn down, with many many rooms. The kitchen consisted of a huge freezer, a sprawlingly large pantry, bins full of fresh vegetables and staple items, and a massive gas stove to cook on. There was a big living room, another five or six bedrooms and a set of otherwise unused rooms full of discarded clothing down in the basement.

One of the older guys, Tom, was an old Brooklyn tough guy who had fully embraced the gospel according to eating vegetables. He was always wanting to cook for people or treat them to the latest harvested fresh vegetables, cooked or raw, asking "Isn't that good? Isn't that so much better than anything you ever had from the outside world?"

A conventional lefty woman named Maggie was probably the main advocate for getting out there and touching the growing things, and she wanted everyone to have the delightful organic experience of harvesting, of sticking one's hands down into the soil or breaking things off their stems. Doing that would restore your soul. I noted that it would also result in the garden being picked, but that was only as it should be. I ended up staying a couple months.

I was in the living room one evening and one of the other travelers, a blonde girl, was sitting cross-legged on the floor there, and I drew her into conversation. We chatted about our travels and experiences prior to finding ourselves here, about this place and what we thought of it. She was confident and smiled easily, and talking felt good.

She mentioned having sore shoulders from the backpack and I made massaging motions in the air with my hands and nodded gleefully affirmative nods at her. She scooted over to sit directly in front of me and I massaged her shoulders and back and neck as we talked. She leaned back against me after a moment, snuggled and squirmed her body into mine. After a beat or two she glanced back playfully, took my hand, and said, "Let's find a room where we can be private." I stood up with her and we slipped down into the basement and chose an empty bedroom and started making out.

She had neither that chip-on-shoulder smoldery-challengey thing like the girl Annette had down in the UNM piano practice room, nor any of the tentative surface vulnerability I'd felt from Linda or Olivia. It was simpler, more casual in a relaxed easy way: this stuff feels good, so let's do it.

I was ambivalent. I wanted it to happen and yet I wanted it to...oh, I don't know, mean something. I actually did want it to be sort of a big deal, I guess, if only because it had been so long getting to this point. "Umm, listen," I mentioned, "I'm a virgin." She smiled and said "Oh, it's easy, here..." and she took control and guided me into place. I was self-conscious and not very relaxed, but it was nevertheless finally happening, and if it didn't quite feel absolutely fantastic, it at least felt close and pleasant. It was really happening at last.

"So, umm, what's your name?" I asked her as we untangled from each other and began searching for our underwear. "Kay Marron," she said. A twinge of sadness, a bit of regret, hit me. I wanted a girlfriend, but this person and I, we hadn't exactly created much of a connection and I wasn't sure how to tell her I was open to getting to know her better, that maybe we'd like each other and care about each other. And do it again, of course. I didn't know if she wanted any of that kind of stuff to happen. Maybe I wasn't someone she'd want to maintain ongoing contact with, as opposed to having been "of the moment." I mean, I hadn't relinquished my virginity conditionally or anything.

I asked if she'd like to hang out somewhere, just sit with each other, and she said yes. We went up to one of the outbuildings. We talked for a while and it came out that she was planning on hitting the road with her traveling companions. I didn't feel like I could just invite myself to come along if she wasn't inviting me to do so, nor did I know whether I'd want to.

That was the problem. I didn't know her. If I could spend some time with her for several days, getting to know her, well who knows? Maybe I could mean something to her, and she could mean something to me aside from what she already meant to me. But she was leaving with her friends, and I didn't have the kind of connection with her that would cause us to hold on to each other.

So perhaps it hadn't been the all-time most passionate and heart-touchingly profound movie-climax sort of first time, but, even so, in just a matter of months after sorting out my sexual identity I had finally lost my virginity on an honest-to-God hippie commune. Which is not even much of a dramatic comedown from having lost it on the violent ward of a loony bin.

PART FOUR
FROM THEN ON

A TIME AFTER

The alert timer application in my menu bar beeped at me. I closed the browser window and yawned and stretched. "Okay, I need to be in motion."

Jean hugged me and then pulled on the hair-tendrils from either side of my forehead, tugging my face nose to nose with hers. "You text me when you land. I want to know your cute little feets are on the ground safely and that you took the right plane and aren't stranded in Cincinnati or Atlanta or something."

I giggled. "I think the days when you can waltz onto the wrong plane are a bit behind us now. But I'll text you, I promise."

I hoisted my overnight satchel and computer bag and stepped out onto the sidewalk. The cold winter air bit through my wool skirt and stockings. Maybe not the garments best suited for the weather but sometimes it's all about the presentation. I had an audience to consider. I put my gloved hand in the air and extended a hopeful finger and after a few minutes a city cab pulled over to give me a ride.

On my way to the airport, I reviewed my notes. I'd been asked to speak to a book club that met at Boston College. They'd recently read my 1991 feminist theory paper, "Same Door, Different Closet: A Heterosexual Sissy's Coming-Out Party" (*Feminism and Psychology* 2(3) 1992.) and wanted me to present and lead a discussion about alternative gender identities.

At the venue, I wandered around the room and found electrical outlets and plugged in computer and microphone. I had been making these presentations for a while now, but whenever I was about to address an audience, I still felt nervous and like I had to pee.

On a bookshelf I spotted bright yellow bookmarks which had the initials LGBTQ in dark black letters. Lesbian and Gay, the original Stonewall-era components, and the often-disparaged Bisexual; and Transgender, about which there was now much more awareness—and now Q. *Queer.* Not a restatement of gay and lesbian (which is what "queer" had meant throughout my childhood and early adulthood), but queer in other ways, such as "genderqueer." People for whom the constructs of male or female are insufficient or problematic. Something not reducible to gay or lesbian or bi or transsexual. Something else. I picked up the bookmark and began my presentation.

"The acronym has gotten longer," I said. "People who are affirmatively tolerant on gay and lesbian issues, even transgender concerns, often still ask, 'Why do we need to add another letter? Isn't anyone who isn't heterosexual and cisgender already covered by gay, lesbian, bisexual or trans? I understand not liking rigid categories but seriously, do we need this term?'"

There were nods of agreement. They'd heard this too.

I continued, "There are transgender people who say that the 'Q' is unnecessary. They say that 'transgender' includes anyone whose gender is different from what people originally assumed it to be, and so they've already got people like me covered. But when transgender activists speak about the issues affecting their community, they talk about surgery and hormones, and medical coverage and bathroom access, and they don't discuss the existence of people like me when they do public education. And, meanwhile, there are other transgender people who say that if you're not going to make an effort to present as and be perceived as female, if you don't plan to transition, you *aren't* transgender. They feel that including people who aren't in their situation is just going to dilute what it means to be transgender. Can't say I blame them.

"I'm more comfortable calling myself genderqueer. There isn't a whole lot of agreement about exactly what it means, but in practice, it just means 'something else' as in, 'Please indicate on this form if you identify as straight, gay, lesbian, bisexual, transgender, or something else.' It's kind of like saying *et cetera*.

"Among those of us who identify as genderqueer there are *genderfluid* people, whose identity varies over time, and there are *agender* and *nonbinary* and *neutrois* folks who feel that they're outside of gender, or at least outside of the classic either/or of male and female.

"I refer to my own specific form of being genderqueer as being a *gender invert*. Basically who I am, who I historically have been all my life, is a male girl, or a male woman, with neither the male part nor the gendered identity being wrong and in need of fixing. So as you can see, we genderqueer folks are a pretty diverse group.

"A lot of folks think we're phonies. That we all hopped on the bandwagon to be different and edgy and trendy, but that if being genderqueer wasn't already out there as a cultural phenomenon, none of us would come up with it on our own, from our own experience."

I paused to organize my thoughts for a moment, then continued. "There are advantages to having a category that basically means 'it's something else.' Getting an unabridged listing that doesn't leave anyone out is impossible. For that to be possible we'd have to think of all the possibilities. And we can't, because there's no way to recognize what you haven't thought of, what you've never encountered, and realize that you forgot to include it."

I glanced from face to face. The book club members and other guests were mostly paying real attention; some seemed to be taking notes. And there was a hand in the air. I gave a nod to the young audience member and gestured for her to proceed. "Your article is heavily based on feminist theory," she said. "Can you say a few words about the relationship between feminism and gender identity movements?"

"Sure," I said. "Feminist theory points out how all the interactions between men and women are organized to centralize the male appetite, the male interests and wishes. It's all about him, in other words. She's reduced to being a desirable commodity and doing other things that help him in his interests and wishes. That's your basic Power 101 level of analysis. Then feminist theory goes on to say that because sexuality is very much organized along these principles, the male-female power disparity, and all its particulars, becomes eroticized for us. Catharine MacKinnon once said that women's subordination is made erotic. 'We get off on it somewhat' she wrote, 'if nowhere near the extent that men do.'"

"You ever wonder why patriarchy would impose a barrage of restrictions on men, telling men how they cannot be allowed to behave? Seems like odd behavior for the ruling side of a social oppression, doesn't it? Power defines appropriate gender identity, defining both the powerful and the oppressed. Power itself is a relationship, not a substance that one possesses, and all the participants to the relationship get defined by it."

I looked into their faces to make sure that they were still following what I was saying. Elbows were propped on desks, and people were leaning forward. An engaged group. It felt heady and powerful to have their ears like this.

"So you have this polarized oppositional thing between men and women that's the blueprint of patriarchal sexuality...gay people threaten the situation. If you've got a pattern established where sex is defined as *man the appetite fucks woman the commodity*, obviously that definition is threatened if the people involved are of the same sex. Less obvious, perhaps, is that *it also threatens the definition because the participants are not rigidly assigned to a specific role*. Think about it. Even in a gay or lesbian relationship where one person is the butch and the other person is the femme, you don't start out where each person is automatically assigned to being the butch or the femme because of what sex they are. It may be a negotiation between the two people, or perhaps a person comes to feel that the butch role or the femme role is the one that fits them best. And of course lots of relationships don't use butch and femme at all.

"Now add in genderqueer and transgender people and consider their impact. Suddenly, it's not just gay and lesbian people. You've got other people whose role is also no longer defined ahead of time by their biological sex."

A young person wearing a diaphanous top called out, "So are you trying to say there wouldn't be any people transitioning to the other sex if things happened the way you were talking about, where a person could just be understood as a male woman or a female man?"

I answered, "I began this presentation by saying that what you'd hear tonight would just be *my* take on things, and the way I presented material would be shaped by my own experiences. If you went to hear a different speaker talking about being genderqueer you'd hear a different presentation. I do tend to emphasize the social over the biological. But imagine someone who is male-bodied and totally masculine in all the traditional ways, and attracted to feminine women, an extremely conventional kind of guy. Except that Karen isn't a guy. Karen says this male body is just wrong. It has the wrong parts. So she is transitioning to female, at which point she will be a very masculine person in behavior and personality, with conventionally male interests, but a female body, and she will live her life as a lesbian. Being understood as a male woman isn't going to help her a bit—she simply doesn't feel right being male.

"There may be some people who have transitioned in order to be perceived more accurately but who could present as a female man or a male woman and be understood that way, if the world comprehended gender inverts. Just as back in the era before reassignment surgery was a possibility, there were people who lived as gender inverts and feeling dysphoria about their bodies all their lives.

"I think it would be a bad mistake to assume that one single pattern would be the case for everyone. If that 'body sense' still makes their body feel terribly wrong, they are still going to need to accommodate that by transitioning.

"I want to increase the options and the range of expressions available to people like me, not take other people's options away or tell people that, you know, in their personal definitions and expressions of gender they're doing it wrong."

Someone else had his hand up, so I called on him. "I just wanted to tell you that your article, the 'Heterosexual Sissy's Coming-Out Party,' really changed my life. It was the first time I'd ever seen anything written that said there were people like me out there. So, I was wondering...would you mind telling us a little about what it was like to come out when there wasn't anything like the modern idea of trans or genderqueer to come out as? I mean, it must have been pretty hard explaining to people."

So I talked about myself. About what it was like. Growing up me. Gradually figuring out that who I was was problematic and disturbing to other people. Not fitting in. Not connecting, being isolated and lonely and left out. I *ummmed* and *uhhhed* and trailed off in mid-sentence a lot. They didn't seem to mind. They were listening and chimed in at times and asked additional questions in mid-narrative. It was a long way from being one of the best public speaking occasions in my life. And yet it was one of the most fulfilling.

I originally met Jean via a dating site. When you're an exception—not just to the rule, but an exception to the exception to the exception to the rule—internet dating is a wonderful tool for finding and meeting the rare and equally unusual people you're likely to connect well with.

She'd written to say that she was a very high match with me, and she had read my profile and my answers to the questions and found me interesting. I wrote, "They really do seem to have a creative approach to this stuff, don't they?" and we set up a date to meet each other.

On one of our early dates, she asked me if I'd heard of BDSM, and what I thought of it. I admitted that I tended to find it a bit silly, based on what I knew about it. "It seems kind of formulaic, with everyone dressing identically in those odd black leather outfits or high spike heels and, you know, Victoria's Secret style underwear. Then they pretend to tie each other up and hurt them but the 'whips' are soft and the 'handcuffs' are velvety Velcro things. Me, I'm interested in appetite and playing with someone or being played with, teased, you know. I think men are weird when they complain about cock-teases. I *like* being made all full of cravings, and I like doing it back in return for that matter. But no, I've never gotten into the whole whips and chains scene."

I told Jean about my sense of self and my experiences with sexual identity issues. To her my pinings to be done unto and be subject more often to my partner's appetite were best explained in BDSM terms: "It sounds to me like you want to be the sub."

I had never thought of it in such terms myself. But, well, it *was* about power and control. A lot of sexual behavior, and the roles and rituals of courtship and flirting and of making sex happen, *are* about power. And it's usually very specifically gendered (male power, male domination, male sexual aggression). But under the auspices of BDSM, power could be played with. And hence allocated differently.

I'd always seen the sexual-initiative issue in terms of, "I want to feel like I can be the desirable one, and feel her appetite for me." Jean had a gift for simplifying and clarifying: "You're a girl, so you want someone to do things to you. You want to be topped." She then proceeded to demonstrate her point and convince me.

I still don't consider BDSM to be a defining characteristic of my identity; it's not The Answer to how and with whom people like me are most likely to connect, or anything like that. But it's another good tool for upending conventional roles and assumptions. It places a lot of emphasis on negotiation and discussion of expectations.

And although I don't always need my partner to play sexual predator while I'm the prey, I definitely need it to not always be the other way around.

In the six months that followed after that Christmas on my parents' porch, when I finally began figuring things out, I found a new way to relate to girls, a way that worked for me. I was a different gender than the other males (I wasn't a boy) and that made my sexuality different too (it wasn't heterosexuality in the normal sense). I finally had opportunities to explore sexual possibilities.

But I was stepping into those opportunities inexperienced, without any more of the skill set for sustaining a mutually fulfilling relationship than any of us have when we're young and starting out. I was a few years behind other people my age in that respect.

I caught up. By the time I met Jean, I had been in several relationships and had learned how to be a good partner. We have a good thing.

A *gender invert* is someone whose gender is the opposite of the gender associated with their physical sex, and who accepts both their physical sex and their unexpected gender as natural and correct. Male girls. Female boys. I'm a male girl and I identify as a gender invert.

Havelock Ellis popularized the term "gender invert" back in the late 1800s. At the time, he was promoting the notion that homosexual people were essentially people who possessed a bunch of characteristics of the opposite sex. That notion got challenged and discarded. Most researchers now agree that being a feminine male, or a masculine female, is not what causes a person to be a gay male or a lesbian. So the term "gender invert" was basically discarded and left to rot on the sidewalk.

I'm reclaiming it. Just because it has nothing to do with causing sexual orientation doesn't mean that gender inversion itself doesn't exist. Or that it isn't a useful term. Our society is now familiar with male-to-female and female-to-male transgender people, transitioners who address their situation by bringing their sex into compliance with their gender. "Gender invert" can be used to refer to a similar person who continues to live a life as a male girl or a female boy, someone who embraces the disparity between their sex and their gender instead of feeling obliged to fix it.

As much as I appreciate finally having a term I can use, I'm not satisfied with "umbrella" terms like *transgender* and *genderqueer*. Like lesbians who felt more erased than included by the use of the term "gay," and preferred to see the word "lesbian" to reflect an awareness of them, I would like to see *gender invert* spreading as a concept and as a terminology.

By the way, being a gender invert is not another way of saying you have a masculine or feminine "side." All of me is feminine. Side, back, front, top, bottom. I'm not less feminine in my gender than some other kind of person. A gender invert is not someone halfway inbetween a person who is cisgender and a person who is transgender and getting hormones and surgeries. I find the "side" thing, and the assumptions that I'm only semi-feminine, to be negating and insulting.

I had become obsessed with virginity—my own and its role as a gatekeeping function—in the process of coming to terms with my atypical gender identity. I'd been astute enough to recognize a significant part of the game for what it was ("a way of keeping boys like me out") and yet I'd swallowed other parts of it unquestioned. A couple years after the events described in this book, a lesbian student pointed out to me: "Just what is it that me and my partner would ever do that would make us non-virgins to you? Virginity is all about penetration, virginity's a heterosexist concept."

There is nothing so centrally important to erotic, romantic and emotional intimacy about penis-in-vagina sex that should make other forms of sex not count. But that's not an assessment that a virgin can easily make, given the lore to the contrary. A lot of what I was actually concerned with was the search for a mutual intimacy, but there's still no denying that I bought into a conventional definition of what constitutes sex.

When people ask "Is it social, or is it biological?" my inclination is to reply "Neither one. It's geometric."

Imagine, if you will, that you have a mango snowcone in one hand and a mint snowcone in the other. Hurl the mango snowcone at the nearest wall from a distance of five feet. You get a massive splatter of orange ice a couple feet in diameter. Now hurl the mint snowcone, aiming about six inches to the right of where you threw the mango cone, and now you have a second large splatter that substantially overlaps the first one but skews to the right.

Even assuming there are built-in differences between the sexes, that's the best way to think about gender: that there is more variation within each population than there is on average between the two populations, and that there is a lot of overlap.

I am the equivalent of a spot of mango ice over in the portion of the wall that's mostly occupied by mint green ice-flecks.

Any time you have two populations where there's a lot of variation within each population and a lot of overlap between them, there are going to be such points. There can't *not* be. And it isn't necessary to come up with an explanation for how they got there that differs from how the *other* points got to *their* locations.

I'm one of the girls. That's my gender. I'm male. That's my sex. I'm attracted to females. That's my orientation. My experience was different from anything else I'd ever heard of. I wanted to write it down so there would be a book showing what it is like to grow up like this. I didn't have any such book available to me as an adolescent and young adult. I had to figure out everything for myself and when I did, I swore that other people who were like me should not have to do that entirely on their own. And maybe now they won't have to.

READERS GUIDE

1. Throughout the book, Derek alternates between attempting to fit in and be accepted and trying to be true to what he sees as his real self. Our society has a storehouse of advice for people who don't fit in (both in general and specifically as males who don't exhibit many masculine characteristics). Some of this common advice encourages the idea of "joining them and then beating them on their own terms" and some of it emphasizes the importance of staying authentic at any cost. Can you give some examples of these kinds of advice? What do you think of the ways in which Derek attempted to handle his situation as a misfit during junior high and high school?

2. Initially, Derek tends to become indignant, outraged, and furiously angry when singled out for hostile attention. Later in the book, he is less often shown to be having those reactions. What do you think is causing this? Is the author neglecting to include Derek's internal emotional state? Or has the character's emotional life in such situations changed in some fashion?

3. Were there scenes in the book where you felt that you were perceiving aspects of the situation that Derek himself was oblivious to? Or scenes where it seemed that other characters were picking up on things that Derek was not aware of? Give some examples.

4. Feminism, in the 1970s, was associated with the notion of having "unisex" standards and expectations instead of believing men and women had fundamental built-in differences in personality, thought, and behavior. In what ways does Derek find this concept useful? Derek eventually decides that he is a "sissy," or a "male girl"—how is this different from believing that the same standards should apply equally to male and female people? What is gained by and lost by switching from the attitude "I don't have to conform to sexist notions of what a guy should be like" to an attitude of "I am different from the other boys, I'm like one of the girls instead"? Did you end up perceiving Derek as different from (most) other males, or did you view him more as a person who held that notion of himself?

5. How was this story different from stories you have heard about people growing up transgender and then transitioning and/or presenting so as to be perceived as a sex other than the one inscribed on their birth certificate? How was this story different from stories you have heard about growing up gay, lesbian, or bisexual? In what ways was this story similar to those other coming-out/coming-of-age stories?

6. The author has commented that *genderqueer*, as an identity, is often dismissed as a trendy bandwagon phenomenon that, if it weren't being written about and tweeted and posted about, would not be something that young people growing up would come up with on their own; that it isn't legitimate and real in the same sense that being gay or being transgender are real. What was your familiarity with the term and the identity "genderqueer" before reading this book? Do you think of it differently in light of this testimonial?

7. When Derek is thrashing around with these ideas immediately after listening to the Pink Floyd album, there is a mention in passing about having originally thought of himself as "nicer" than other boys/men. Are you familiar with any rhetoric regarding males who think of themselves as "nice guys"? In what ways is Derek an example of this phenomenon? How is his perspective or behavior different from the beliefs and attitudes and behaviors that are attributed to "nice guys"?

8. A major theme in the book is the question of sexual aggression, and specifically of Derek's not wanting to be perceived as a sexual predator or a sexual user. How do you see this experience and attitude in light of such things as the #metoo movement against sexually intrusive misbehavior or issues of sexual harassment and objectification? Do you see Derek's complaint being primarily about sexist propaganda that created the illusion that males have to be sexually aggressive in order to function as heterosexuals, or do you think there are actual real difficulties for a heterosexual male who does not engage in sexual initiative-taking?

9. The transgender woman Michelle, in the diner, says that the male body she had originally been incorporated in had been "a lie—it was lying to everyone about who I am. It was lying to them; it was lying to me. That body was a lie. I'm telling the truth now about who I am." Derek does not seek to be perceived as female. Should he, if he identifies as a girl or woman? Do you think he is being reasonable if he expects acceptance in the world as a male girl or male woman?

10. The gay activist Rafael took issue with Derek emphasizing that he was not gay. "You don't need to be denying that you're gay. It sounds to people like that's the main point you're making, that you're not us." Do you agree with Rafael? Do you think Derek should have found a less divisive way to come out as a femme or sissy, or was his inclusion of his sexual orientation a necessary and relevant part of his identity as a marginalized person?

CPSIA information can be obtained
at www.ICGtesting.com
Printed in the USA
BVHW031139180221
600499BV00006B/62